Organized Interes

Organized Interests and the State
Studies in Meso-Corporatism

Edited by Alan Cawson

Sage Series in Neo-Corporatism
Series Editor: Philippe C. Schmitter
SAGE Publications · London · Beverly Hills · New Delhi

SAGE Publications Ltd
28 Banner Street
London EC1Y 8QE

 SAGE Publications Inc
275 South Beverly Drive
Beverly Hills, California 90212

SAGE Publications India Pvt Ltd
C-236 Defence Colony
New Delhi 110 024

British Library Cataloguing in Publication Data

Organized interests and the state: studies
   in meso-corporatism.
   1. Corporate state
   I. Cawson, Alan
   321.9   HD3611

Library of Congress Catalog Card Number 85 050949

ISBN 0-8039-9718-3
ISBN 0-8039-9719-1 Pbk

Printed in Great Britain
by J. W. Arrowsmith Ltd, Bristol

Contents

Preface

Philippe C. Schmitter and Wolfgang Streeck

'Corporatism' seems unwilling to go away — either as a subject of inquiry or as a practice of governance. Denounced as a momentary fad insufficiently distinct from its academic predecessors, pronounced as an unstable arrangement incapable of surviving economic scarcity and overcoming class conflict, and announced as a priority target for extinction by crusading liberals and right-wing governments, it has nevertheless continued to capture the attention of scholars and politicians. When the concept was disinterred ten years ago from the crypt where fascism and various authoritarian experiences had buried it, corporatism was but a spectre of ill-defined and ill-known presence. Over the years, it has proved to be a powerful analytical instrument that was fruitfully applied to an astonishing variety of arenas and countries.

Given this persistence of interest, we organized the Fifth Summer School on Comparative European Politics of the European University Institute in Florence around the topic of 'Class Interests, Neo-corporatism and Democracy'. The Summer School was held from 20 June to 16 July 1983, and attracted 31 participants from a wide variety of countries and disciplines. The 'staff' was equally varied. In addition to the two of us, several scholars were able to spend as much as a week or more with the participants: Reinhard Bendix (University of California, Berkeley), Claus Offe (Universitaet Bielefeld), Victor Perez-Diaz (Universidad Complutense de Madrid) and Marino Regini (Università di Milano). An even larger number came for shorter periods. This extensive collaboration with outsiders, combined with the excellent preparation and the enthusiasm of the participants, prepared the ground for a lively exchange of ideas which, far beyond the original objectives of the Summer School, resulted in the emergence of new, common themes of systematic inquiry.

Two of these themes surfaced with special intensity and frequency. The first was that the neo-corporatist literature had been excessively centred on the phenomenon of comprehensive 'social pacts' involving national peak associations of capital and labour and the national state (e.g. incomes policies), and had tended to overlook highly significant — if less visible — developments at the meso-level of specific economic sectors or policy arenas. Second, the previous discussion had focused on relatively few countries — usually ones governed by social democratic parties — and it was rightly emphasized that it had ignored the experiences of other Western European polities where neo-corporatist arrangements had emerged in different political and social contexts.

This volume is a product of that Summer School experience. Many of its essays were originally presented there, and they have subsequently been circulated for comment and criticism among participants. Alan Cawson accepted the difficult, and at times thankless, task of moulding them into a coherent volume. Where 'gaps' were identified and significant scholarship was found to fill them, the editor has gone beyond the original participants, and commissioned essays for inclusion.

To a substantial extent, these two Summer School volumes represent a 'second generation' of research on neo-corporatism. They follow the 'first generation' of conceptual speculation and exploratory empirical study collected in the volumes edited by Gerhard Lehmbruch and Philippe C. Schmitter on *Trends Toward Corporatist Intermediation* and *Patterns of Corporatist Policymaking.* As participants in those early efforts, we are particularly pleased that Sage Publications has continued to support this line of inquiry. Indeed, two more collections of essays will be forthcoming soon under its imprimatur: Wolfgang Streeck and Philippe C. Schmitter (eds), *Private Interest Government: Beyond Market and State;* and Philippe C.Schmitter and Claus Offe (eds), *Corporatist Practices and Democracy.* We hope that, with this sequence of publications, we may be beginning to approach something which is unfortunately rare in the social sciences: a research tradition which is cumulative in its ability to build upon previous work, and critical in its ability to discern enduring insights from ephemeral enthusiasms.

Finally, we would like to join with the editor of this volume in thanking the European University Institute for the generous support it has given to this project since its inception, and in expressing our admiration for two persons without whose competence and dedication it would never have materialized: Henrietta Grant Peterkin and Constance Meldrum.

1
Introduction
Varieties of corporatism: the importance of the meso-level of interest intermediation

Alan Cawson

Introduction

The last ten years have seen a considerable growth of interest in the concept of corporatism, and this must surely be taken as evidence of considerable dissatisfaction with previous theories of interest group politics. In spite of recent protestations to the contrary (Almond, 1983; Martin, 1983), corporatism is more than simply a variation or enlargement on the theme of pluralism, and its popularity is not to be dismissed as the product of the latest intellectual fashion. There remains, however, considerable semantic confusion, as well as inevitable theoretical diversity, within the literature (Panitch, 1980: 159), and this chapter contends that the concept can be made clearer, and more useful in research, if three different levels of corporatism are distinguished.

The main part of this introductory chapter is given to this task, but first, it is necessary to identify the salient features of corporatism, which are common to each of its different levels, by way of a brief review of the recent literature, in order to illustrate the significance of the research reported in this book. In my concluding chapter I will comment on the present state of research on corporatist interest intermediation, and suggest some implications of these essays for future research.

Corporatism in political theory

As is more generally true of theorizing in politics, there is some disagreement about whether the strategic task for the development of corporatist theory should be concerned with a holistic explanation of political systems, or with the formulation of 'middle-range' generalizations about political processes. Examples of the first include the continuing effort to rank nation-states along a continuum of degrees of corporatism (Lehmbruch, 1982, 1984); the second includes attempts to locate corporatism as a universal sociological principle of association, alongside community, market

1

and state (Streeck and Schmitter, 1984; Schmitter, 1985). The focus of this book is on the analysis of political processes at a middle — or meso- level — which involves the interaction of state agencies and interests organized on a sectoral basis. Our concern is not with the comparison of national political systems, but with the explanation of policy-making of a more limited scope where interest organizations do not aggregate broad class interests but reflect the more specific concerns of particular interest categories.

The macro-focus of much of the corporatist literature tends to downplay the importance of corporatism as an explanatory concept for the analysis of politics in countries, such as Canada and Britain, where tripartite bargaining at the macro-level over incomes policies or economic planning has been either non-existent or unstable and short-lived. Despite the low ranking that such countries achieve on international comparisons (Wilensky, 1976; Schmitter, 1981; Lehmbruch, 1982, Schmidt, 1982), the middle-level corporatist hypotheses explored in this book, which link policy effectiveness to meso-corporatist associational systems, are richly suggestive, and question the premature foreclosure of discussion which follows from identifying the utility of the corporatist paradigm solely with its manifestation at the national level (Salisbury, 1979; Cox, 1981; F.L. Wilson, 1983; Cox and Hayward, 1983).

Whatever the level chosen for study, it remains true that the appeal of corporatist theory is in part a product of the manifest theoretical problems and empirical inadequacies of alternative paradigms of state–society relationships. The other two main contenders are varieties of pluralism and neo-Marxism, and while the challenge of corporatism is relatively recent, it is possible to identify a number of reasons for its appeal. Pluralism has proven to be deficient because of its underlying assumptions of a competitive political marketplace, its voluntarism and methodological individualism in its implicit theory of interests, and especially in its portrayal of a neutral state which is disengaged from interest conflicts at the same time that it preserves an institutional and ideological boundary between public and private spheres. Neo-Marxist theory correctly identified many of the weaknesses of pluralist analysis, especially in its emphasis on the necessity of constructing a theory of the state (Macpherson, 1977), and on developing a concept of interest beyond the simple aggregation of the subjective preferences of individuals (Connolly, 1972).

But neo-Marxism suffered from a tendency to reduce political processes to their alleged economic bases, and from the prior assumption that political interests are structurally given by economic class relationships. The consequence of these two factors is seen in the specification of the role of the state as either the instrument of a dominant class, or the arena in which class struggles are fought out (Miliband, 1969; Poulantzas, 1973). In both versions the autonomous impact of the state is downgraded, and the empirical relationship between class organizations and state power is preempted by the theoretical assumptions. (But see Miliband, 1983, for a version of neo-Marxism which recognizes the distinct basis of state power.) The evident fragmentation of class loyalties and the undeniable importance of non-class interests proved difficult to accommodate within the limitations of classical theory; attempts to do so (Jessop, 1982a) proved to be vulnerable to criticism on the grounds that the distinctive focus of Marxism was lost (Offe, 1983) — a charge that even that author found difficult to refute from within Marxist assumptions (Jessop, 1983).

This tension between pluralism and neo-Marxism has added to the appeal of corporatism as a possible synthesis, but has also led to the danger of expecting too much from corporatist analysis. The aims of the authors of the subsequent chapters are relatively modest. The reader will find no claims to explain the totality of the relationships between state and civil society in capitalist countries; he or she will not find within these pages an analytical philosopher's stone. Nevertheless, the authors do share a conviction that corporatist theory promises a more useful set of tools with which to examine such relationships than is offered within the perspectives of pluralism and neo-Marxism, and their findings substantiate the claim that much of importance is left out in pluralist and neo-Marxist analyses. They believe both in the commitment to empirical research which is the strength of pluralism, and in the theoretical self-consciousness (Connolly, 1974) which has been a hallmark of neo-Marxism.

Many of those living in neo-corporatist tents are refugees from these opposed traditions within political theory, and are trying to build a more solid structure. The following remarks are a 'structural survey' of corporatist theory, from which the reader can judge whether the property ought to be demolished, or is capable of refurbishment.

Individuals, organizations and interests
The basic concept of interest within pluralism is individual preference; that within neo-Marxism is class consciousness. While it is true that both approaches recognize the importance of groups and organizations, theoretical development of collective action is constrained by their central assumptions. Offe (1981: 123) argues that there are three perspectives from which interest groups can be analysed: that of the individual, that of the organization and that of the social system. Pluralist approaches focus only on the first;

neo-Marxist ones (he might have admitted) concentrate on the third. By recognizing that interest group politics can be explained only by combining all three perspectives, Offe points towards the particular contribution of neo-corporatism: the treatment of organizations as collective actors which relate to their members' individual interests in a dialectical fashion: organizational interests are shaped by individual interests, but at the same time fashion and control those interests (Cawson, 1982, 63–4).

While interests are organized within a framework of opportunities, they are not givens which can be read off from an account of socioeconomic structure (Berger, 1981: 9), as in neo-Marxist theory, which allocates 'objective' interests to classes and then explains political outcomes as contingent upon the effective expression of those given interests. But equally, not all interest organizations are simply aggregates or containers into which congruent individual preferences are poured. Certain kinds of organizations have developed a semi-compulsory character; they constrain and discipline their members and often make exit from the organization difficult if not impossible. Moreover, this social control capacity has often been promoted or licensed by the state (Schmitter, 1974: 93), and used as a means of implementing public policies.

A central part of the corporatist research agenda has been the effort to identify what kinds of groups develop these characteristics, and how this process is affected by the scope and activities of the state. A reliable empirical generalization seems to be that most of these are groups constituted on the basis of their function in the social division of labour, rather than, say, on their member's preferences for certain collective ends, or on the basis of common characteristics such as ethnic identities. Moreover, within this distinction producer groups (including trade unions as well as employer and professional organizations) are more likely than consumer groups to develop significant corporatist relationships with state agencies (Beer, 1969).

Power relations between organizations
At the heart of the pluralist paradigm lies the assumption that inequalities in power between groups are not cumulative, and that a competitive political marketplace guaranteed by democratic institutions ensures equality of opportunity for groups to exercise power, even if not a final equality of outcome. By way of critique, and with a diametrically opposed starting point, neo-Marxism asserts a structurally guaranteed dominance for the class interests of capital through the institution of the state. Evidence of state policies which

favour non-capitalist interests is rendered by some theorists consistent with this assertion by way of the tortuous logic of the idea of the 'relative autonomy of the state' (Poulantzas, 1973).

By contrast, neo-corporatist theory builds on the manifest concentration and centralization of functional interests which in part has been the outcome of the processes of pluralist competition. The group marketplace is hierarchical, segmented and asymmetrical, and the organizations within it tend to seek monopoly representation of their constituent interest category. There is a lively debate within corporatist theory about how differences between various types of interest organizations can be conceptualized and explained, and those who come to it from neo-Marxism tend to stress the importance of class distinctions. Most would agree with Berger (1981:13) that organizations representing the interests of labour and capital are not simply pressure groups like any other (and hence would disagree with Martin, 1980). Not all would follow Panitch's insistence that there is a structural asymmetry in the power of organizations of labour and capital (1979a: 125), or with the view that labour and capital organize according to different logics of collective action (Offe and Wiesenthal, 1979).

The organization of class interests and the interrelationships between class organizations and the state have been central to neo-corporatist analysis (especially, as I shall argue below, at the macro-level), but not all corporatist organizations have their basis in a class interest. One approach is to pursue the hypothesis that groups in monopolistic exchanges with state agencies, whether they represent doctors, farmers or industrial workers, have more in common with each other then they do with competitive pluralistic voluntary associations (Cawson, 1982: 64), and that the dualism between competitive and corporatist processes is an increasingly important cleavage in contemporary capitalist democracies (Cawson and Saunders, 1983). The term 'corporatization' may be an ugly one, but it can be useful to signify an organization's capacity both to represent its members' interests and to discipline them as part of a negotiated interaction with other groups. But it is important to stress that this approach differs from more conventional organization theory, in that the process of corporatization is not argued to be a property of the organization itself; it is, rather, a description of a specific type of relationship between interest organizations, and with the state.

This brings us to one of the crucial aspects of corporatist theory: the question of the state. While the state has been identified as constitutive of corporatist relationships, and empirical studies of corporatism have provided more insights into the economic

managerial role of the modern state than either pluralism or
neo-Marxism (Held and Krieger, 1984: 13), there has yet to emerge
from corporatist writing a distinctive theory of the state (Schmitter,
1985; Cawson, 1985). It is clear from the conceptual definition
proposed below (p. 8) that corporatism always involves the state,
but the failure to agree what is unique about state activities or state
actors, or to explain the changing patterns of state organization,
amounts to a debit on the surveyor's report which may well deter
potential purchasers. The crucial issue of whether there is a state
interest which is integral to corporatist relationships, and how that
interest can be theorized, is as yet unresolved in corporatist writing.

State–Organization relationships
The useful term 'interest intermediation' was coined by Schmitter
(1977) to capture the reciprocity of the relationship between
corporatist organizations and state agencies. The modern state has
adjusted to the development of rival centres of power and
quasi-public decision-making by selectively incorporating nominally
private interest organizations into public decision-making, and in
doing so the state has excluded other kinds of (competitive)
organized interests. In addition, the implementation of public
policies has frequently been carried out by delegating public
authority to corporatist bodies, which exercise control over their
members to secure acceptance of negotiated agreements. Thus,
corporatist organizations not only represent the interests of their
respective interest categories, but also play a part in the governance
of those categories.

It is not, however, easy to distinguish state agencies from other
collective actors on the basis of what they do, or how they do it
(Schmitter, 1985), precisely because of the inter-penetration of
public and private power. But it does seem that there is good reason
to follow the implications of Weber's view that 'Today legal
coercion by violence is the monopoly of the state' (1978: 314). The
control exercised by organizations over their members in a process
of interest intermediation is underwritten by state coercion,
sometimes directly (when we may speak of 'state corporatism' —
see Coleman, chapter 6 below), sometimes indirectly, under the
explicit or implied threat of legal regulation if corporatist agreements break down (Crouch, 1983a).

While some writers in the corporatist debate (e.g. Winkler, 1976)
have misleadingly defined corporatism in terms of a directive role
for the state, most have taken the view that the growth of
corporatism has chipped away at the sovereignty and autonomy of

the state, and has made the employment of its coercive capacity more problematic (Cawson, 1982, chapter 4). The recognition of relatively privileged categories of interest within corporatist relationships has either created new hierarchies or licensed existing ones, and this has undermined the universality of citizenship and transformed the democratic character of the state. This is not to argue that there was once an egalitarian and democratic 'golden age' which has been superseded by the growth of corporatism, but rather to make the point that corporatist practices are in effect suspensions of universalistic norms, justified frequently on the grounds of expediency, and that the issues this raises for democratic theory have hardly begun to be discussed (but see Cawson, 1983; Schmitter, 1984).

Political exchange
The relationship between corporatist associations and the state within 'liberal' or 'societal' corporatism comprises a process of political exchange, whereby bargains are struck in which favourable state policies are traded for compliance and enforcement of those policies by the associations. It is not a relationship in which the state directs the interest associations (state corporatism), or one in which state agencies are captured by private interests. It implies that the state is sufficiently powerful to be able to bargain in a situation where its partners know that the alternative to reaching agreement may be coerced compliance or legal–bureaucratic direction. But the state is not powerful enough, or has insufficient specialized knowledge, to formulate and implement policy without the agreement of the partners (Birnbaum, 1982b). These kinds of political exchanges we may describe as 'power dependence' relations, to emphasize that both the interest associations and the state enjoy some measure of autonomy, although within a set of constraints.

Actual corporatist arrangements often involve more than one interest association, and most frequently the organized representatives of labour and capital. In such tripartite corporatism, the issue of political exchange and power dependence between associations is very important, and the role of the state may be to induce agreements between these groups. An important part of the corporatist research agenda comprises the uncovering the rules, or logic, of collective action where exchanges take place across the threshold of public power (Crouch, 1982). Under what conditions will particular collective actors accept the probability that self-restraint will become a rule followed by all parties, and that the policy consequences will be of benefit to all? (see Boston, chapter 4 below). Neo-corporatist political exchanges are premised on the assumption that power is not always zero-sum, and that it is possible, in cases of interest conflict, for both sets of interests to benefit from collectively negotiated policy.

Where such exchanges are not ephemeral, ad hoc responses to particular short-run policy perceptions, but are institutionalized in the structure of the political system, they tend to be inclusive and involve a system of encompassing interest associations which brings together a wide variety of interests (Marin, 1983). In other cases, such as in Britain, corporatist relationships may be seen as privileged, and as being the result of a process of social closure (Parkin, 1979) around specific interests which at the same time exclude other kinds of interests that are not equally capable of organization and closure (Harrison, 1984). The relatively stable examples of such exchanges may be confined, as in Britain or France, to sectoral bargaining arrangements (Keeler, 1981; Grant, 1983a).

A conceptual definition of neo-corporatism
Summarizing these observations, and the extensive literature from which they are drawn (Cawson and Ballard, 1984), we can identify as the essential feature of neo-corporatism a distinctive concep-tualization of the relationship between the modern state and society. Corporatism is a specific socio-political process in which organizations representing monopolistic functional interests engage in political exchange with state agencies over public policy outputs which involves those organizations in a role that combines interest representation and policy implementation through delegated self-enforcement.

This concept combines two key features: the intermediation of functional interests (representation/control) and a specific mode of public formation (intervention). It is the combination of these features that is the hallmark of corporatism; it is their separation that is central to parliamentarism (Jessop, 1979). Schmitter (1982: 262) suggested that it might have prevented some confusion in the literature had these aspects been separately identified as corporatism$_1$ (interest intermediation) and corporatism$_2$ (policy concertation), but that would be to diminish the importance attached to the fusion of the two (Lehmbruch, 1982: 8). In short, corporatism *is* corporatism$_1$ and corporatism$_2$ together.

The elaboration of conceptual definitions of corporatism has been one of the most common features — some would say, weaknesses — of the literature. The definition offered here clearly distinguishes corporatism from pluralism, and implies a rebuttal of the arguments put forward by recent critics (Almond, 1983; Jordan, 1983; Martin, 1983) that corporatism is merely a variety of pluralism in which the most powerful and significant interest groups are the organizations of capital and labour. What is distinctive about corporatism, however, is the process of closure (rather than competition) which can lead to monopoly interest representation, and the form of the political exchange (representation/control/delegated self-enforcement) which takes place between corporatist associations and the state. To my knowledge, nowhere in the literature on interest groups written from a pluralist standpoint is stressed the reciprocity of the relationship between interest groups and the state, which holds true only for some organizations (in the corporatist sphere) and not for others (in the competitive sphere).

Corporatism can develop at different levels, and the organizations which represent functional interests can vary in the scope of their membership and the degree of inclusiveness of the collective definition of their interests. Much of neo-corporatist theoretical analysis and empirical observation has been concerned with the important macro-political questions of system stability through bargaining between the state and 'peak' organizations of labour and capital (tripartism); some authors (e.g. Panitch, 1979a; von Beyme, 1983) insist that tripartism is the constitutive feature of corporatism. But recently, as reflected in the concerns of the authors of the chapters that follow, more attention has been paid to the meso-level (Wassenberg, 1982), in which the relevant collective actors are not peak class associations, but organizations which close around and defend specific interests of sectors and professions. Their power dependence relationships with state agencies are monopolistic and exclusive, but not necessarily tripartite.

Corporatist interest intermediation at the meso-level may be part of a broader system which also includes peak bargaining, or in other cases may be relatively isolated within a system where pluralistic interest politics and parliamentarism remain the most important policy determinants. A separation of the meso-level of analysis permits intersectoral comparisons of the particular 'mix' of policy modes and associational systems within a single national case (Cawson, 1982; Atkinson and Coleman, chapter 2 below), or comparisons of sectoral processes in different countries (such as those presented in this book by Grant and Streeck, Rhodes, and Schneider).

In addition, some industrial policies may involve political exchanges of a contractual kind between state agencies and individual firms exercising monopoly power in the market. In such cases these firms are powerful enough not to have to rely on sectoral or peak associations to represent their interests, and to be able to bargain directly with the state, which suggests that for producer interests meso-corporatism occurs in particular kinds of product markets dominated by medium- to large-sized firms organized into monopolistic interest associations. There is a case for describing direct bargaining between firms and state agencies which involves delegated self-enforcement on the part of those firms as 'micro-corporatism'. Some writers would argue that such processes should not be included as varieties of corporatism, because differentiated interest organizations are not the principal actors; this issue is taken up below.

Macro-level corporatism

For some writers, what is a 'macro-bias' in the literature (Wassen-berg, 1982: 86) is its great strength: the rigorous and quantitative comparison of nation-states according to various indices of neo-corporatist development. Three main hypotheses have been advanced: (1) that macro-corporatism can explain the differential 'governability' of advanced capitalist countries (Schmitter, 1981); (2) that it can explain their different unemployment rates (Schmidt, 1982; and (3) that it lies behind the variation in the extent of 'tax–welfare backlash' experienced by states facing rising fiscal burdens (Wilensky, 1976). From such limited explanatory objectives, some have sought to refine macro-corporatism as an alternative paradigm to macroeconomics (Tarantelli, 1983), and further to suggest, in a dubious normative extension of a secure empirically based generalization, that, if countries such as Italy or Britain were to adopt neo-corporatist concertation policies and industrial relations practices, they might better be able to secure stable economic growth. (See Schmitter, 1981: 318–24, for a critique of such views.)

What does seem clear from these important studies is that those countries which had already developed intensive corporatist policy networks have proved better able to withstand the harsh international economic climate of the 1970s without enforced deflation and the creation of mass unemployment. But equally clear is the fact that fiscal retrenchment and the adoption of some form of monetarist policy, however unwillingly, puts a severe strain on even the most highly developed macro-corporatist systems such as Austria's.

In this sense, macro-corporatism has been a 'fair-weather creature', built up during the boom years of the 1950s and 1960s, when organized labour traded 'social peace' for a governmental commitment to full employment and an increased share of national resources. Such arrangements have indeed proved resilient in hard times, and the experience of countries which have tried to implement macro-corporatist bargains in difficult times (Boston, chapter 4 below) bodes ill for the advocacy of neo-corporatism as a specifically counter-recessionary strategy. This is not, however, to accept the argument that neo-corporatism is a form of 'institutional sclerosis' which can explain the propensity of mature capitalist countries to experience faltering growth rates (Olson, 1982; see the critique by Crouch, 1983b).

Nevertheless, macro-corporatism is on the wane, and the claims of 'Modell Deutschland' or 'Modell Osterreich' as successful blueprints for other countries to emulate are looking increasingly hollow. The three players in the tripartite game must all believe in a non-zero-sum outcome, and if one player demurs then the game is over and the 'prisoner's dilemma' reasserts itself. It may be premature to conclude that macro-level corporatism was a unique postwar historical phenomenon, and that it cannot be reconstructed short of a return to the historical conditions that gave it birth, but certainly the normative tendencies within the neo-corporatist literature seem not to rest on secure empirical foundations. More promising, and in keeping with the theoretical dissatisfaction at the level of explanation which attended the emergence of the concept, is the shift in attention towards the more limited objective of the development of corporatist theory in the analysis of specific policy outcomes and inter-organizational relationships at the sub-system level. Hence the objective of this book is to contribute towards theory and empirically based generalizations at the meso-level.

Meso-level corporatism
Meso-corporatism refers to the fusion of the processes of interest representation, decision-making and policy implementation with respect to a more restricted range of issues than the 'system-steering' concerns of macro-corporatism. There is no presumption that meso-corporatist arrangements are tripartite in form, or that the interests they embrace are restricted to capital and labour. The range of collective actors which enter into meso-corporatist political exchanges with state actors includes trade unions and sectoral associations of business interests. But other groups are potential partners, including professional and managerial interests, as long as they have developed the organizational capacity to monopolize the representation of a distinctive interest category.

In practice, it is commonly observed that those organizations which do negotiate meso-corporatist bargains with the state are the representatives of producer/provider interests rather than consumer ones. There is thus a general empirical correlation between the corporatist sphere and those associations whose members produce goods or provide services. This is clearly related to the terms of political exchange within corporatism: such groups may have the capacity to deliver their members, or to invoke sanctions (strikes, non-cooperation, refusal of information). The crucial prerequisites of meso-corporatism can be located both in terms of organizational capacity and in terms of an unwillingness or inability on the part of the state to assume a directive role, or to rely on market processes to produce desired ends.

The characteristics and properties of interest organizations at the meso-level can be studied by identifying a 'logic of membership' (relationships between the organization and members' interests) and a 'logic of influence' (relationships between the organization and state actors), and analysing the organization itself as subject to both sets of opportunities and constraints (Schmitter and Streeck, 1981). Where conditions are favourable for the development of stable meso-corporatist arrangements, writers associated with the comparative research project on the organization of business interests have found it useful to refer to these arrangements as 'private interest governments' (Streeck and Schmitter, 1984) in order to emphasize the extent to which public purposes are served by essentially private organizations licensed but not directly controlled by the state.

Sectoral and trans-sectoral corporatism
Lehmbruch (1984) proposes a useful way of distinguishing between varieties of corporatism according to whether the political exchanges in policy formation and implementation are negotiated within a single sector or, as in tripartite peak bargaining, across all or a range of sectors. This distinction is particularly useful in the discussion of industrial policy, and complements rather than conflicts with the three levels of corporatism suggested above. Sectoral corporatism can never be macro-corporatist, but there can be a shift between meso- and micro-levels, as suggested in the case of the steel industry by Rhodes (chapter 10 below). In addition, meso-level interest organizations can be concerned with trans-sectoral questions (such as the industrial training example discussed by Vickerstaff in chapter 3 below); and multi-product firms which operate in different sectors may engage in trans-sectoral bargaining with state agencies. The macro/meso/micro distinction concerns the level of interest organization, 'meso' referring to those organizations which operate between peak national associations and individual firms or members. The sectoral/trans-sectoral distinction refers to the definition of the scope of policy bargaining.

The usefulness of the latter distinction would seem to turn on the problem of defining the concept of 'sector', and here we run into some difficulties reflecting different concepts. The following is offered as a preliminary attempt to clarify what lies behind the use of the term 'sector'.

The conventional usage treats 'sector' as equivalent to a branch of industrial production, and we can break down the whole economy into an almost indefinite number of sectors reaching at the limit the markets for single products. Most empirical research makes use of various standard industrial classifications to describe the sectoral differentiation of industry. For the purposes of this discussion, however, such distinctions are only a starting point for the investigation of sectoral interests, where actors themselves identify a collective sectoral interest, and organize to defend or promote it. To examine the relationship between structure, organization and political action it may be useful to borrow from Marxist analysis the equivalent of the concepts of 'class-in-itself' and 'class-for-itself'. Like class, sector is a structural concept, and sectoral identity is a necessary but not a sufficient condition for political action. Neither classes nor sectors *as such* act politically; class and sectoral interests are identified, promoted and defended through organization. Under certain conditions, as yet imperfectly understood, firms competing in the same market may perceive a common sectoral interest and form an interest association, sometimes in response to organizations of workers. In certain cases these sectoral interests may be perceived as conflicting with the interests of capitalists in other sectors, so that sectoral identity may weaken class loyalties and the cohesion of peak associations.

In this sense, 'sector' is a 'vertical' concept, whereas 'class' refers to 'horizontal' social relationships between actors occupying a common position in a hierarchical structure. Classes are divided by sectoral identifications; sectors are marked by class distinctions, antagonisms and conflicts. Within broad class groupings we should expect to find varying degrees of sectoral consciousness, which in peak organizations may take the form of intra-organizational conflict. Intersectoral comparisons will reveal different class organizations of varying strength which may go some way towards explaining differences in sectoral politics.

An analysis of class and sectoral organizations and their relationships with state agencies may reveal important clues about the linkages between macro- and meso-levels of corporatism. So far we lack reliable data with which to test meso-corporatist hypotheses, but it is worth speculating a little about the conditions where meso-corporatist arrangements will obtain, and under what circumstances the level of corporatist intermediation shifts from macro- to meso-level. I will first discuss economic and industrial policies, and then turn to the issue of social welfare.

The relationship between macro-corporatism and economic growth discussed earlier implies that peak class organizations can negotiate and implement bargained agreements more easily where class frictions are lubricated by an expanding economic product. A deep economic recession such as that experienced since the mid-1970s creates crises in specific sectors, and in certain circumstances meso-corporatist industrial policies may be negotiated on a sectoral basis, sometimes in the form of crisis cartels for 'sunset' industries. Economic aid from either the state or the banks may be made conditional on a negotiated agreement in such areas as reduced production capacity, layoffs and plant closures. A highly developed 'sectoral consciousness' and an effective associational system, which allows the costs of restructuring to be shared between a number of firms and the state, may prove a less conflictual means of industrial adjustment than a 'no lame ducks' policy, or forced contraction through the instrument of nationalization.

Sectoral meso-corporatism seems not to require the same degree of associational capacity on a class basis that is a prerequisite for macro-corporatism. For this reason the argument discussed above (pp. 10–11), that macro-corporatism cannot be seen as a possible policy strategy for governments to adopt in response to economic recession, may not hold so strongly for corporatism at the meso-level. But as Atkinson and Coleman (chapter 2 below) point out, some sectoral associational systems are unsuited to meso-corporatism, and in some cases state agencies lack relevant expertise and are too weak to bargain independently. Nevertheless, in addition to examples of stable and persistent meso-corporatist practices which exist in the absence of any significant degree of macro-corporatism, there are examples of governments choosing to adopt meso-corporatist sectoral policies.

Welfare and consumption sectors
So far, the discussion has concentrated on sectoral interests as emerging from market differentiation in the sphere of industrial production, and the contributors to this book are concerned exclusively with this sphere. But it is worth mentioning, if only very briefly, the relevance of sectoral analysis in the welfare field. Here, sectors are differentiated much more in relation to the specific historical process of the involvement of the state in social provision, and welfare sectors correspond closely to the division of tasks within the state system. Education, social security, health services, social work and housing are among the sectoral divisions of welfare, and

in an earlier study (Cawson, 1982) I argued that an intersectoral comparison of welfare reveals different degrees of corporatist interest intermediation.

The variations were dependent in part upon the whether the sector is concerned with allocative or productive activities (Offe, 1975), and in part were a consequence of the extent to which professional groups had managed to monopolize the representation of particular producer interest categories. A common characteristic of welfare sectors in Britain is that consumer interests are relatively weakly organised, and that the politics of producer interests is divided internally along class lines. Sectoral consciousness is strong in some cases, for example in the National Health Service, where the defence of levels of spending has led to inter-class interest alliances. The strength of producer interest monopolies in social provision permits us to identify a distinctive form of welfare corporatism (Harrison, 1984) at the meso-level. Such developments are arguably less likely in countries where macro-corporatism is the prevailing mode of economic management, because in such cases social policies tend to form part of the agenda for tripartite negotiation (Wilensky, 1976), and peak class organizations are more likely than professional bodies to have a decisive voice in welfare allocation. If, as in cases of welfare corporatism, social provision is effectively controlled by the providers of welfare, the effective representation of consumer interests depends upon the welfare priorities of political parties.

It should be emphasized that this concept of sectoral divisions refers to the organization of welfare services and not to the political implications of the 'consumption' of welfare. It is distinct from the argument concerning 'consumption sectors' advocated by Dunleavy (1979, 1980a, 1980b) and others, who have suggested that the political processes of collective consumption produce sectoral cleavages according to the relation of different interest categories to the means of consumption. Dunleavy's analysis suggests that social closure around interest monopolies in the sphere of consumption is unlikely, if not impossible, and that a fluid competitive pattern of conflicting interests is the norm. The combined effects of market concentration, state provision and collective forms of consumption create interest categories that are not organizable into corporatist forms of interest intermediation, thus producing a tendency to dualism both in the sphere of consumption and the sphere of production (Cawson and Saunders, 1983; Goldthorpe, 1984).

Micro-level corporatism
The characteristic feature of corporatism at the macro-level is the involvement of peak organizations in global policy concertation; at

the meso-level it refers to political exchange between state agencies and more specialized interest associations. Much less discussed, and often not acknowledged in the way the concept has been developed, is the possibility of corporatism at the micro-level. The reason for this is that those who focus empirically on specialized interest organizations have neglected the processes by which interests can be aggregated, and interest conflicts resolved, at the micro-level of the firm without the necessity of formal interest organization. But there are good reasons for including within the scope of corporatist analysis direct bargaining between state agencies and firms, as long as we can distinguish specifically corporatist bilateral relationships from other types, such as those that Atkinson and Coleman (chapter 2 below) refer to as 'sponsored pluralism', or which others have identified as 'clientilism' or the 'franchise state' (Wolfe, 1977). In the latter cases state authorities are so weak that they depend upon firms or interest groups for vital information, and conceive of their own task as one of serving the interests of their client groups (Lapalombara, 1964: 283, 274).

The examples I have in mind are those where state agencies have a considerable degree of autonomy and bargaining power, but pursue specific policy aims by negotiating planning agreements with individual firms rather than with interest associations. Recent industrial policy in France has involved this form of intervention (Green, 1983; Estrin and Holmes, 1983a, 1983b), in which firms have signed non-legally-enforceable contracts which bind them to specific investment and employment strategies in exchange for economic assistance from the state. It may be hypothesized that such policies are adopted where a considerable degree of monopoly obtains in particular sectors, and where those sectors are identified by state actors as requiring priority intervention (to prevent collapse or to induce growth). Openly discriminatory treatment between firms in a sector (unlike the meso-corporatist crisis cartel, which is specifically designed *not* to discriminate between firms) cannot easily be negotiated by an association which defends a collective sectoral interest. But in some cases (such as that reported by Rhodes in chapter 10 below), micro-corporatist contractual agreements may follow a plan negotiated with the sectoral association.

The process of negotiating a micro-corporatist agreement is likely to involve trade union participation, which is facilitated when there is plant bargaining instead of industry-wide agreements, and thus presupposes that both peak and sectoral trade union organizations are weak. We must be careful not to identify all examples of plant-level bargaining as 'micro-corporatist' (see Bonnett, chapter 5 below). As elsewhere in corporatist arrangements, state agencies are centrally involved, either in actively securing agreements at the micro-level or in making such agreements a precondition of subsidy, assistance or support.

Such a process was envisaged in Britain under the 1974–79 Labour government's industrial strategy, where it was expected that trade unions would agree with individual managements on the terms of a planning agreement to be signed by both parties and the government (Winkler, 1975). According to the theory developed by Holland (1975), the market power of these large firms would force other firms in the industry to follow suit, thus enabling industrial policy to be implemented without the need for large-scale nationalizations. Micro-corporatism of this kind remains an important part of Labour's Alternative Economic Strategy, and a version of such planning agreements on a smaller scale is an important part of the Greater London Enterprise Board's attempt to harness private industrial power to public purposes.

There has been some discussion of a similar process of contractual bargaining between state agencies and individual firms in the area of land-use planning at the local level in Britain. Jowell (1977) reported a tendency for local councils to use their power to withhold planning permission for new development to initiate bargaining over public facilities to be included in private developments. Such arrangements (often undisclosed) were argued by Jowell (and later by Reade, 1982) to be part of a corporatist trend in British planning administration, and are specific examples of the more general form of non-bureaucratic administration discussed by Winkler (1977). Those, like Winkler, who identify corporatism with a mode of policy implementation rather than as a process of interest intermediation may have little hesitation in describing such processes as 'corporatist', but those who see it as the mediation of conflict between interests through the intervention of the state may insist that intermediary organizations are a necessary part of corporatism.

It is worth pointing out, however, that the conceptual definition advanced on p. 8 above reflected the argument that the constitutive feature of corporatism is the fusion of representation and control in securing policy which is implemented by delegated self-enforcement. The act of persuading firms to honour agreements which are not legally enforceable by granting them certain monopoly powers — which is what is involved in this case — seems to me to be consistent with the generic concept, and also seems substantively an important development which raises a number of questions concerning how formally democratic state institutions conduct their business — questions which, if not unique to the corporatist debate, are certainly central to it.

If we resist the temptation to foreclose by definition the existence of corporatism at the micro-level, we can pursue the issues related to the organization of interests within the firm. Some corporatist theory takes interest organizations as its central concern and insists that, for corporatism to be present, there must be interest intermediation through specialized and differentiated organizations. Firms in a sector are then treated theoretically as individual members of such organizations. There seem to be a number of problems with such an approach, but the most important is the failure to pose the question of the relationship between contractual agreements involving single firms and state agencies and corporatism at meso- and macro-levels. In the case of industrial policy, sectoral aims might be pursued through a 'national champions' or 'backing winners' or 'nursing lame ducks' policy of a micro-corporatist kind. State assistance may then be made conditional upon specific agreements at plant level between management and unions. We might then hypothesize that such an approach is likely, either where macro- and meso-corporatist solutions have broken down, or where the interest associational preconditions did not exist in the first place.

Conclusion
This chapter has been concerned with the theoretical task of devising ways in which the evident variety of corporatist practice may be distinguished. Previous work suggested distinctions between state and societal variants, between corporatism as interest intermediation and corporatism as policy concertation, and between sectoral and trans-sectoral types. I have argued that the second distinction is unhelpful, at least in so far as we are dealing with policy-making in capitalist democracies where concertation requires intermediation (but see Coleman, chapter 6 below). The first distinction was originally devised to capture the differences between authoritarian and democratic regimes, but its utility is not limited to that. In the following chapter Atkinson and Coleman find it useful to distinguish between different corporatist arrangements at a sectoral level.

The distinction between sectoral and trans-sectoral corporatism is important, particularly when we link it to the levels of corporatism identified in this chapter. Macro-corporatism is inherently trans-sectoral — perhaps we should say pan-sectoral — in that it involves encompassing class organizations which aggregate interests across sectors. Trans-sectoral policy-making may, however, be limited to a more restricted range of issues than those which arise from the interrelationships at the level of the whole political economy, and

FIGURE 1
Varieties of corporatism in economic/industrial policy

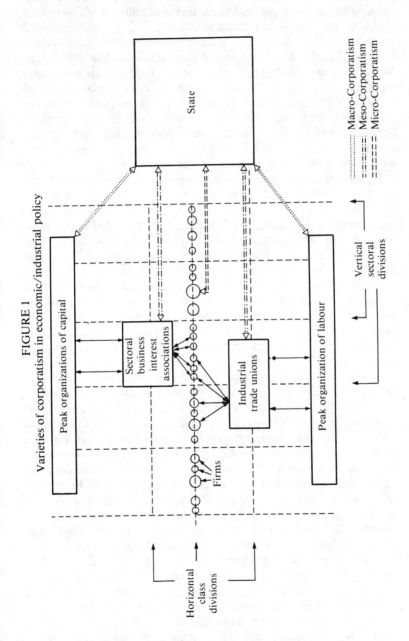

may involve limited collaboration between sectoral interest associations as well as peak organizations. But in examining the conditions under which macro-corporatism obtains, and in analysing such trans-sectoral policy issues as industrial training or incomes policy, the importance of the meso-level becomes clear. As Boston and Vickerstaff demonstrate in subsequent chapters, the effective maintenance of class organization among both workers and employers which is necessary to sustain macro-corporatism can be undermined by factors operating at the meso-level. The distinction between sectoral and trans-sectoral policy-making, and that between macro-, meso- and micro-levels, are both necessary if we are to capture the variety and complexity of neo-corporatism.

Figure 1 is a graphical representation of the distinctions between sector and class, and between different levels of corporatist intermediation, which are important to the understanding of industrial policy-making. It adds nothing to what has been said in the text, but two points are worth making. First, the line between capital and labour is drawn through the middle of the firms. Corporatist practices blur this line through sectoral and trans-sectoral class-collaborative arrangements, but when their limits are exposed in economic crises, there is a tendency for the level of engagement to shift back to the micro-level, but not to the unfettered market, for the state remains a major presence. Second, the links between collective actors are drawn as being two-way so as to emphasize that corporatism is a process of political exchange — although not free exchange — and that corporatist interest organizations define as well as defend their members' interests.

The chapters which follow present case material covering seven industrial sectors, and two trans-sectoral issues crucial to industrial policy — training and incomes policy — in seven countries. The scope is wide, but it would be idle to suggest that the comparisons made allow us to reach exhaustive conclusions concerning the causes, effects or conditions of meso-corporatism, or the fit between institutional patterns and policy outcomes. Indeed, as I shall argue in the concluding chapter, 'the state' remains something of a mystery, and it is important that some of the attention which has so far been given by students of corporatism to interest associations and private interest government should now be diverted to the study of the internal organization of the state. The following chapters suggest that considerable progress has been made in refining corporatist theory and examining corporatist practice in some of the relatively 'hidden' reaches of capitalist democracies. We cannot yet, with any confidence, suggest comparative measures of meso-corporatism, but at least its existence is beginning to be acknowledged and the foundations uncovered. The structure appears to be sound, although we must note on the surveyor's report that some improvements need to be made.

Note

This chapter was written, and the book was edited, while I was a Jean Monnet Fellow at the European University Institute in Florence. I would like to express my thanks to the Institute, and, for comments on and discussion of this chapter, to Philippe Schmitter, Bill Coleman, Peter Saunders, Wolfgang Streeck, Erling Rasmussen, Jelle Visser, Wyn Grant and Kevin Bonnett.

2
Corporatism and industrial policy

Michael M. Atkinson and William D. Coleman

Persistent inflation, lagging productivity and high levels of unemployment are problems that have been common to most Western
industrialized countries during the 1975–85 decade. With varying
levels of enthusiasm and consistency, the state in each of these
countries has experimented with different economic formulae in an
effort to restore the postwar economic boom. No one seems to
doubt that the state has some responsibility in this regard. One of
the reasons that the present economic malaise has been referred to
as a crisis of the state is the widespread belief that activities of
industrialized states are in large measure responsible for the arrest
of economic growth.

Among the most prominent of the economic solutions urged on
the political leadership of Western industrialized countries is that of
industrial policy. While macro-economic management policies are
used to plot the broad course of economic development, industrial
policies are sectoral in nature. They urge the strategic deployment
of selected policy instruments to achieve goals that are specific to
each industrial sector (Magaziner and Reich, 1982). Two types of
industrial policy will be discussed in this chapter. The first will be
termed 'positive adjustment policy' and will refer to measures
adopted to facilitate movement of labour and capital from the
production of goods and services in declining demand to the
production of those where demand is increasing, from less to more
efficient forms and locations of production, and from production in
which other countries are gaining a comparative advantage to new
competitive lines of production (OECD, 1979:82). The second type
will be called 'large-scale restructuring' and will involve not
abandoning a sector but staying with it and changing radically its
structural base. Such a policy will normally be complemented by
attempts to stabilize profit levels in the sector through the
introduction of controls on inputs, whether these be raw materials
or labour. In either case, the state is drawn more and more into
long-term production decisions.

This type of economic policy-making has always had more
support in some countries than in others. Japan and France, for

example, have traditionally placed greater emphasis on economic growth through the transformation of key industrial sectors than have, say, Britain and the USA, where commitment to a liberal international economy has meant reliance on commercial and monetary policy instruments. Peter Katzenstein (1978) has suggested that the willingness of countries to adopt particular economic policies depends on the composition and stability of the ruling coalition; the capacity of countries to do so depends on the centralization of society, the centralization of the state and the degree of differentiation between the two. This latter set of factors, which Katzenstein refers to as the policy network, conditions, he suggests, the choice of policy instruments in any given country.

In this chapter we will outline three types of policy networks which might be associated with the introduction of industrial policy — pressure pluralism, sponsored or clientele pluralism and corporatism — and argue that of these three corporatism is the arrangement most conducive to the successful pursuit of industrial policy. While it has been appreciated for some time that the success of particular economic policies is often contingent on the presence of congenial systems of public sector–private sector relations, research on industrial policy has not been informed by recent theories of corporatism (but see Zysman, 1983). This is partly because corporatism has been viewed primarily as a total society phenomenon and not as a sectoral one. We will argue, however, that the political economy of industrial policy forces a serious consideration of corporatist structures because these will reduce the likelihood of social conflict but still permit orderly change. What corporatism offers is a means whereby the capitalist state can manipulate the system of interest representation both to structure and to lower demands. Broad appeals for self-restraint and self-discipline can be replaced by negotiated settlements among producer groups and the state.

Part of the reason for the reluctance with which some capitalist states approach industrial policy is that the conditions for corporatism, which are likely to enhance its prospects for success, are not present. Corporatism is not a necessary condition for the pursuit of industrial policy, but it will enhance the prospects for putting such a policy into place. Other types of policy networks cannot sustain the intensive collaboration needed for the pursuit of an industrial policy. None the less, there is every reason to expect that corporatist forms, which are specifically created for such collaboration, will develop more rapidly and more completely in some sectors than in others. In an argument that parallels Katzenstein, we will suggest that corporatism will develop in those sectors in which there

is a strong demand for industrial policies, where the state
bureaucracy is centralized and autonomous, and where the political
organization of the private sector permits major socioeconomic
producer groups to contribute to the development and implementation of these policies. This chapter will detail the conditions under
which sectoral corporatism can be expected to develop and then will
illustrate the importance of these conditions by comparing policies
in two industrial sectors — dairy and pharmaceuticals — in a single
country — Canada.

Policy networks: from pluralism to corporatism
'Policy network' is the term we will employ to denote relations
between the state and organized interests in the private sector. As a
means of distinguishing among different types of policy networks we
will concentrate attention on the structures of interest representation, their relationships with other groups and the role they are
expected to play in the policy process. On the basis of these three
dimensions, several types of networks might logically be posited,
but in reality three are dominant: pressure pluralism, sponsored or
clientele pluralism, and corporatism.[1]
  Of these, the most widely recognized is pressure pluralism.
Celebrated in volumes on interest group activity in the USA,
interest groups operate largely on their own, failing to integrate into
encompassing systems of representation. They have highly differentiated, narrow, very specialized and overlapping domains and
are often competitive with one another for members as well as for
the ear of the state. The dynamics of the system of associations
foster individual rather than concertative group activity and
increasing differentiation and specialization. In their relations with
the state, associations in a pressure pluralism network meet the
state independently of other groups and remain outside the formal
policy-making process. One short step removed from the electoral
process, these associations are typically more attentive to politicians
than to bureaucrats, and they search constantly for means of
applying political pressure.
  In a sponsored or clientele pluralism network, the associational
system shows the same structural pattern noted above: little formal
integration, high differentiation of domains, and competition
among member associations. Associations meet the state on their
own rather than in concert with other groups. The dynamics of the
system favour differentiation rather than integration and concertation. However, unlike pressure pluralism, sponsored pluralism
involves the incorporation of groups into the processes for
formulating and implementing policy. Individual groups dealing

with a weak state agency are able to secure these privileges through political clout or having a monopoly on expertise. Alan Wolfe (1977) has described this practice as the franchise state and identified the 1920s as the high water mark of its popularity. According to Theodore Lowi (1979), the franchise state has yet to lose its appeal in the USA. Under the name of 'interest group liberalism' it constitutes for Lowi a Second Republic, having replaced the First Republic which was built around the practice of federalism, a strong Congress and the politics of patronage and subsidy. In the new Republic the state, faced with the growth of irreconcilable demands, seeks to keep organized interests apart by delegating to each some measure of public authority. Among the by-products of this practice is a system of privilege in which certain groups are accorded special status by virtue of their association with the activities of the state. This, as Lowi (1979:60) points out, is not merely pluralism, but *sponsored* pluralism. Somewhat similar practices in Italy have been noted by Lapalombara (1964), who invents the term 'clientela' to capture the phenomenon.

Plagued by definitional disputes, corporatism will be understood here to be both a mode of interest organization (Schmitter, 1982) and a means for making and implementing public policy (Lehmbruch 1979, 1982; Buksti and Johansen, 1979). Unlike our first two policy networks, associations are vertically integrated into encompassing systems which seek to concentrate the representation of interests into a few organizations which are themselves centralized, highly representative bodies with a monopoly on representation. Unlike pluralist systems, the dynamics of the system favour increasing integration and concentration.

In fact, corporatism bears only a surface resemblance to sponsored pluralism in that in both policy networks associations are incorporated into the processes of policy formulation and implementation and may be delegated certain state powers. In addition to the different structural properties of associational systems and distinctive dynamics to these systems, the policy process itself is different in the two cases. In corporatism, more than one economic interest is being represented at the policy table, and these economic interests are in conflict (von Beyme, 1983). The network is established to mediate and contain this conflict. These several economic interests may be represented by separate associations; or, in some cases where the conflict is among different fractions of the same class, they may be represented by a single, more encompassing, association. A corporatist network will function successfully only if the state is strong and autonomous and not open to capture, as in the case of sponsored pluralism. The state is capable of exacting a promise by the associations to control their members (Crouch, 1983a), something it cannot do in sponsored pluralism. Corporatism is installed as a complement to territorial representation, one based on negotiated consensus among producer groups and the state, rather than on institutionalized conflict among political parties (Lehmbruch, 1979:180–1).

Observers of corporatism have tended to treat it primarily as a macro-level phenomenon, that is, as a property, to a greater or lesser degree, of particular states.[2] Seen as either an alternative to capitalism (Winkler, 1976) or a political structure within capitalism (Panitch, 1979a), the stress has been on the system-wide functions that corporatism performs. Chief among these have been the disciplining of wage labour in the administration of incomes policy (Lehmbruch, 1979; Panitch, 1979a) and the enhancement of regime governability through the control of demand overload (Schmitter, 1981; Offe, 1981). Thus the tripartite board responsible for developing macroeconomic polices, from tax expenditures to wage restraints, has come to be seen as *the* classic corporatist institution.

Efforts to create tripartite structures for political mediation in Canada have been infrequent and generally unsuccessful (Panitch, 1979b). The system of labour organizations in Canada meets virtually none of the organizational requirements for corporatism (Adams, 1982), and the several peak business associations either have no relation to sectoral associations, and are therefore incapable of aggregating interests, or are, at best, loose federations. There have been no social democratic governments at the national level to create and legitimize corporatist arrangements, and relatively high levels of unemployment have encouraged business to concentrate on securing guarantees from the state rather than labour. In short, the structural conditions associated with corporatism are, in Canada, conspicuous by their absence.

These observations are valid, however, primarily at the macro-level of analysis, that is at the level of nationwide politico-economic structures. Information on corporatism in various sectors of the economy is largely unavailable, not only in Canada but also in other OECD countries. This is mainly because of the total society perspective which has dominated studies of corporatism. However, there also exists, as Wassenberg (1982:85) has recently emphasized, a meso-level which includes the more or less institutionalized entity of complete industries, regional public authorities and the industry-wide and regional managerial machines of trade associations and labour unions. It is his argument that, where the macro-level is used for acts of symbolic polarization among groups and where there is class confrontaton at the micro- or firm level, the meso-, or sectoral, level is likely to become the place for bargaining. For this reason industrial policies, which are inherently sectoral in nature, will meet fewer obstacles than policies cast at either the micro- or macro-levels.[3]

Wassenberg's emphasis on the meso-level in the study of corporatism would appear to be particularly attractive for countries like Canada or the USA, where the macro-level has been chàracterized by considerable posturing among producer groups through the medium of weak organizations on both the labour and business side. On the micro-plane, labour unrest has been among the highest for OECD countries. It may suit all parties, in such circumstances, to attempt to contain group conflict by transferring it to the sectoral level where it can be compartmentalized and quietly managed by sectoral bureaucrats representing producer groups and the state (Wassenberg, 1982:94–5).

Changing the focus of attention from the macro- to the sectoral level will necessitate a reconsideration of the factors conducive to corporatism. At bottom, of course, the purpose of corporatism remains the same at both levels: to mediate political differences and achieve consensus on economic goals among major producer groups. The need for inclusive, hierarchical and non-voluntary organizations will be just as pressing at the meso- as at the macro-level. But the likelihood of achieving this type of structure and the incentive for attempting to create corporatism will vary by sector. This variation, we will argue, depends on the institutional structure of the economy and the organization of the state in each sector.

Conditions for sectoral corporatism

Corporatism will be closely associated with industrial policy because the success of the latter is dependent on how readily producer groups will agree to accept the inevitable dislocations associated with economic adjustment. As a distinctive policy network, corporatism promises to deliver consensus on the goals and instruments of policy and to be a vehicle through which the state can share responsibility for implementation as well as policy direction.

Sectoral corporatism then becomes more likely when industrial policy itself is a viable option. This requires, in the first place, that the dominant policy problem in a sector be defined in terms of the long-term viability of the sector as a component of the national economy.[4] It also requires that, as a means of addressing the problem, the state employs sector-specific policy measures as well as macroeconomic policies or such horizontal policy instruments as competition legislation and research and development incentives.

None the less, industrial policies of the positive adjustment or large-scale restructuring sort will almost inevitably entail severe economic and social dislocation for some capitalists and, even more likely, for some groups of workers. Thus these policies hold out the prospect of discontent and perhaps severe social conflict. In sectors which are deemed to require such policies, corporatist political structures therefore become a serious option for the state. They provide the means for creating a policy community which extends beyond the borders of the state. As in the classic models of corporatism at the macro-level, the emphasis is on achieving consensus among producer groups and the state, with the former ultimately bearing much of the burden of implementation. This represents an attractive alternative to the extremes of neglect and coercion, and one implicitly endorsed by the OECD (1979:87): 'The need for adjustment will ... be better understood and more readily accepted where there are effective arrangements for consultation between social partners, both bipartite and tripartite, from the earliest possible moment.'

In spite of this, the creation of corporatist arrangements and the decision to pursue an industrial policy need not occur simultaneously. Indeed, each can develop without the other. However, corporatism and industrial policy are complementary state strategies. The state is more likely to encourage the development of corporatist arrangements if it is committed to an industrial policy, or more likely to pursue an industrial policy if corporatist arrangements are in place.

If the dominant policy problem in a sector is defined in such a manner that some form of industrial policy is deemed to be a reasonable response, under what conditions can the state expect to develop or nourish corporatist institutions that will facilitate this policy direction? We will argue here that it is conditions peculiar to each economic sector that are crucial to the development of what might be called 'sectoral corporatism'. Specifically, sectoral corporatism requires, first, economic conditions conducive to a 'developed' associational system and, second, a centralized, autonomous state bureaucracy.

A developed system of interest associations is one which is centralized, integrated and highly representative of the sector (Marin, 1983). The fate of corporatism in a given sector will depend in some measure on whether the institutional structure of the economy in that sector can contribute to a developed associational system. Three aspects of this institutional structure are particularly important. The first of these is the degree of foreign control in the sector. In sectors where there is a mixture of foreign and domestic firms, there will be significant obstacles to associative action because of the conflicting needs and orientations of these two types of firms. Moreover, if a sector is greatly dominated by foreign firms, this fact alone may restrict the range of policy instruments that can be employed. Investment decisions, profit levels and even wage increases may not be subject to influence by the host state.[5] If government policies are unable to influence the behaviour of major private sector actors, then neither corporatism nor an industrial policy may be viable options for the state.

Second, the international competitiveness of firms in the sector will affect the integration of the associational system. The more internationally competitive firms are in a sector, the more difficult it will be to create an integrated associational system. Such firms will favour free trade policies and minimal state intervention. Associative action in this case is likely to be irregular and less formal, and many firms will prefer to engage the state on their own behalf rather than rely on intermediaries. On the other hand, firms oriented to and subject to strong competition for the domestic market are more likely to engage in associative action (Schmitter and Streeck, 1981:22–8; Olson, 1982). They will seek protectionism, and once the measures are in place will need to defend against attacks on them.

Finally, the development of the association system will also depend on the degree of concentration in the sector. Sectors that are oligopolistic will be in a better position to engage in and reap the benefits of associative action (Schmitter and Streeck, 1981:22–8). John Zysman (1977:69–73, 201–8) has shown, for example, that in the French steel industry oligopoly facilitated a corporatist-like restructuring of the firms in that sector.[6]

The presence of a developed associational system is a necessary, but not a sufficient, condition for sectoral corporatism. Equally important is the organization of the state in each sector. Pierre Birnbaum (1982b) has argued persuasively that most of the recent discussions of corporatism have ignored the question of what institutional characteristics the state should possess if corporatism is to develop and be sustained. For him, it is essential that the state possess a significant degree of autonomy from society, an autonomy which is likely to occur only where the state bureaucracy is well developed and self-contained. It is this autonomy which permits the bureaucracy to develop and defend a conception of the public interest which is more than the sum of particular interests. In a similar vein, Katzenstein (1978:308) has argued that the degree of differentiation between state and society will have a profound effect upon the policy network constructed to link the two. Without some differentiation, efforts to induce cooperation among producer groups are likely to culminate in the type of de-bureaucratization associated with sponsored pluralism.

Under what conditions will a bureaucracy develop autonomy or become differentiated from society? Three conditions seem particularly important.

1. The bureaus involved in a given sector should have a clearly defined conception of their role and a value system that supports that role. This property is likely to be enhanced when a bureau has been given a functional mandate rather than one which demands the representation of a particular clientele.[7] There is less likelihood in the case of a functional mandate that bureaucrats will adopt the industry's norms and expectations as their own. Autonomy will be further enhanced if the personnel in the bureau tend to be drawn from a specialized professional group with well-developed professional values (for example, engineers, medical doctors, physical scientists). The professional ethos of the group will further enhance bureaucratic autonomy if it is distinct from the ethos which prevails among professionals in the industry.

2. The bureau administers a corpus of law and regulations that defines barriers between itself and the sector. These rules will clearly reflect a set of values and principles, and will not be open to the type of bargaining associated with sponsored pluralism. Again, such a body of law will likely be housed in a bureau with a functional mandate rather than a representative one. To the extent that the values and principles of the rules are clearly defined, they are likely to become values and principles with which the bureau identifies, thus reinforcing the role definition and distinctive value system of the bureau.

3. The bureau itself generates the information, technical and otherwise, which it needs for the pursuit of its mandate. Information of a technical sort is vital to industrial policy-making in advanced economies (Mayntz and Scharpf, 1975). If the bureau is unable to generate the information it needs for policy-making, it becomes dependent on firms or sector associations. The development of in-house information may take place in one of two ways: legislation may exist forcing firms and unions to provide the details the bureau needs, or the bureau may have the expertise among its own staff to create the information base it requires. If this in-house capacity should exist, it is likely to coincide with the presence of a professional group within the bureau.

In addition to autonomy, Katzenstein (1978:324) has stressed the degree of centralization of the state for understanding the policy networks that are likely to develop. For sectoral corporatism to exist, the state agents belonging to a corporatist structure must possess the wherewithal to agree on a decision and bend the government to it. The consensus needed for corporatism is most likely to emerge when a single agency or bureau dominates, bureaucratically, a given sector. A hegemonic bureau of this kind would be capable of aggregating authority from regional decision points, thus making decisions binding on a nationwide basis. The presence of multiple agencies, on the other hand, with overlapping jurisdictions and engaged in bureaucratic competition, makes corporatism rather more difficult to achieve.

The presence of a hegemonic bureau in a sector is not a sufficient condition for corporatism. Given the long-term nature of the policies that are likely to be applied, some stability in the state structure is also highly desirable. At any given time there may be a hegemonic bureau for a sector, but the actual bureau playing this role might change relatively frequently. At the sectoral level this translates into a bureaucracy that has little autonomy from firms and associations. Such a bureaucracy can be expected to transform itself frequently to match changes in the sector, be open to capture by the sector and, in short, fall into the classic pattern of sponsored pluralism. Such a bureaucratic structure will also encourage pluralism in the associational system and hence will lead to a decline in the capacity of the private sector to engage in corporatist decision-making.[8]

It is important to emphasize that the implementation of industrial policy will place significant stress upon the bureaucratic organization of the state, and this may prove to be the primary impediment to its introduction. Positive adjustment or restructuring policies will typically involve the application of *multiple* policy instruments in a *coordinated* manner. In most Western states, these instruments normally have been housed in different departments and agencies. For the state to achieve the bureaucratic coordination and centralization which are necessary for corporatism, well-entrenched, bureaucratic vested interests may need to be removed. The state organization prerequisites for corporatism often may be the most difficult to satisfy and therefore the most important reason why corporatism does not develop in a sector that otherwise would appear to be admirably suited to it.

In the following sections we amplify upon our argument by showing how corporatist institutions have developed in the dairy sector of the Canadian policy system and how sponsored pluralism is the dominant network in the pharmaceuticals sector. This discussion will parallel the argument up to now by focusing on the organization of the state and on the impact that the institutional structure of the economy has on the association system in each sector. Although these cases can only illustrate our argument, they will underline our basic contention that corporatist arrangements will be available to facilitate the pursuit of industrial policy only in sectors where the conditions identified above are met.

Industrial policy in the dairy processing sector

The dominant structural characteristic of the Canadian dairy processing industry is its vulnerability. Except for the fluid milk part of the industry, where perishability and transport costs provide some insulation from competitive forces, most products of this industry, particularly cheese, butter and powdered milk, are susceptible to international competition. Since the 1930s, successive governments have recognized that if a Canadian dairy industry was to be retained it would require a large measure of protection.

In the late 1960s, in the face of rising political action by farmers and the evident discontent of processors, the state declared its intention to provide this protection and stability.[9] Domestic requirements for processed dairy products and fluid milk would be met as much as possible from Canadian sources; there would be price stability and a reasonable level of return for dairy producers; and Canadian consumers would have an assured supply of 'high-quality' dairy products (Stonehouse, 1979). The dairy industry would become almost exclusively a domestic one with the home market reserved for domestic producers. To reduce the negative consequences of such a blatantly protectionist policy, a transformation of the dairy industry was also undertaken. Milk production was to become more efficient, which meant that the number of dairy farms would have to be reduced and their relative size increased. The processing sector was to be rationalized through the elimination of numerous small establishments in favour of large, more specialized and efficient concerns.

By the late 1970s progress had been made in all areas through the manipulation of supply quotas and prices (Barichello, 1981:48ff.; Mitchell, 1975:123–32). By 1978 dairy was essentially a domestic industry: only 2.3 percent of the market was served by imported dairy products, and dairy exports amounted to only 2.5 percent of production.[10] The number of establishments manufacturing dairy products dropped from 1413 in 1965 to 416 in 1981; the number of dairy farms fell from 308,980 in 1961 to 67,889 in 1981. At the same time the number of large farms (over 93 cows) increased by more than ten-fold (Statistics Canada; Barichello, 1981:7).

To achieve these goals it was necessary for the state to arrange a concordat between usually warring farmers and processors in which both sides would tolerate major structural changes in their respective sectors in return for order and stability. It was under these circumstances that the 'corporatist temptation' arose. To relieve the stress occasioned by major structural change, the state sought to absorb producer and processor associations into a system in which they would participate in the design and administration of the instruments of industrial policy. In the service of their own long-term interests, broad-based producers' associations would be harnessed to goals already articulated by the state. Such a use of corporatist structures in the Canadian dairy industry is similar to practices in many Western states (Grant, 1983a; Traxler, 1983; van Waarden, 1983).

The most important goal of industrial policy in the dairy sector has been the management of the milk supply. Through a federal cabinet order and the delegation of similar provincial powers to marketing boards, the governments in Canada set the total amount of milk to be produced in the country in a given year. The amount of industrial milk (milk for processed dairy products) to be produced is decided upon by an organization called the Canadian Milk Supply Management Committee. This committee is composed of delegates from the Canadian Dairy Commission representing the federal government, from provincial departments of agriculture represent-ing the provincial governments, and from provincial marketing boards representing the dairy farmers. In addition, the National Dairy Council representing the dairy processors on the federal plane, and the Ontario and Quebec dairy councils representing processors on the provincial plane, are ex officio members of the committee. This quasi-corporatist organization is complemented by more pure corporatist forms at the provincial levels. The provincial marketing boards have been delegated responsibility under the dairy policy for fixing the price of milk sold to the processors and for allocating quotas to individual plants. These decisions are taken by committees of the marketing boards that are fully tripartite in that farmers, processors (through their provincial associations) and the government are all full members.

The remaining policy instruments — including import controls, income stabilization and subsidies for exports — all complement supply management. The state retains ultimate authority for their exercise, but by virtue of the corporatist arrangements that prevail in supply management, tripartite consultation is a regular feature of decision-making. No decision on these matters would be taken by the state agency concerned — the Canadian Dairy Commission

(CDC) — without first referring the matter to its Advisory Committee which includes associations representing both farmers and processors. In addition, dairy processors participate in the maintenance of quality control in the industry since dairy products must be of sufficiently high quality to justify insulating the market. In short, the state has no interest in pursuing a course of action in this sector independent of the industry and its sector associations. When asked about the regularity of consultation, one official replied: 'All the time, all the time. I think our lesson has been that we wouldn't want to put out any piece of legislation that industry hasn't laid its hands on.'

The economic structure of the dairy industry has facilitated the development of an associational system along corporatist lines. Dairy producers in Canada are represented by one association at the national level, the Dairy Farmers of Canada (DFC). This association has 19 member associations including the nine provincial milk marketing boards. These boards are completely representative of farmers in the respective provinces because dairy farmers must be members if they are to market their milk. Hence the DFC represents every dairy farmer in Canada and suffers no competitors when it comes to the formulation and implementation of dairy policy on the national plane. The system of associations is only a little weaker on the processors' side. The National Dairy Council (NDC) is seen to be the sole representative of the dairy processing industry on the federal level. It claims to have firms representing 95 percent of the industry on its rolls and adds that the two firms outside its membership are usually briefed on developments (interview, December 1981). The success enjoyed by the NDC in its organization of the industry is due in some measure to the relatively high level of industry concentration and the fact that foreign firms in the industry are, like Canadian-owned firms, simply producing for the domestic market.[11]

We have argued that two aspects of government organization — the presence of a hegemonic bureau and the existence of a bureaucracy autonomous from the sector — are also necessary for the development of sectoral corporatism. If we examine the five groups of instruments being used to implement the Canadian dairy policy, in four of these — import controls, market management, stabilization subsidies and export programmes — the organization of the state meets the first of the requirements; the Canadian Dairy Commission (CDC) effectively controls and coordinates these crucial instruments. It is the fifth instrument group — quality control — where the state presents a less than united front. Three federal departments are involved in this area: Agriculture (product grades and standards, and plant registration), Health and Welfare (compositional and processing standards) and Consumer and Corporate Affairs (packaging and labelling).

Even here, however, the bureaucracy is not as divided as it might appear because the Department of Agriculture plays a coordinating role. The regulations under the Canada Agricultural Products Standards Act administered by that department incorporate directly the compositional and sanitation standards developed by Health and Welfare under the Food and Drugs Act. This practice has the dual effects of presenting one set of guidelines to the industry and of lessening considerably the possibility of competition between the two bureaus in their areas of overlap. Similarly, Agriculture Canada has a formal agreement with the Department of Consumer and Corporate Affairs whereby the latter department has delegated to the former its responsibilities for packaging and labelling as they are administered to the processors at the point of manufacture. Consumer and Corporate Affairs then exercises its responsibilities only at the retail level.

In the application, then, of each of these five groups of policy instruments, the state speaks, more or less, with one voice. However, in order for corporatism to develop, the state must also be able to coordinate these several instruments. In the Canadian case, the potential exists for considerable coordination, again through the Department of Agriculture. Given this department's pre-eminent position in the quality control area, and given further that the Canadian Dairy Commission is an agency for which the Minister of Agriculture is responsible, that Minister is theoretically in a position to coordinate directly the application of the instruments in all five groups. Relatively speaking, the Minister of Agriculture has had some success in that the various policy instruments in play have been coordinated and have not worked at cross purposes. On the other hand, the CDC is a crown agency and not directly part of the Department of Agriculture. This lessens somewhat the control exercised by the Minister over the CDC, and the two have been known to be in conflict in recent years. If this sort of conflict were to become more intense, associations would be drawn in as pressure groups, policy coordination would be weakened, and corporatist arrangements would be undermined.

When it comes to the autonomy of the sectoral bureaucracies, the situation, at first blush, does not appear conducive to a corporatist policy network. The Food Production and Inspection Branch of Agriculture Canada, which administers the Canada Agricultural Products Standards Act, does not define its role and responsibilities in a manner which guarantees its autonomy from the industry. Its personnel are often recruited from industry, and the bureau has reconciled itself to the marketing orientation that the Department of Agriculture adopted in the late 1970s. This orientation, which has also influenced the behaviour of the CDC, predisposes the department to treat the industry as its client.

None the less, the autonomy of the state bureaucracy is considerably enhanced by the corpus of law and regulations in effect in the sector. The Food and Drugs Act is very precise and comprehensive in what it defines to be appropriate properties of foods, although as we shall see, the same does not apply in the case of drugs. The independence of the sectoral bureaucracies is also encouraged by the fact that most of the technical information for application of the instruments in question is generated within the state. The several departments involved in quality control have their own inspectors and laboratories for assessing compliance with the regulations. Economic information on the industry is provided by the government statistics bureau. These data are of sufficient quality that, not only do the government departments use them effectively, but so do the associations, which for this reason do not maintain their own statistical programmes.

In summary, a heavily interventionist set of policies has been utilized in the Canadian dairy industry to insulate the domestic market from international competition and to restructure the farming and processing sectors. These policies have been implemented through corporatist political structures. The use of corporatist forms was made possible by an industrial organization and by policy instruments that have encouraged the strong collective organization of producer and processor interests. The state organization dealing with the sector is quite centralized, and its corpus of regulations and information-gathering capacity have allowed it to differentiate itself from the industry. These properties have provided fertile ground for the growth of sectoral corporatism.

The pharmaceuticals sector
In the pharmaceuticals industry in Canada, there is currently no industrial policy in effect or being planned. It is, of course, not inconceivable that such a policy might be countenanced at a later date. If this were to take place, pursuit of the policy would not be facilitated by the existing policy network in this sector, which is one of sponsored pluralism. We turn now to an examination of this network.

The international pharmaceuticals industry is dominated by approximately 100 firms who produce and sell pharmaceuticals on a world-wide basis. World trade in pharmaceuticals is relatively unencumbered by tariff barriers but a significant amount of foreign direct investment has none the less placed the plants of final dosage manufacturers in most OECD countries. Research and development is normally concentrated in a single country, usually the country of origin, but the manufacture of fine chemicals, the active ingredients of ethical (or prescription) drugs, can be manufactured anywhere that the technical skills are available. This makes the industry relatively 'footloose', able to migrate to those countries which offer tax or other inducements.

In Canada the pharmaceuticals industry is, in a rather pronounced fashion, multinational. By 1975 the subsidiaries of 'foreign' firms (that is, less than 50 percent domestically owned) had captured 85 percent of the domestic market (Canada, Industry, Trade and Commerce, 1979:7; Gordon and Fowler, 1981), a proportion among the highest in OECD countries. The industry in Canada devoted approximately 3 percent of sales to R&D in both 1968 and 1976, significantly less than half of the R&D spending in the USA (Gordon and Fowler, 1981:79). The bulk of this spending, moreover, has been devoted to satisfying the clinical and pre-clinical testing requirements of the Department of Health and Welfare. Virtually all of the fine chemicals used in the manufacturing process in Canada are imported, as are an increasing number of finished products (Gordon and Fowler, 1981:47). As a result, in 1978 Canada exported $60 million of pharmaceuticals but imported $264 million. In short, the multinational pharmaceuticals industry does virtually nothing in Canada which it does not do elsewhere, and the national industry is too small and fragmented to consider seriously the development of export markets.

The policy objective of the Canadian government in this sector has been simply to ensure the availability of drugs that are safe, effective, and reasonably priced. Behind this rather assuring formula lies a particular view of drug use and deep-seated contradictions with respect to objectives. Following the pattern in the USA, the emphasis on safety has led to a movement away from self-medication (through the use of proprietary drugs) and towards medication by doctors through prescription drugs (Temin, 1982). The importance of efficacy is a more recent requirement and one which has reduced the range of drugs available to doctors. The contradictions in the policy emerge from the emphasis on safety and efficacy on the one hand and price on the other. The research required to ensure the former, particularly efficacy, is not always conducive to low prices. Moreover, the instruments chosen by the government to pursue these objectives are not easily coordinated, as we shall see below.

The type of policy network that emerges in this sector is sponsored pluralism: rather than enhancing its capacity to pursue long-term adjustment policies through collaboration with several major producer groups, the state abdicates its authority in certain limited policy areas to a single, narrowly specialized producer group. A sponsored pluralism network is found in both the prescription and the proprietary drug industries. For the sake of brevity, we shall examine several policy instruments affecting the former industry to illustrate this pattern of concertation.

The association representing the prescription drug industry in Canada is the Pharmaceuticals Manufacturers Association of Canada (PMAC), and the agency most actively devoted to the government's objectives is the Health Protection Branch (HPB) of the Department of Health and Welfare. The sponsored pluralism network joining these two actors is based on two general consultative mechanisms. In the first of these, officials from the HPB are drawn together in joint committees with representatives from PMAC committees. At the most senior level the assistant deputy minister responsible for the branch has an advisory committee of officials which meets with the Board of Directors of the association twice yearly to discuss 'major impending regulatory change and major impending policy determination' (interview, HPB official, 1982). At lower levels several joint committees meet regularly to work out regulatory changes and guidelines. In addition to joint committees, the second consultative mechanism used by HPB has been the information letter. Changes envisaged by officials are detailed in a letter to the industry and reactions are solicited. These comments are usually furnished by the association following a discussion with its members. This rather formal description of the information letter approach probably overstates the initiative taken by the government. As one official in HPB reported, 'We consult with the association before we even go out with the original proposal to discuss with them.'

The successful development of these consultative mechanisms had led the state to experiment with the delegation of authority. Two examples can be cited to illustrate this aspect of the sponsored pluralism network in this sector.

1. *Safety and good manufacturing practices.* Under the terms of the Food and Drugs Act, since the mid-1950s government inspectors have been empowered to enter manufacturing establishments for purposes of inspecting operations for cleanliness and such requirements as dosage accuracy. While so empowered, these same inspectors receive little guidance from the Act on standards that can be used for making judgements. In the presence of this void, a joint

committee with industry was formed and guidelines drafted for the inspectors' use. These guidelines are published 'by the authority of the Minister of Health and Welfare' but carry no legal force. At this point, PMAC becomes a self-regulating agent: companies sign and agree to accept these guidelines as a condition of membership in the association. If the guidelines are broken, members can expect expulsion.

2. *Efficacy and drug advertising.* In pursuing the objective that drugs be effective, the government has been particularly concerned that advertising reflect accurately to physicians the virtues of any given drug. When a drug is approved by HPB, it is accompanied by a product monograph developed by the firm, 'which is totally non-promotional, non-advertising, and is up-to-date with all the good and all the bad that is known of that drug' (interview, HPB official, 1982). Another condition of membership in the PMAC, then, is that firms agree to abide by the association's 'Code of Marketing Practice'. This Code states: 'Claims for a products shall reflect accurately and clearly the intent and spirit of the Product Monograph as accepted by the Health Protection Branch...' (PMAC, n.d.:2). The state and association have jointly delegated responsibility for enforcing this agreement to a private actor, the Pharmaceutical Advertising Advisory Board. This board is composed of representatives from the PMAC, from the medical and pharmacists' associations and even consumers. A representative from HPB sits as an ex officio member. The board then approves advertisements by comparing them with the product monograph. This is a clear example again of industry and government being 'co-responsible', to use Schmitter's (1982:26) term, for the formulation of policy, with industry representatives primarily responsible for its implementation.

What we have described is a sponsored pluralism network because only one producer group, and a narrow one at that, is working with the state and the state is simply relinquishing some of its authority. In addition, the underdeveloped character of the association system is consistent with a sponsored pluralism network. This underdevelopment is rooted in the institutional structure of the pharmaceutical sector.

The Canadian pharmaceuticals industry, like its counterparts in other Western countries, is divided into three sub-sectors: prescription, proprietary and generic drugs. Based on opposing philosophies of medication, the first two have been fiercely competitive for close to a century. The third group, the generic manufacturers, competes directly with the first two by copying and mass-producing their most successful drugs. A degree of intensity is added to this competition by the fact that the generic industry is almost completely domestically owned in Canada while the prescription and proprietary industries are highly foreign-owned. As a result, there is no encompassing or integrated system of manufacturers' associations in this sector. Each sub-sector has its own association, with a domain carefully drawn to exclude the other two. One is left with three isolates and the possibility of, at best, ad hoc cooperation on particular issues. On the labour side, the pharmaceuticals industry is largely non-unionized, with the consequence that there exists no collective voice for articulating the labour perspective. Finally, the Consumer's Association of Canada, which is the only group that might be called upon to speak for consumers in this instance, is notoriously weak, over-extended and under-funded.

If the institutional structure of the economy contributes to the association system side of this equation, the properties of the sectoral bureaucracy contribute to relationships between association and bureau. Turning first to the degree of centralization in the state, the conflict between safe and effective drugs on the one hand and cheap drugs on the other has been reproduced in the organization of the federal government. The primary instruments for safety and effectiveness are contained in the Food and Drugs Act entrusted to the HPB. The most important policy instrument for reducing drug prices was a change to the Patent Act, introduced in 1969, which required manufacturers of prescription drugs to issue a licence to manufacture to any firm that wished to produce a generic counterpart. This instrument, normally referred to as 'compulsory licensing', is housed in the Department of Consumer and Corporate Affairs.

The foreign-controlled prescription drug sector is naturally hostile to compulsory licensing. It has enlisted the support of the Department of Regional Industrial Expansion in its fight against this instrument. Officials in HPB also tend to be sympathetic to the industry on this score. The generic industry, on the other hand, has lined up solidly behind Consumer and Corporate Affairs, as have many provinces which are major purchasers of drugs. The result is that contact between these bureaus is minimal, and no effort has been made to coordinate the employment of these instruments, in spite of the fact that compulsory licensing has created a new set of problems for drug safety and effectiveness. The coordination of policy required for sectoral corporatism is virtually impossible under these conditions, and, as predicted by Lowi (1979), a decline of authority over the sector has occurred.

The presence of a sponsored pluralism network in this sector is also very much a product of the lack of differentiation between the industry and the sectoral bureaucracy, especially in the area of safety and efficacy. The first and most striking fact about HPB is its almost overwhelming reliance on the industry for information. Decisions on safety and particularly efficacy are based on research done by the firms themselves and supplied to the government. The agency does little of its own research in-house; it evaluates the research done by firms. Because of staff shortages, there is a need to transfer even more of this evaluative work to the drug companies. A lack of differentiation is further created by the relatively weak character of the regulations themselves. In the classic pattern of sponsored pluralism they tend to be general, leaving much open to negotiation and discussion. An official in HPB described the situation in the following manner:

> They [the regulations] are not that great now. There are about six or seven pages and that covers all there is in Canada about new drugs. In the usual way, following the old British tradition, we keep things very vague. For example, what is your regulation for testing the safety of a new drug? Well, what's asked for in our regulations is submission to us of details of the test carried out to establish safety. That's the extent of the regulation.... So we need to have and we do have a fair amount of guidelines explaining what we interpret that regulation to mean.

In short, the nature of the regulatory system means that the state must rely on practices developed by the industry.

Finally, the lack of differentiation is encouraged by a shared set of values among the industry, the government and the medical and pharmacist professions on the use of drugs. These professions dominate both the sectoral bureaucracy and the industry. State officials do not have a point of view that questions or is independent of the prevailing views in industry and the professions on the appropriate way to medicate. Industry is not on the outside of the process, as one would expect in pressure pluralism; the state is not autonomous, as is required by sectoral corporatism.

To review, there is no industrial policy in this sector. The state has limited itself to regulating drug quality and prices. The sponsored pluralism network that we have described here, with its fractionalized associational system and its decentralized, dependent and competitive state agencies, is not conducive to the development and conduct of such a policy. If the state were to embark on an industrial policy in this sector, it is our view that it would either have to proceed without working through the associational system or would have to significantly reorganize that system. In either case, the state's own organization too would need to undergo some dramatic changes.

Conclusions

In bringing this analysis to a close, two general points emerge, the first relating to the differences among our three policy networks and the second to the types of industrial sectors in which each network is likely to prevail. Katzenstein (1978:323–32), in his characterization of the factors likely to affect the type of policy network (and the policy instruments used), identified three conditioning variables: the centralization of the state, the centralization of society, and the degree of differentiation between them. We have relied upon three analogous variables at the sectoral level: the centralization of the sectoral bureaucracy, the integration and comprehensiveness of the association system in the sector, and the autonomy of the sectoral bureaucracy from the sector.

The differences among the three policy networks that have been developed in this paper can now be summarized in terms of these three variables (see Table 1).[12] Sectoral corporatism differs from both forms of pluralism in the degree of organizational development on both the state and society dimensions. The sectoral bureaucracy is unified and is able to lay its hands on a wide range of policy instruments: the association system is integrated, centralized and highly representative of the sector. Strength begets strength in this policy network. For the pluralist forms, the sectoral bureaucracy is divided with competition among departments and agencies and an uncoordinated deployment of policy instruments. Associations tend to be narrow, specialized and competitive, with little if any cooperation among them.

The contrast between sponsored pluralism and pressure pluralism relates to the relative autonomy of the sectoral bureaucracy. In the

TABLE 1
Policy networks and conditioning variables

	Pressure pluralism	Sponsored pluralism	Corporatism
Centralization of the sectoral bureaucracy (state)	Weak	Weak	Strong
Centralization of the sectoral associational system (society)	Weak	Weak	Strong
Autonomy of the sectoral bureaucracy (differentiation between state and society)	Strong	Weak	Strong

case of pressure pluralism, both the state and the industry are relatively independent of one another. The industry has little need for state assistance and the bureaucracy guards its autonomy in order to deploy its instruments in as neutral a fashion as possible. By contrast, sponsored pluralism is based on a strong mutual dependence between the bureaucracy and the sector. The bureaucracy has little independence in policy formulation and can proceed only hesitantly in implementing policy without information and assistance from both firms and sectoral associations. The regulatory system that one often finds in sponsored pluralism is needed by the industry to ensure fair competition and stable market shares.

These various differences between sectoral corporatism and sponsored pluralism culminate in distinctive patterns of delegation from the state to sectoral associations. In the case of corporatism, several socioeconomic producer groups are involved and the decisions taken in conjunction with the state have the capacity to change fundamentally the structure of the economy. In the case of sponsored pluralism, however, one fairly narrow economic interest is involved, and decisions are being taken to preserve and protect the structural bases of that interest.

One can expect, then, that certain types of industrial sectors will be associated with each of the three policy networks. The sectors likely to be dominated by the pattern of pressure pluralism are those that James Kurth (1979:33) has termed 'the free trade' sectors. Robust in the face of international competition and considerably less dependent on state financing, these sectors will generate associations that lobby for incentive measures, support for export promotion and freedom from tax burden. Corporatism is unlikely here, not only because the state prefers not to intervene but also because the sector is unlikely to generate the associational forms required.

Sponsored pluralism will occur in sectors like pharmaceuticals, which are stable in the face of international competition. The balance of trade may be negative but is not poised for a precipitous decline. The sector is mature and relatively concentrated. Regulations have been developed gradually to protect the interests of the sector and are perceived as such by the state, individual firms and interest associations. Sectoral corporatism is not likely because the viability of the sector has not reached the policy agenda.

In the case of sectoral corporatism, the suitable sectors will be relatively old and established sectors on the verge of crumbling in the face of international competition. The state in these cases can adopt a laissez-faire attitude, but this choice will likely be politically unpalatable. It can move to protect the sector without any adjustment measures, but this is a position made increasingly difficult under the GATT. Finally, it can choose an industrial policy; it can reach for competitiveness by radically restructuring the sector, or it can orchestrate a rational withdrawal. In making either of these choices, the corporatist temptation will arise.

Notes

This research has been supported by the Social Sciences and Humanities Research Council of Canada, Grants 410-78-0716, 410-80-0280, 410-82-0180 and 410-83-0499. An earlier version of this paper was presented to the Sixth Colloquium of the European Group for Organization Studies, Firenze, 3–5 November 1983. We would like to thank Alan Cawson, Wyn Grant, Leon Lindberg, Philippe Schmitter and Wolfgang Streeck for their comments on this version.

1. A classification which overlaps somewhat with the one proposed here can be found in Schmitter (1982:263–4). We are more sanguine than Schmitter about the prospects for sponsored pluralism. An alternative classification based on different criteria has been done by Crouch (1983a).

2. For an effort to rank-order Western European countries on a corporatism scale see Lehmbruch (1982:16–23) and Schmitter (1981).

3. Wassenberg's view contrasts with that of Cawson presented in the introductory chapter to this volume. Cawson leaves room for corporatism at the micro-level whereas Wassenberg does not.

4. On the importance of problem definition for the study of policy, see Anderson (1978).

5. On the subject of internal markets and the control exercised by parent firms over their subsidiaries, see Buckley and Casson (1976), Rugman (1981) and Hennert (1982).

6. However, this corporatist arrangement broke down after the oil crisis hit. See Martin Rhodes's chapter 10 below.

7. For a similar distinction, see Lowi (1979:79–91).

8. Developments in the state influence developments in the association system. As G.K. Wilson (1982:224) has observed: 'It seems reasonable to suppose that a strong, united state produces interest groups which are themselves united and cohesive.' For a counter-hypothesis, see Schmitter and Streeck (1981:84–106).

9. For a discussion of the political circumstances surrounding the introduction of the policy, see Hiscocks (1981).

10. These calculations are based on data supplied to the authors by Statistics Canada.

11. In 1976, 37.6 percent of production in the dairy processing sector was by foreign-owned firms (Statistics Canada, 1981).

12. We realize that these policy networks do not constitute an exhaustive classification. For example, the cases of France and Japan are not covered for most sectors. There, the centralization of state and society would appear to be strong but differentiation between the two less so. The inter-penetration of business and political elites in both societies lessens the differentiation, and thus the autonomy of sectoral bureaucracies. This observation is admittedly preliminary and subject to revision when more information on our three sets of variables becomes available.

3
Industrial training in Britain:
the dilemmas of a neo-corporatist policy

Sarah Vickerstaff

'Neo-corporatism' is still a contested concept, but this has not prevented a healthy growth of concrete empirical work in the field. This work, however, necessarily mirrors the continuing theoretical debates within the literature. Three main areas of contention continue to dominate the discussion: the initial question of the scope of the concept; the nature and demarcation of 'functional groups'; and the role of the state. Before looking at the concrete case of industrial training in Britain, a few remarks must be made on these central dilemmas in the theory of neo-corporatism.

The neo-corporatist critique of both pluralist theory and cruder Marxist formulations of the relationship between the state and the economy focused on three interrelated empirical developments found in varying degrees and combinations in many contemporary Western European societies. Put simply, these developments were: (1) the organizational growth, centralization and political dominance of functional interest associations (especially those of capital and labour), and the growing (formal or informal) collaboration between such groupings, in contrast to the politically weaker position of 'common interest' lobbies; (2) the recognition of these functional groups by the state in the form of (formal or informal) institutionalization of regular collaboration between these groups and the state, often through the vehicle of tripartite bodies; and (3) the growth of state intervention in the economy beyond Keynesian techniques, through concertation with functional groups, involving attempts at both macro-level economic planning or steering and at selective intervention in areas such as industrial policy, industrial relations and employment policy, which had the consequence of the blurring of the boundaries between the state and the economy and the public and private spheres.

These developments suggested the need for an alternative to the pluralist view of competitive (market model) interest group politics and challenged the view of the state as a disinterested arbitrator in the political process. It also questioned the adequacy of cruder

Marxist models of the state as a simple (structural or volitional) agent of 'capital in general'.

The role of neo-corporatist theory as critique has tended to falter, however, around the central theoretical debates noted above. Much of the early work on neo-corporatism concentrated on a discussion of the concept's scope, on whether we were witnessing the development of a new type of society or a new form of the state, or if, in fact, neo-corporatist developments were much more fragmentary or were confined to specific areas or policy issues, such as 'interest intermediation', 'industrial relations' or 'incomes policy' (Winkler, 1976; Panitch, 1979a; Schmitter and Lehmbruch, 1979). Quantity of opinion rests on the latter, but we are now seeing a further division among those who agree that neo-corporatism is a more partial development. Schmitter (1982) has argued for a differentiation between work concentrated on the 'input side' of the political process, in the study of 'interest intermediation', and that focused on the study of policy formation, on the output side'.[1]

This suggested division of labour has already been questioned on the grounds that the neo-corporatist paradigm points precisely to those developments within advanced liberal democracies in which a radical distinction between the 'input' and 'output' sides of the political process is theoretically and empirically difficult to sustain (Jessop, 1979:189; Pempel and Tsunekawa, 1979:231–3; Crouch, 1977: Part 1; Cawson, 1982:38–40; Johansen and Kristensen, 1982:208; Lehmbruch 1979:149–50). If this division of labour were taken up, it could easily reduce neo-corporatism to merely a new interest group theory or a new policy formation theory rather than a means for developing an understanding of the historically changing relationship between both these aspects of the political process, which empirically provided part of the impetus for the critique of pluralism.

The concentration on 'input' factors in some contributions is related to the other two central dilemmas in neo-corporatist theory: the precise nature of functional groups, and the role of the state. By focusing on 'interest intermediation' it has been hoped to demarcate more precisely the specific nature and dynamics of functional groups, and to avoid a monolithic and unitary view of the state as implied in the traditional concept of state corporatism. This attempt, though laudable, all too easily leads us down the interest group theory road and helps to produce the dichotomy between 'top-down' and 'bottom-up' explanations of neo-corporatist development, i.e. state-induced versus interest-group-induced explanations. A rejection of this division of labour need not have the consequences of either embracing a macro-societal scope for the concept, or effectively giving the state the prime role in neo-corporatist development.

A recent contribution by Lehmbruch begins to open up the possibilities of an approach that can combine both 'input' and 'output' questions and reject the *a priori* assumption that it is either the state or functional groups that 'cause' neo-corporatism.

Lehmbruch (1984) makes a distinction between 'sectoral corporatism' and corporatist concertation or 'trans-sectoral corporatism'. The distinction is used primarily, though not exclusively, to demarcate historically between the 'relatively old phenomenon' of functional groups within different sectors, organized with a view to controlling access, entry and representation of that sector, and to acting as the main mediation between that sector and the state, and 'trans-sectoral corporatism', a more recent development, in which such functional sectoral groups are involved in the formulation and implementation of trans-sectoral macroeconomic policy (Lehmbruch, 1984). Thus the distinction also refers to the scope of public policy and provides a simultaneous concentration on the historical development of both the nature of interest group intermediation and the scope of state intervention, providing a means for historically (rather than analytically) distinguishing the relationship between 'input' and 'output' functions in the political process.

Lehmbruch's conceptualization can be taken further and may also begin to provide a means for a more satisfactory understanding of the nature of 'functional groups'. Within the neo-corporatist literature there is a continuing debate between what Panitch (1980) has characterized as 'group-theoretical' and 'class-theoretical' approaches. This demarcation, however, tends to perpetuate a rather sterile concentration on the argument over whether functional groups are or are not 'really' class groups, rather than on the more interesting and fruitful question of the relationship between class and functional groups. The sectoral/trans-sectoral distinction may provide a means for developing this more interesting question.

Even if a distinction between 'functional' and 'preference' groups is stressed, if all functional groups are theorized as essentially the same, that is if they are all equally groups formed within the social division of labour, then as Panitch points out this is to deny that 'One of the great putative advantages of the corporatist over pluralist approach is that by using it one need not reduce all group interests, group conflicts and group state relations to the same salience and the same plane' (Panitch, 1980:169). And we progress no further in understanding why some functional groups (critically, those of capital and labour) seem to be more involved in neo-corporatist developments than others.

Equally, however, as Cawson points out, if all functional groups are seen as 'really' being class groups, we encounter extreme difficulties in understanding professional groups such as the British Medical Association (BMA), who fit 'badly' into a straightforward class analysis (Cawson, 1982:44, 52–4). Cawson correctly makes a distinction not only between 'voluntary associations' or preference groups and 'functional' groups, but also within functional groups, between class-based groups and vertically organized functional groups such as the BMA. He argues: 'Those areas of state policy which impinge directly on the relationships between capital and labour in capitalist production will involve corporate organisations — of capitalist owners and managers and workers — which directly represent class interests' (Cawson, 1982:53–4). Thus, he begins to provide clues as to which functional groups will relate to which policies, and which classes will be involved in policy 'directly related to capital accumulation', that is, 'issues relating to the social relations of production'; whereas in areas such as social policy (consumption as opposed to production policies), we might expect vertical functional groups to be involved as well (Cawson, 1982:44; 52–4, 64; Cawson and Saunders, 1983).

This is an advance over the debate as to whether functional groups 'really' are classes, but it still leaves us with at least two critical problems. The conceptualization of policy relating to 'capital accumulation' is not fine-grained enough; it potentially points to a range of public policy stretching through incomes policy and nationalization to the reorganization of training practice in the knitwear industry, which blurs the insight of many authors that the specific scope of different kinds of public policy conditions the organization and impetus of functional groups. In other words, it fails to locate the specificity of the 'neo-corporatist' option.

Cawson, correctly, points out that in analysis one cannot reduce 'corporate organizations directly representing class interests ... to those same class interests' (Cawson, 1982:54), but he does not develop this to pose the critical question of the relationship between functional and class interests within functional organizations based on class.

To explore fully the relationship between functional and class associations, it is not enough to distinguish between them; we must also ask how public policy relates to this division of interests, and how groups with both class and functional bases manage the tension between these potentially competing demands. The sectoral/trans-sectoral focus allows us to make a distinction between functional groups which are simply 'sectoral', or functionally specific, such as the BMA, and those whose scope is potentially or actually trans-sectoral, such as the National Union of Mineworkers (NUM), the Trades Union Congress (TUC), the Engineering Employers Federation (EEF). The latter groups are derived not simply from their functional position within the division of labour but also on the basis of their class position in the production process. What joins both the doctors and the miners is that, if organized, they possess defensive strength in their own sectors; put another way, they have a threat potential to any attempts to 'interfere' with their sector by other groups or the state. Equally, the development of the welfare state required BMA involvement and acquiescence, just as attempts to restructure the mining industry must confront NUM defensive power. The BMA, however, is sectorally based and largely confined; in contrast, the NUM represents not only miners' interests in the mining industry, but also potentially the more general interests of industrial workers. Theoretically, any functional group might develop a trans-sectoral role, but in the context of an advanced capitalist society we can expect that some functional groups are in a better position to do so than others.

The threat potential of functional groups differs just as some groups of workers are sectorally stronger than others. The defensive strength of any functional group would seem to be dependent upon at least three critical features: (1) the degree of organization and centralization; (2) the historically specific importance of the sector in question, in relation to a specific policy or set of policies; and (3) the extent to which the potential is sectorally confined or circum-scribed. Class-rooted functional groups' orientation towards, and potential for disrupting, trans-sectoral policy initiatives can be expected to be greater than that of groups formed solely on a vertical sectoral basis. This observation, however, does not absolve us from the task of investigating in concrete cases the conditions under which class-based functional groups will act on a trans-sectoral basis.

If, as many have suggested, the re-emergence of neo-corporatism is closely related to the development of trans-sectoral state policy (e.g. Lehmbruch, 1984; Panitch, 1979a), our demarcation between functional groups would seem to provide one clue as to why some groups, for example organizations of capital and labour, are much more involved, positively or negatively, in neo-corporatist develop-ments than others.

This formulation extends Cawson's distinction between class-based and vertically organized functional groups and points to the central feature of neo-corporatist, as opposed to other state/interest group, relations as one outcome of the increasing threat potential or defensive strength of functional groups in a highly centralized and concentrated economy, while also focusing on the fact that the particular policy issue is a critical variable. This approach also raises a series of questions about the relationship between and within functional groups. In class-based functional groups, such as trade unions and employers' associations, we can expect tensions between sectoral (or functional) and trans-sectoral (or class) interests. Combined with Lehmbruch's insight into the increasingly trans-sectoral role of public policy, it allows us to pose questions about the 'strategic' options of the actors in the neo-corporatist drama (Lehmbruch, 1984). As others have argued, there has been a tendency to ignore the question as to why certain functional groups, especially the trade unions, are willing to be involved in the neo-corporatist option (Regini, 1982; Roche, 1982:58; Boston, chapter 4 below). Related to this is another tendency to assume that functional groups and the state can be treated as unitary blocs. Introducing the dynamic of the relation between sectoral/trans-sectoral organization, interests and policy, we can perhaps begin to dissect more satisfactorily the contingent, conflictual and constrained nature of the involvement of functional groups and the state in neo-corporatism. This is especially important in regard to business organization and the structure of the state; there has been a tendency in the literature to assume that organization of these two corners of the tripartite triangle is unproblematic or unitary, with the corollary that the 'sticky' actor in neo-corporatist development is seen necessarily to be labour. If the sectoral/trans-sectoral dynamic is a tension for all participants on the neo-corporatist stage, then it opens up the possibility that employers or even the state might in certain cases be the 'sticky' element.

The debate around the three central dilemmas of neo-corporatist theory will no doubt continue, and indeed it is fruitful that it should. These necessarily brief remarks offer some possible suggestions as to how we should proceed. It seems necessary to abandon a radical distinction between 'input' and 'output' factors and to concentrate instead on the development of the political process, in terms of the historical relationship between interest representation and policy formulation as necessarily related features of the same process. We should also refuse to make an a priori assumption as to whether the state is or is not the trump card in the corporatist pack, and concentrate instead on understanding the historically specific strategic options of all the actors within neo-corporatist settings.

Postwar industrial training in Britain[2]
Prior to the 1964 Industrial Training Act (ITA), training in Britain had been firmly embedded in the British tradition of voluntarism in

industrial affairs. Following the second world war it was assumed that, with the dismantling of controls, the labour market would resume its 'natural' functions in allocating manpower to where it was needed. Neither side of industry was motivated to challenge this view in the training field. The trade unions concentrated on consolidating the old apprenticeship system and maintaining their defensive control over conditions of entry to skilled trades, and although shortages of skilled labour, especially in engineering, became more pressing as the 1950s continued, employers, in conditions of relative prosperity, were prepared to offer the wages needed to poach the skilled labour that they lacked from their competitors. It was left to educational groups to lobby periodically for a more national, trans-sectoral approach to training (Perry, 1976; Kennedy et al., 1979).

In 1958, the Carr Report was the first postwar attempt to look at training as a whole. The Report was the work of a tripartite committee set up to review training arrangements in the light of a forthcoming bulge in the number of school-leavers (Ministry of Labour and National Service, 1958). It lamented the absence of a national organization with an overview of training arrangements and proposed a voluntary bipartite National Apprenticeship Council (Ministry of Labour and National Service, 1958: para. 3). The ethos of the Report, however, was firmly voluntarist, eschewing a national executive body to overlook training (Ministry of Labour and National Service, 1958: para. 87). A bipartite Industrial Training Council (ITC) was set up by the British Employers Confederation (BEC), the TUC and the boards of nationalized industries to fulfil a 'trouble-shooter' role, inviting industry to review its training practices. Though far from a radical departure from previous thinking on training, the setting up of the ITC did mark the growing realization that existing industrial training practice might have implications for wider economic performance.

In the late 1950s and early 1960s, it was not only training that was receiving renewed attention; the role of the state in the economy in general was under consideration in the debate about economic planning and incomes policy. Increasingly, reliance on 'stop–go' policy as the basis of the state's economic management was meeting with criticism as Britain's economic performance relative to its Western competitors was deemed poor.[3]

The popular base of the postwar social democratic compromise rested on the commitment to full employment (Keynesianism) and the development of the welfare state. In industry this meant voluntarism, which was accepted and defended by the state and industry. In Britain in the 1950s, social democracy had to be reconciled with a competing base for policy, the interests of money capital. The policy objective of money capital was 'sound finance', which in practice meant a balanced budget, the maintenance of London's role as a centre for world banking, and the lynchpin: sterling stability. The result of these competing bases for state action in the 1950s was the policy of 'stop–go'. This policy integrated the opposing interests under the ultimate hegemony of financial capital. It worked by satisfying popular demands for social reform (namely, the welfare state, full employment and rising living standards), by leaving industry to get on with its own business, and by applying the economic brake if either seemed to threaten the stability of sterling.

For most of the 1950s the 'stop–go' policy provided an integrative mechanism for reconciling competing (and antagonistic) demands on the state, but by the end of the 1950s its integrative potential was beginning to break down. The policy of full employment and voluntarism in industrial affairs had significantly increased the defensive strength of the trades union movement in industry. By and large, industrial capital, in conditions of relative economic prosperity, posed no challenge to economic orthodoxy, but simply pursued its own interests. As international economic conditions tightened at the end of the 1950s, however, British industrialists found themselves squeezed between money capital's hegemony over economic policy and the trade unions' defensive strength in industry, between restrictive deflationary economic policies and rising wage costs. It seemed clearer by the end of the 1950s that the particular mix of policy that 'stop–go' involved was having detrimental effects on Britain's industrial competitiveness. Industrial capital started to challenge economic orthodoxy and countenance the need for a degree of state intervention in the economy. (Radcliffe Committee, 1960: vol. 2). In doing so, it revealed that it had immediate interests in common with the trade unions, who also sought an end to the 'stop' part of policy and the development of a concerted policy of economic expansion.

In the training field voluntarism had allowed industry to maintain traditional practices; along with other voluntary industrial policy in the 1950s, it had not provided a strategy congruent with trans-sectoral needs. Continued skill shortages were beginning to be perceived as a potential (or actual) brake on industrial expansion. In the context of full employment, poaching of skilled labour was seen less and less as a viable option for individual employers; it was an unpredictable and ad hoc way of managing their labour supply, and in the harsher economic reality of the early 1960s this inflationary way of attracting labour ('jobs were chasing men' — BEC, 1957, 1958), appeared less defensible.

In 1962 the government published a White Paper, the contents of which marked a substantial shift from the voluntarism of the Carr Report four years earlier (Ministry of Labour, 1962; Hansard, 20 November 1963: vol. 684, col. 1016). The White Paper identified three objectives for a training policy: to make training more responsible to wider economic needs and technological developments; to improve training standards; and to spread the cost of training. It proposed a bill giving the Minister of Labour statutory powers to set up training boards in industry, and, most radically, it introduced the idea of imposing a training levy on employers to be raised by the training boards and paid back to industry in the form of grants for improved training.

The voluntary attempt by the ITC to foster employer awareness of the economy's broader training needs had failed. Only the state could orchestrate a trans-sectoral policy by means of a carrot and a stick. The stick was the degree of compulsion in the levy/grant system. The potential carrots were the spreading of training costs more evenly throughout industry, the possibility of breaking down some of the trade unions' defensive strength over the form of apprenticeships, and the introduction of a greater degree of flexibility in the labour market, all of which were in the trans-sectoral interests of employers as a whole.

A trans-sectoral training policy also needed to secure the acquiescence of the trade unions, who, through their defensive strength on the factory floor, had considerable potential for disrupting attempts to modify the traditional apprenticeship system. As with other state intervention of the period (e.g. incomes policy, 'planning'), the trade union movement found itself in a contradictory position, jealous of its sectoral interests as reflected by its strength in industry, but historically wedded to calls for social reform by the state, reflecting the trans-sectoral interests of the movement as a whole. The trade unions had long voiced the opinion that, if laissez-faire failed to produce economic expansion, then the state should intervene to ensure it (Jenkins and Mortimer, 1965).

The Industrial Training Act, passed in 1964, set up an advisory Central Training Council (CTC), including six employers and six trade union representatives, and empowered the Minister of Labour to set up statutory Industrial Training Boards (ITBs) to operate the levy/grant system.

Following the passage of the Act there was a period of rapid institutional expansion in the training field, and by 1969, in general, a case could be made that the Act and the ITBs had acted as a spur to industrial training (Lees and Chiplin, 1970; Giles, 1969; Page, 1967: 83–101, 143–327). The Act was not without its critics, however, and the main debate centred around the role of the state in training. The TUC wanted an extension of the Act to all industries and services and an independent National Training Council to take over the role of the Department of Employment and Productivity (TUC, 1969: 665 and 182). Employers were divided on the merits of the existing set-up, there was unease over what was felt to be undue state interference (MacDonald, 1969: 36). The CBI lamented the lack of progress in reforming apprenticeships and developing adult training but generally agreed that the Act was a sound development (CBI, 1968). The main criticisms of the Act came from the ranks of small businesses, who felt that the training boards were biased against their traditional 'on-the-job' training (Lees and Chiplin, 1970; Kennedy et al, 1979; Tavernier, 1968; Giles, 1969; Stretch, 1969), a situation, it was felt, to be explained partly by the lack of representatives of small firms on both the ITBs and the CTC.

The CBI's concern over apprenticeships was echoed in the Report of the Royal Commission on Trade Unions and Employers Associations, which criticized 'restrictive traditions' in British industry (Donovan Commission, 1968: paras. 357–9). It recommended the abolition of time-serving, unofficial restrictions on entry to skilled trades and the introduction of standardized training programmes and formal qualification.

By the early 1970s it was clear that, although the Industrial Training Act could claim some credit for an upsurge in training, it was failing in certain broader aims and was becoming increasingly unpopular with small firms. The Act had attempted to foster a neo-corporatist consensus in industry over the need both to increase training and to train for wider economic needs. It heralded an unprecedented form of state involvement through the levy/grant system, but by no means introduced a centrally directed and planned training system. The institutional structure of the policy, the industry-by-industry training boards, tended, in fact, to perpetuate training in industry-specific skills, instead of fostering the vaunted flexibility in the labour market, and it was quite unsuitable for the development of trans-sectoral skills, such as commercial training.

By the early 1960s it had become obvious to all concerned that the voluntary training framework was inadequate for general economic needs. Three possible policy options were on the agenda: to leave things as they were, but recognize that industry did not seem able or willing, voluntarily, to transcend its immediate sectoral needs in favour of a trans-sectoral approach; to impose a state-directed policy on industry, which would have risked non-compliance from industry and probably have entailed substantial expenditure; or, third, to attempt a collaborative, theoretically self-financing, policy in which industry might be induced to develop a trans-sectoral consciousness. The adoption of the last alternative, the neo-corporatist collaborative policy, presented itself as a way of trying to overcome the defensive strength of industry and its apparent inability to generate a voluntary trans-sectoral policy, without, on the other hand, riding rough-shod over the accepted British tradition of voluntarism.

The neo-corporatist framework was a strategic option for all the actors involved; for employers it offered the possibility of increasing labour market flexibility; for the trade unions, 'training for all' could be sold as an economic and social benefit for all workers; and for the state it was a cost-effective way of inducing a trans-sectoral approach without having to take on a vastly expanded role in the field, with all the possible organizational and legitimation problems 'naked' intervention might have posed. The industry-by-industry organization represented the soft edge of state intervention, allowing industry to retain a large measure of control. As the 1960s progressed, however, it became increasingly clear that the economy's trans-sectoral training needs were not being met and that training effort in industry was being organized with a view to getting the grant back rather than because of conversion to the importance of the 1964 Act's objectives.

The state faced the perennial problem, in trying to coordinate a trans-sectoral policy, of how to make industry do its bidding — in this instance, improve training. As one trade unionist pointed out, 'There is no compulsion to train under the Industrial Training Act, only compulsion to pay the levy' (TUC, 1969:523). On the trade union side, the progress of the Act had had contradictory effects. It had done little to challenge trade union control over apprenticeships and thus had not really challenged traditional sectoral interests; on the other hand, it had served to raise trade union aspirations in the training field. The TUC wanted a more aggressive national policy since it believed employers would train only if forced to.

It was by no means obvious, in the early 1970s, how training policy could be reshaped. The CBI continued to tread its path between the divergent views within industry, criticizing the Act but retaining basic support for it (CBI, 1971). It wanted the benefits of a trans-sectoral training policy — greater labour market flexibility, better manpower forecasting — but not the costs. The particular grievances of small firms received more unqualified recognition in the proceedings of the Bolton Inquiry on Small Firms (Bolton Committee, 1971).

The small firm sector had found itself progressively marginalized politically during the 1960s. The formation of the CBI in response to the new interventionist state had been resisted by small employers (Strinati, 1982:100). The 'new' economic policies of the 1960s and the neo-corporatist framework of some of them had isolated the interests of small firms. The success of the neo-corporatist attempt, symbolically and practically, was dependent upon the mobilizing capacity of the trade unions and employers associations to bring their constituents into a consensus. The prime players were inevitably the best organized trade unions and employers who could glimpse the possible benefits of trans-sectoral policies. The impetus towards neo-corporatism derived from the recognition that voluntarism had failed and that a new form of accommodation between capital and labour was required. Small industrial capital recognized neither, and was, in any case, largely incapable of delivering the latter.

The Bolton Committee was much less hesitant than the CBI, and concluded that small firms should be exempted from the levy/grant system (Bolton Committee, 1971: paras. 14.22–15.24). In February 1972 the government published its consultative paper, *Training for the Future*, which represented an attempt at a new compromise. The levy/grant was recognized as a necessary 'shock treatment' which had fulfilled its catalyst role but should now be phased out (Department of Employment, 1972: paras. 30, 43). The document pointed to the problems of the industry-by-industry structure which failed to give a national picture, and proposed a National Training Agency (Department of Employment, 1972: paras. 75–8, 82, 40).

On the practical side, the decision to expand the government Vocational Training Scheme into a new Training Opportunities Scheme (TOPs), heralded the growth of countercyclical training provision and the recognition of the need for public expenditure in training facilities for industry (Department of Employment, 1972: para. 63).

In the ensuing Employment and Training Act 1973, a Manpower Services Commission (MSC) was set up, including three trade union and three CBI representatives, to act as an executive agency for the management of employment and training services, responsible to the Department of Employment (Department of Employment, 1973: paras. 2–7). Subsequently, a Training Services Agency was set up as the MSC's executive organ in the training field. The levy/grant system was replaced by a levy/grant/exemption system, whereby small firms, or employers training adequately, could be exempted from the levy (Department of Employment, 1973: paras. 62–3).

The Act followed many years of debate about the role of the state in training. The establishment of the MSC brought together, in a somewhat contradictory form, the differing views that had abounded in the previous years. Like many other aspects of Conservative policy at the time, it was a compromise; faced with the need to devise an industrial policy to aid the restructuring of an increasingly faltering British economy, the dilemma was between more state involvement or less, which, in the context of the early 1970s, translated itself into a debate over more corporatism or less.

Paradoxically, the result was both an extension of, and a withdrawal from, neo-corporatism and, as such, amplified its contradictions. Industrial capital, in the guise of the CBI, could not agree on the neo-corporatist option; it wanted the payoffs but not the costs, and the immediate interests of small and large capital often diverged. For the trade unions the neo-corporatist alternative offered the possibility of greater influence over policy, and, like much state intervention in trade union spheres of action, it served to increase demands from trade unions, which had largely been absent prior to the state involvement.

The Employment and Training Act was both an attempt to rationalize the state's dealings in the field, extending central planning and forecasting capabilities in the labour market, and a rear-guard action against aspects of the 1964 Act that had become unpalatable to sections of industrial capital. It simultaneously extended tripartite coordination and legitimation at the central national level in the MSC and undermined the practical effectiveness of this new central cohesion by denuding its lower echelons — the ITBs — of some of their powers.

It is clear that the policy was not derived in any straightforward fashion from the interests of industrial capital. Indeed, no 'general interest' of capital existed *vis à vis* training, and individual employers consistently pursued their immediate sectoral interests over wider trans-sectoral concerns. The trade unions, however, were better placed to pursue the logic of a trans-sectoral training policy than was industrial capital. Sectoral interests notwithstanding, the trade unions could mobilize nationally in favour of a policy of training for all, with the possible economic and social benefits for their members of improved labour market position and improved quality of work experience. At the local level, collusion between employers and trade unions over accepted custom and practice meant, along with a policy that did not in any case descend to this level, that the trade union leadership's ability to sell training for all as a shop-floor reality was not really tested. The industry-by-industry structure of the 1964 Act had attempted to generate, through the 'carrot and stick', a practical neo-corporatist consensus for pursuing a more rational trans-sectoral policy; but the structure had tended to reinforce, rather than overcome, sectoral interests. With the creation of the MSC, policy moved away from the attempt to create a meso-level neo-corporatist consensus, opting instead for a national tripartite legitimating body, and, effectively, heralding a more active role for the state.

Contrary to the theoretical expectations of much of the corporatist literature, the central dilemma of neo-corporatism in both policies was less the acquiescence of the trade union movement than the compliance of industrial capital in a trans-sectoral policy.

Following the establishment of the MSC, state expenditure in training grew rapidly (MSC, 1974: 8). In 1971–72, the state had stepped in, via the ITBs, to finance apprenticeship award schemes 'to make good the cutback in recruitment' (Department of Employment/MSC, 1976: para. 4.10), and by 1976 the MSC could claim that this scheme had effectively made good the shortfall in apprenticeship training arising from the recession. State financial and practical support for industry's training needs have never been so great (Ridley, n.d.; Rees and Atkinson, 1982; MSC, 1976; 1977b).

A joint Department of Employment/MSC consultative document of 1976 pinpointed, as it turned out all too clearly, the problems of the system as it had evolved. *Training for Vital Skills (TVS)* put forward radical proposals for the collective funding of the initial stages of training in transferable skills, as a means to ensure a stable supply of skilled workers in key sectors. It commented:

> Various measures have been made to find a means both of subjecting the overall volume of recruitment to influences going beyond the employers' short-term needs and of removing from individual employers all or part of the financial burden which acts as a major disincentive to recruitment. In the past none of these attempts has been completely successful. (Department of Employment/MSC, 1976: para. 1.3)

It recognized that the 1964 Act had failed because the ITBs had no means of ensuring that the volume of training was in line with longer-term trans-sectoral needs, and it concluded that the 1973 Act was also unlikely to remedy this situation (Department of Employment/MSC, 1976: paras. 4.5–4.6). It also pointed to the dilemmas of public funding in the training field: the risk that employers would cut back their own recruitment in expectation of government provision, and that government aid might tend to increase pressure for further central expenditure (Department of Employment/MSC, 1976: paras. 4.3, 4.11, 5.20). The document raised the idea of training contracts between companies and the ITBs or similar bodies.

In short, the document was a detailed critique of both the industry and state role in training. It pinpointed the problems that the 1973 Act had unsuccessfully grappled with, and suggested a remedy which the Act had specifically abandoned under pressure from industrial capital. The collective funding idea of *TVS* was not pursued, however; employer opposition to it was total (MSC, 1977c: para. 1.4). Instead, the MSC set up a tripartite Task Group on Vital Skills to examine the other ideas of *TVS*.

In effect, the MSC was doing in abundance what it was singularly well-placed to do: produce detailed plans and schemes, set up working parties, but in practice introduce ad hoc, pragmatic, special measures. The MSC involved a national neo-corporatist consensus for making plans, but no detailed neo-corporatist machinery for putting them into practice. The result was a series of unconnected expediencies that did not require detailed industrial acquiescence. In the meanwhile, state expenditure on training mushroomed but little was achieved in restructuring the training system at the level of the firm (*Department of Employment News*, issues 32 (1973), 36 (1976), 40 (1977); MSC, 1977a; 1976). On top of this, as the 1970s progressed the MSC was increasingly having to deal with a problem it was not specifically created to cope with: unemployment. The training system was under pressure; state provision seemed to be allowing industry to cut back its own training provision; and as 'special measures' abounded, much of the MSC policy seemed unplanned and uncoordinated (MSC, 1977a: para. 3.17; 1977b: paras. 2.17, 2.31–2.32; 1977c: para. 3.9).

Remedies for these problems were as numerous and contradictory as they had been in 1963 or 1973. Attention was increasingly being drawn to the 'need' for flexibility in the length of training and age-entry requirements and for the introduction of recognized training standards (MSC, 1977c). The neo-corporatist element in policy was symbolic, rather than practical. The MSC acted as a talking shop where a broad consensus could be reached but little else. The peak organizations of capital and labour were content to be involved in endless working parties, producing plans, but the extent to which either could sell these plans to their respective memberships was questionable (and to a degree untested). As Offe has pointed out, this general problem is perhaps more acute for employers' organizations than for trade unions (Offe, 1981: 147–50). Industrial capital's capacity for acting collectively depends upon the particular 'game' under consideration; with regard to employees, collective action is easier than in the 'market game' where each individual employer is necessarily seeking competitive advantage. The CBI could not force individual employers to train with trans-sectoral needs in mind; private industry, however, was quite happy to let the state provide training and training services for them at minimal direct cost. On the trade union side, the increased visibility of training policy served to raise their demands, from a relatively ambivalent attitude to a national training policy in the early 1960s, to regular TUC demands for more training, more state involvement and more expenditure by the late 1970s.

The effect of symbolic neo-corporatism was not to raise industry's commitment to actual trans-sectoral training needs on the ground, but to raise expectations of state provision and the self-interested use of public provision by industrial capital. The MSC could identify trans-sectoral training needs but had no means for making industry do anything about them.

In the absence of a base within industry for a concerted policy that worked at the level of the firm, the state's options were limited, so long as direct compulsion was eschewed. In the worsening economic conditions of the late 1970s, this was something of the worst of all worlds. The basic 'problems' of inflexibility in the labour market remained, and added to this was growing unemployment; in the context of stagflation, a training system which was most effective in generating demands for increased expenditure was thought to be increasingly problematic.

As the recession progressed the possibilities for another attempt to revitalize a workable neo-corporatist policy on training were being rapidly undercut. Deepening recession has the effect of lessening private industry's already weak commitment to maintaining recruitment levels, and undermining appeals for industry to spend more money on training. Growing unemployment was to bring the contradictory position of the trade unions into stark relief; recession would harden sectoral interests and a defensive protection of skilled workers' positions, while simultaneously increasing the demands at national level for trans-sectoral measures to deal with unemployment.

In the late 1970s the focus of the training debate changed; increasingly, Britain's training 'problem' was seen to be less an effect of the inadequacies of the training institutions than a product of restrictive work practices (R. Taylor, 1980; MSC, 1980; Central Policy Review Staff, 1980; British Institute of Management, 1980). The failure to reform apprenticeships was not surprising, given the particular form of the neo-corporatist bargains, which had served to obscure questions about the nature and implications of the training system as manifested on the factory floor. The 1964 Act had focused mainly on industry-specific shortages and had been aimed primarily at influencing employers to increase the quantity of their training. The 1973 Act and the MSC had moved the legitimating consensus to the national level in an attempt to focus more clearly on trans-sectoral training needs, but, operating through state counter-cyclical training provision and ad hoc crisis management, it had partially abandoned the attempt to create a working neo-corporatist consensus at the industry or factory level. The terms of both variants of the neo-corporatist compromise failed to have detailed impact at the level of the individual company.

Outlook on Training, published by the MSC in 1980, suggested a radical overhaul of the system. It proposed that there should be no statutory limit to the levies ITBs could raise and, further, that the operating costs of the ITBs be charged to industry (MSC, 1980: Rec. 10, paras. 9.8, 9.9). The CBI rejected both ideas, wanting to control the ITBs but not pay for them. A solution soon appeared with the institution of a review of the ITBs, with a view to abolishing some of them. Following the review, the government announced that 16 of the 23 ITBs were to go, and that Exchequer financing of those that remained would be phased out. Both the MSC and CBI argued that financing should continue, and the trade unions called it a 'training disaster' (*Financial Times*, 13 October 1981).

If the logic of the new policy was not immediately clear, the White Paper issued in December 1981 revealed what the attempted policy was going to be: it set a target date of 1985 for the reform of the apprenticeship system. The MSC was to remain 'the main agency through which the Government initiates action' (Department of Employment, 1981: para. 51). The policy was an attempt to circumvent and overcome the problems that the neo-corporatist approach to training had generated. The new programme was couched in the rhetoric of laissez-faire as a return to voluntarism; in fact, it was a new mix of an old recipe — state intervention and private provision. The policy aimed to bypass the levels at which the two earlier attempts at neo-corporatism had been situated: the meso-level ITBs and the macro-level MSC. Henceforward, policy would be generated explicitly by government rather than the MSC at the macro-level; and, through collective bargaining at plant level, the continuance of public support for skill training in industry was to be contingent on proof that industry was mending its ways in the field of apprenticeships (Department of Employment, 1981: paras. 47, 58, 42, 2). The proposals also involved a commitment to greatly increased spending on a new Youth Training Scheme to replace and extend the previous Youth Opportunities Programme (Department of Employment, 1981: paras. 1, 2; MSC, 1982: chapter 5).

Conclusions

The 1964 Act showed that a limited neo-corporatist consensus could be achieved at meso- (industry) level but that this did not translate either to the level of the firm or to the level of trans-sectoral needs. The meso-level focus of the policy tended to entrench rather than overcome sectoral interests. The more general tendency for neo-corporatism to aggravate the tensions between sectoral and trans-sectoral interests within the organizations of capital and labour was less critical for the trade unions at this point. The meso-level of training policy served trade union organization fairly well; the neo-corporatist consensus on training appeared to work best in industries with a high degree of organization on both sides, such as engineering, but it did so without significantly challenging traditional sectoral interests; it worked badly in poorly organized sectors and industries such as hairdressing. This situation furnished the trade unions with the opportunity to lament the particular plight of workers in small industries and to argue the case for extending neo-corporatist organization without contradicting the sectoral interests of workers in well organized industries.

In effect, the ITB structure failed to overcome trade union rank-and-file defensive strength, or to induce a trans-sectoral training consciousness in industrial capital. It was a policy incapable of generating a working basis for manpower planning.

The second phase of neo-corporatist training policy aimed at producing a trans-sectoral training strategy, but failed to overcome the problems of the neo-corporatist option in the British case. The MSC as a macro-level neo-corporatist legitimating body was capable of inspiring plans but not any means for ensuring the translation of these to the level of action in industry. The effect, in worsening general economic conditions, was simply to increase the state's financial and practical support for private industry's training effort. The MSC took refuge in ad hoc practical policies that did not necessitate detailed industrial acquiescence.

The conclusion reached by the late 1970s was that public expenditure was being directed at the wrong problem. The last, and continuing, phase in the development of training policy has witnessed a partial withdrawal from the neo-corporatist option and an attempt by the state to overcome the dilemmas of previous policy by shifting state involvement directly to the problem of 'rigidities' in labour market organization. In the wider economic conditions of stagflation employers' already conditional support for neo-corporatism, as a strategic option, is increasingly undercut. Motivated to reduce costs, employers might be convinced that the answers to the problems of an inflexible labour market lay not in accommodation with the unions, but with state support for restructuring of the labour supply. It is in employers' immediate interests to re-commodify labour, to break down the 'rigidities' in the labour market. Critical to the waning of neo-corporatism as a strategic option for both the state and employers is the abandonment of full-employment policy, which serves to undercut the defensive strength of the trade unions. In a sense, the micro-level focus of some of the present policy is a backlash to the failure of the neo-corporatist attempt to harmonize the interests of both sides of industry in order to restructure the training system trans-sectorally. It is too early to say how successful the reform of apprenticeships will be. Indicators at present point in opposite directions.[4] There is still trade union and employer involvement in the MSC and in the management of the Youth Training Scheme (YTS), but this role is becoming increasingly difficult for the trade unions, as unemployment rises and the YTS is seen by some trade unionists to be part of a larger attempt to reduce trade union influence over the form and remuneration of industrial training (AUEW/TASS, 1982; NATFHE/AACE, 1983).

The fact remains, however, that even with centrally directed policies like the YTS, the aim of providing 70 percent of trainee places within industry makes the scheme dependent to a degree on the compliance of both industrial capital and the trade unions, who still have the sectoral power to threaten the delivery of trans-sectoral policies.

The concrete experience of the neo-corporatist option in training policy may not necessarily be replicated in other policy fields. Lehmbruch and others are correct to point to the increased possibility of neo-corporatism in the context of the development of trans-sectoral economic policies (Lehmbruch, 1984; Cawson, 1982: 38–41; Panitch, 1979a). But the designation 'trans-sectoral' need not apply only to the 'grander' attempts at economic planning or incomes policy; it also allows us to focus on changes within particular policy areas such as training and employment. The British experience of trying to generate a trans-sectoral training policy illustrates that the neo-corporatist option is by no means guaranteed to be successful; our analysis suggests that neo-corporatism can be a strategic option for various groups for quite divergent reasons. We have focused attention on the need for a more concrete understanding of 'functional' groups and policy options. It is necessary to look at the interest dilemmas of class-based functional groups and to avoid the a priori assumption that 'trade unions' or 'employers' associations' can usefully be analysed as unitary blocs. In policy issues that impinge directly on the 'market game' of individual employers, the 'sticky' element in neo-corporatist development may frequently be the employers. In Britain, at least, employers' commitment to the neo-corporatist option seems weak, and both they and the trade unions seek to 'work the system' to their own advantage. It is clearly important to look at the level and scope of policy — for example, whether it is sectoral or trans-sectoral, and if it is pitched at the macro-, meso- or micro-level; both critically affect the ability of functional groups and the state to pursue the neo-corporatist option. Perhaps more than anything else, the British case highlights the importance of recognizing that an apparent neo-corporatist consensus at macro-, or even meso-, level may be far more symbolic than effective in practice.

Notes

1. P.C. Schmitter has sanctioned this division of labour with the designation 'corporatism$_1$' (e.g. 'interest intermediation') and 'corporatism$_2$' (e.g. policy concertation) (Schmitter, 1982: 262–343). In a later article Schmitter is forced to split his original definition of 'corporatism' (Schmitter, 1979a:16) to maintain the distinction between 'corporatism' and 'concertation'. The role of the state in recognizing and licensing functional groups then becomes part of 'concertation' (Schmitter, 1983).

2. The following section on industrial training is taken from a longer and more detailed account of postwar training (Vickerstaff, 1983). In the following discussion I deal only with industrial training; for reasons of space it has not been possible to discuss the important development of Youth Training Schemes in the 1970s and 1980s.

3. For further discussion of the economic planning debate and the wider economic context of these discussions, see Jessop (1980); Leruez (1975). The proceedings of the Radcliffe Committee (1960) on the Workings of the Monetary System provide many examples of the growing discontent of industrial capital to the policy of 'stop–go'.

4. For example, negotiations in the engineering industry over abolishing time-served apprenticeships broke down (*Financial Times*, 4 May 1983), though negotiations in the electrical contracting industry resulted in a reduction in apprentices pay (*Financial Times*, 7 January 1983). It is possible to hypothesize, however, that, as unemployment rises, trade union bargaining power seems likely to diminish. The debate over apprentice and trainee pay has been a critical element in the introduction of the Youth Training Scheme. Some unions have negotiated YTS trainee rates well above the Scheme's specified allowance, for example the Transport and General Workers Union with Massey-Ferguson Ltd (*Financial Times*, 1 November 1983).

4

Corporatist incomes policies, the free-rider problem and the British labour government's social contract

Jonathan Boston

Introduction

For many decades, but especially since the world-wide wage explosion of the late 1960s and early 1970s, there has been intense debate among economists and other interested scholars concerning the causes and consequences of inflation and the 'best' means — which is to say, the most economically and socially efficient means — of achieving greater price stability. Broadly speaking, the main division of opinion lies between those macroeconomists, mostly post-Keynesians (Galbraith, 1978; Layard, 1982; Mayhew, 1983; Weintraub, 1978), who favour an anti-inflation programme involving some (more or less permanent) form of incomes policy, and those neo-classical macroeconomists, mostly monetarists (Brittan and Lilley, 1977; Friedman, 1977; Laidler and Parkin, 1975), who argue that price stability can be secured only by means of firm, non-accommodating monetary and fiscal policies; incomes policies, according to this view, are economically inefficient and in the long-run accomplish nothing. In fact, they may even be counter-productive.

There is not the space here to examine and evaluate the divergent philosophical and economic assumptions which underlie these conflicting policy prescriptions. Instead, this chapter will address two major problems which must be confronted by all those who advocate an anti-inflation strategy based upon, or at least incorporating, an incomes policy, particularly policies of a voluntary, consensual or corporatist nature. First, how can governments secure trade union acceptance of and cooperation with a policy of wage restraint? (The concern here is both with policies to reduce or control nominal wage growth and with policies to lower real wages.) Second, and closely related to this, how can a sufficient degree of compliance be achieved with a centrally agreed wage norm? Or, to put it another way, how can free-riding by individual unions and bargaining groups be prevented, or at least contained within acceptable limits?

The corporatist solution

One solution suggested by many scholars during the past decade or so (Crouch, 1977; Schmitter and Lehmbruch, 1979; and Schwerin, 1980) is a form of policy-making and implementation described variously as societal, liberal or bargained corporatism. As Crouch explains, the 'crucial characteristic ... of corporatism is that interest organisations constrain and discipline their own members for the sake of some presumed "general" interest as well as (or even instead of) representing them' (1983a: 452). Hence, a corporatist incomes policy is a negotiated policy which is enforced primarily by means of moral suasion and private coercion, rather than state coercion. That is to say, compliance with the policy guidelines is maintained largely by the peak organizations of labour and capital, not by state controls and regulations. Essentially, this means that the peak organizations act as their own game-keepers, or, to quote Tarling and Wilkinson (1977: 412), as 'the government's policeman'. One of the advantages of this approach, or so it is claimed, is that it enables governments to pursue policies based upon consent and voluntary cooperation and thereby to avoid both the 'law of the jungle' (monetarism) and the 'jungle of the law' (statutory incomes policies).

Yet if a corporatist strategy is to be successfully implemented, it would appear, at least at first sight, that several important conditions must be satisfied. First, the central organizations of labour and capital must have both the incentive and the capacity to negotiate a bilateral (or multilateral) programme of mutual restraint. This implies, among other things, that the claimed advantages of a corporatist incomes policy — in terms of lower inflation and a higher level of aggregate employment — are regarded as sufficiently attractive to outweigh the perceived disadvantages of such a policy — in terms of reduced bargaining autonomy and the likely enforcement costs. Second, the peak organizations must possess the necessary moral authority and/or coercive resources to deter free-riders, and must be willing to exercise their power.

But it is just at this point that the rationale for a corporatist incomes policy comes unstuck. To start with, relatively few advanced industrialized democracies have the required institutional arrangements in the form of powerful, centralized, hierarchical, peak organizations. Moreover, since institutional reform — especially in the labour market — is usually a slow and hazardous process, it would seem that a corporatist solution to the problems of wage inflation and unemployment is not widely applicable. In any case, the evidence indicates that the mere existence of corporatist institutions and policy-making does not automatically overcome the free-rider problem. One needs only to consider those countries which come nearest to the corporatist model, such as Norway, Sweden and Austria, to notice that free-riding (in the form of decentralized wage drift) presents a continuing headache for sectoral elites (see Addison, 1979; Schwerin, 1980; Flanagan, Soskice and Ulman, 1983). Thus, no matter how powerful the peak organizations are, and no matter how potent the sanctions available, a very high level of compliance with a consensual incomes policy cannot be guaranteed. Quite apart from this, corporatist approaches encounter many other well-known difficulties — uncertain and often small macroeconomic payoffs, asymmetrical payoffs to labour and capital, distributional conflicts, disputed legitimacy, organized resistance and resource scarcity (Boston, 1983: 25–81; Maital and Benjamini, 1980; Schwerin, 1980; Walsh, 1984). Each of these problems must be tackled and at least partially overcome if a corporatist counter-inflation strategy is to be successfully negotiated and executed.

While the existence of powerful, centralized peak organizations representing labour and capital appears to be a necessary condition for stable, longer-term corporatist policy-making, such structural arrangements are not a prerequisite for the effective implementation of short-term consensual incomes policies. Perhaps the most telling reminder of this fact was the Social Contract between the British Labour government (1974–79) and the Trades Union Congress (TUC). This case is notable because the British industrial relations system is among the least well suited to an economic strategy incorporating an incomes policy, however enforced. In the first place, pay bargaining is highly decentralized. Second, there are nearly 500 unions, many of which compete for members, and many of which are characterized by strong sectional or craft-based loyalties. Third, decision-making power is often concentrated at the shop-floor or workplace level; indeed, the extent of workplace bargaining and the strength of the shop steward movement is unrivalled in the West. Fourth, employer solidarity is low, and the peak organizations of employers and employees are weak. Lastly, the union movement is ideologically divided, with a substantial section opposed to incomes policies and antagonistic to state interference in wage determination.

Altogether, these structural and attitudinal features of British industrial relations would be expected to increase the tendency of union negotiators to concentrate on narrow, short-term objectives, to reduce their willingness to subordinate their wage claims in the national interest, and to encourage free-riding. Yet despite this, it proved possible for the Labour government and the TUC to negotiate and implement, at least for two years (1975–77), a reasonably successful programme of wage restraint. During these years, for instance, the rate of wage inflation (as measured by the change in basic weekly wage rates) was reduced from nearly 30 percent to under 7 percent (see table 1). Furthermore, the union movement demonstrated a remarkable degree of unity and discipline: there was little free-riding; there were few open challenges to the authority of the TUC; and there was a surprising degree of rank-and-file acquiescence. Admittedly, from 1977 onwards union support for the Social Contract declined steadily, industrial unrest increased and nominal-wage inflation accelerated, thereby undermining the gains of the mid-1970s. Nevertheless, the Social Contract reveals that, even in a supposedly hostile structural context, a programme of wage restraint can, in certain circumstances, be mutually agreed and successfully enforced.

But what are these circumstances? Or to put the question more precisely, what are the necessary conditions for the effective implementation of a short-term corporatist incomes policy, and how, if at all, can these conditions be created or fulfilled? The hypothesis which will be presented here is that there are two main prerequisites: a relatively low conflict of interest, and a relatively low conflict of values. The meaning and content of these conditions will be discussed later in the chapter. But first it is necessary to consider the economic rationale for an incomes policy and some of the proposed solutions to the collective action problem.

It should be stressed that the argument which follows is highly condensed. Space does not permit a comprehensive treatment of all the relevant theoretical issues and contextual factors. Regrettably, therefore, many assumptions have not been adequately specified or justified, certain objections have not been considered, and many background details relating to the British economy, industrial relations system and political environment have simply had to be taken for granted.

Trade unions and the prisoner's dilemma of inflation
Let us begin by outlining some preliminary assumptions. It will be supposed, initially at any rate, that trade unions act in accordance with the a priori behavioural assumptions of rational choice theory (see Laver, 1981; Moe, 1980; Olson, 1965). That is to say, they are rational; they maximize their expected utility (preferences or wants) subject to constraints; they are economically self-interested; they

have a positive time preference; and their utility functions are stable over time. Next, let us assume that union negotiators are concerned to maximize some combination of real wage, relative wage and employment objectives. This does not mean that they have no other objectives, such as improved fringe benefits and conditions of work, shorter hours, organizational survival, a fair share of national income, improved social services and so forth; but these are sufficiently insignificant to be disregarded for our present purposes. Let us also make the controversial assumption that inflation has real effects and is economically injurious. In other words, a high rate of inflation, say 10 percent or more, is economically inferior to a low rate, say 2–3 percent. (Just how inferior is immaterial at the moment.) Finally, let us suppose that union negotiators are operating in an economy characterized by decentralized wage bargaining, a significant degree of monopoly power in the labour market and a good deal of uncertainty. That is to say, they can not predict accurately the rate of inflation during the currency of their awards; they do not know how other negotiators will behave; they are unsure about the rate of increase in labour productivity; they are unable to distinguish between temporary and permanent movements in key economic variables such as the public sector borrowing requirement (PSBR) and the money supply; and they are uncertain about what changes in fiscal policy may occur and what impact these will have on real disposable incomes.

As should be evident, such a strategic setting is not that far removed from a situation of free collective bargaining in an economy like Britain. Yet notice carefully the implications of this bargaining context for the problem of controlling wage and price inflation. If, as suggested above, pay bargaining is fragmented and decentralized, union negotiators will perceive that their wage settlements will have little influence on the aggregate price level. Consequently, they will judge that, if they act independently to try and reduce the current rate of inflation — by settling for a money-wage increase lower than that obtainable — they will bring neither a positive return to their own members, nor any discernible advantage to the nation. In fact, unless the vast majority of unions also choose to exercise restraint, voluntary pay moderation will be 'rewarded' with a loss of real income and a fall in the position of the union's members in the wage hierarchy. Such action, needless to say, would be quite irrational for self-interested union negotiators and their constituents. Yet, at the same time, if every union fully exploits its labour market power, the outcome will be suboptimal or 'Pareto'-inferior (see Laver, 1980: 495; Oswald, 1980: 12). Stated bluntly, there will be a wage–price spiral which will eventually prove economically damaging to most, if not all, members of the collectivity (with lower investment, lower growth, higher unemployment and so on). Naturally, one solution is for all the unions to coordinate their strategies and agree to settle for smaller wage increases. But the major problem with this approach is that in the absence of altruism, or of adequate penalties and rewards, each union will be strongly tempted to free-ride and thereby secure both real and relative gains at the expense of everyone else.[1] Such a configuration of payoffs — where the cooperative solution yields the greatest aggregate payoff, but where there is an inherent conflict between the individual and collective interest — has been referred to as 'market failure' or a 'prisoner's dilemma' (see Luce and Raiffa, 1957; Barry and Hardin, 1982; Maital and Benjamini, 1980; Sutcliffe, 1982).

Broadly speaking, there are two main ways of resolving a prisoner's dilemma. Either one can change the payoff structure so that it is advantageous for every union to cooperate, or one can modify one's behavioural assumptions to allow for irrational and/or non-self-interested behaviour. With respect to the former strategy, a variety of possible solutions can be identified. One could, for example, attempt to change the payoff structure from that of a prisoner's dilemma into that of an assurance game (Sen, 1974: 59). Essentially, this would entail some kind of conditional promises between union negotiators. Such a strategy, however, would be virtually impossible to apply in the context of decentralized bargaining, numerous actors and minimal trust.

Another option would be for the government to try and alter the payoff matrix by employing various rewards and penalties. These could be of either a general or a selective nature. For instance, the government could offer to reduce direct taxes — and hence increase real disposable incomes — if every bargaining group agrees to abide by certain wage guidelines. Alternatively, it could threaten to impose wage controls or to increase taxes if no agreement is forthcoming or if unions attempt to free-ride. Whichever option is chosen, numerous problems are bound to arise. Resource constraints may severely limit the government's freedom of manoeuvre with respect to fiscal policy. Individual unions may conclude that, regardless of what the government offers or threatens to do, it is still in their interests to free-ride. And the government will have to reckon with the fact that it has relatively few general sanctions available and that some of these may be politically unacceptable, indiscriminate in their impact, ineffective or even counterproductive.

Given the drawbacks associated with the application of general rewards and sanctions, many economists (Layard, 1982; Jackman and Layard, 1982; Seidman, 1978; Weintraub, 1971) have recommended the use of selective incentives. These have the advantage of impacting directly upon the payoff structure of every bargaining group and therefore, in theory at any rate, offer a potential solution to the collective action problem. Undoubtedly, the most widely known and frequently advocated policy employing selective incentives is a tax-based incomes policy (TIP). Such a policy can involve rewards or penalties, and can be applied to either unions or employers. Thus there are four possibilities: a reward or a penal TIP on employees, or a reward or a penal TIP on employers. Unfortunately, no matter which solution is adopted, a host of complex administrative, economic and industrial relations problems are sure to arise. Because of this, no Western government has, to date, embarked upon such an approach.

The remaining option is to amend the wage-fixing system in order to reduce the autonomy of local bargaining units and increase the costs of free-riding. One of the obvious solutions here is to strengthen the peak organizations representing capital and labour and pursue a broadly corporatist strategy. As already observed, this proposal has certain attractions, but it is not devoid of weaknesses.

So far I have considered very briefly, within the confines of rational choice theory, how it might be possible to change the payoff structure for bargaining groups in order to remove their incentive to free-ride. An alternative, but by no means mutually exclusive, approach is to modify one's behavioural assumptions to allow for the fact that individuals (and groups) are motivated by a host of moral, political and ideological commitments (see Alchian, 1973; Collard, 1978; Phelps, 1975; Sen, 1977). Men and women, after all, are not totally self-interested. They are not mere pleasure–pain calculating machines. They do not live, as it were, in a vacuum, completely divorced from a moral-cum-political system. Rather, human beings are simultaneously economic, political, cultural and moral creatures who inhabit an economic system which is, in turn, profoundly influenced by, and in a sense dependent upon, the attitudes, habits, beliefs, aspirations and ethical standards of its members. This is not to deny, of course, that economic self-interest is a primary motivation or that, other things being equal, people prefer more political, social and monetary advantage to less. None the less, it seems perfectly reasonable to assert that man's value structure is complex and heterogeneous, and that people sometimes, if not often, sacrifice their short-term individual advantage because of certain moral and ideological commitments.

But what bearing does all this have for the prisoner's dilemma of inflation? The main implication surely is this: to the extent that normative commitments influence union bargaining behaviour, they may either deter or encourage free-riding. They will probably deter when the union leadership (and membership) accept the rationale for an incomes policy, when they consider it to be their duty to abide by the policy, when they have a strong sense of working-class loyalty (as opposed to craft-based affinities), when they support the government in power, and when the proposed policy is perceived to be fair. Free-riding is more likely to occur, other things being equal, when these conditions do not apply. Consequently, whether or not a union or bargaining group attempts to free-ride will depend not only upon the state of the labour market and the short-run opportunity costs of compliance (what I shall term the union's 'conflict of interest'), but also upon the nature and intensity of the moral and ideological commitments within each union (what I shall term the 'conflict of values'). From this it follows that a union is most likely to free-ride when it faces a high conflict of interest and a high conflict of values (that is to say, when its members are ideologically opposed to incomes policies, are hostile to the government in power, believe the proposed policy to be unjust, and so on). Conversely, a union can be expected to comply with the wage guidelines or pay norm when both the conflict of interest and the conflict of values are low. It is less easy to predict how unions will behave when they experience either a low conflict of interest and a high conflict of values, or a high conflict of interest and a low conflict of values. Nevertheless, it seems reasonable to suppose that a union in a weak bargaining position will be unable to break the guidelines regardless of how opposed it is to the incomes policy. Similarly, one would expect a powerful union whose members were strongly in favour of the policy to abide by its terms.

Given this analysis, it should be evident that a corporatist incomes policy is most likely to be negotiated and successfully implemented when the vast majority of unions, if not all of them, support the policy and when the opportunity costs of compliance are low. In contrast, the policy will be in jeopardy when there are unions or important bargaining groups with a powerful incentive to defect and also a strong desire to do so. But what relevance, it might be asked, does this theorizing have for the operation of the Social Contract? Can it, for example, assist us in explaining why the wage guidelines of the Social Contract were closely observed in 1975–77, but were frequently disregarded in 1974–75 and 1977–79? The contention here is that it does.

The Social Contract: an overview
The Social Contract, which incidentally was not in any sense legally binding, lay at the heart of the Labour Party's political and economic strategy during the 1970s.[2] Fashioned during Labour's years in opposition following its defeat to the Conservatives in June 1970, the Contract involved a broad political understanding between the parliamentary and industrial wings of the labour movement whereby the parliamentary leadership promised to implement a comprehensive set of economic, social and industrial policies backed by the TUC in exchange for a commitment by leading trade unionists to cooperate with a future Labour government, especially in the field of wage bargaining. In its original form, this commitment was deliberately vague and imprecise. No explicit guidelines were laid down, and no principles for the determination of incomes were established. However, with Labour's return to office in March 1974, and in the midst of mounting economic difficulties (sparked by the oil crisis and the collapse of Heath's statutory pay policy in early 1974 as a result of the miners' strike), the TUC came to endorse various limitations of pay bargaining. These culminated in two years of severe restraint between August 1975 and August 1977. While the policies adopted during these years proved effective in reducing the rate of wage inflation, they also contributed to a sharp fall in real earnings (see table 1). This, among many other things, provoked a strong reaction within the union movement. As a consequence, at the TUC Conference in September 1977 the balance of opinion moved against the supporters of incomes policies and the TUC formally withdrew its support for the Social Contract. The Labour government was thus left to devise and implement its own stabilization policies for the remainder of its term. Although this task was assisted initially by a generally acquiescent trade union stance, rank-and-file resistance to the government's pay policy grew in the latter months of 1978 and forced the Cabinet to abandon, or at least heavily modify, its counter-inflation stategy.

Having sketched the broad outlines of the Social Contract, let us now explore the evolution of the Labour government's incomes policy in greater depth.

The wage–price explosion of 1974–75
When the Labour Party under Harold Wilson was returned to power in early March 1974, the economic situation was already deteriorating. Indeed, the prospects for a reforming government intent upon improving social services, eliminating poverty, increasing economic equality and restoring full employment could hardly

have been worse. The world economy was moving into sharp recession. The huge oil price rise of late 1973 had cut real national disposable income by more than 5 percent, imparted a strong inflationary shock into the economy and brought about a serious deterioration in the current external balance (see Barnett, 1982: 23; Cohen, 1975: 52). Furthermore, the union movement was in no mood to accept a strict pay policy. There were two main reasons for this.

First, wage bargaining had been rigorously controlled since November 1972 under the Conservative government's statutory pay policy. This, not surprisingly, had generated a good deal of frustration among pay negotiators and shop stewards, and had sparked repeated calls for a return to free collective bargaining. Therefore, notwithstanding the TUC's desire to assist the new government to curb inflation, the union leadership was in no position to secure rank-and-file endorsement for a rigid pay norm for the 1974–75 wage round. Even reaching agreement on a more general set of guidelines would be difficult enough. Second, all the evidence indicated that there had been an upsurge in the level of rank-and-file militancy and that workers expected sizeable real-wage increases. During the spring of 1974, huge pay claims were ratified by union conferences up and down the country (for example, teachers, 37 percent, farmworkers, 80 percent and builders, 87–107 percent). Many groups of workers rejected their proposed agreements under Stage III of the Conservative government's counter-inflation policy (which continued, at least nominally, until July). And all the indicators of industrial unrest registered increases on the levels recorded in 1973.

Moreover, even if union leaders and their constituents had been more favourably disposed towards pay restraint in 1974, it would still have proved difficult to have prevented a significant rise in the rate of wage inflation. This was because in November 1973 Prime Minister Heath had introduced a form of wage indexation known as the 'threshold system'. In accordance with this, unions were permitted to seek clauses in their pay awards whereby additional payments of up to 40 pence a week could be made for every 1 percent by which the retail price index (RPI) rose more than 6 percent above its October 1973 level. The rate of 40 pence corresponded roughly to 1 percent of average weekly earnings, which meant that all workers on or below average earnings could receive full pre-tax compensation for any unanticipated inflation. Now, as matters transpired, in the year to October 1974 the RPI rose by over 17 percent, 10 percent above Treasury's original forecasts. As a result, 11 threshold payments were 'triggered', thereby increasing weekly earnings for those covered by threshold agreements by as much as £4.40.[3]

Despite the strong sentiment against incomes policies within the union movement and growing shop-floor militancy, senior TUC leaders, such as the General Secretary, Len Murray, and the General Secretary of the giant Transport and General Workers Union, Jack Jones, accepted the need for both nominal and real-wage restraint following the removal of the statutory pay controls in July. Thus, working in close consultation with the government, the union movement developed a set of guidelines to assist negotiators during the new era of voluntary restraint. The guidelines were endorsed unanimously by the General Council of the TUC in June and ratified by the TUC annual conference in September (TUC, 1974).

Unfortunately, the new policy suffered from a number of serious weaknesses. To start with, the guidelines were vague and far too flexible. The TUC's principal recommendation was that unions should, in general, restrict themselves to the objective of maintaining rather than improving real incomes. However, it was not made clear whether this referred to pre-tax or post-tax incomes. Matters were further complicated by the fact that the guidelines explicitly allowed unions either to claim compensation for changes in the cost of living since their previous settlement, or, alternatively, to negotiate arrangements to keep abreast of the cost of living during the currency of their new award. This provision, in effect, gave unions the right to lodge large, anticipatory wage claims and yet still remain within the bounds of the policy. In addition, the guidelines contained various provisions for exceptions which were drafted so broadly that virtually any group could legitimately seek (and probably obtain) improvements in their real wages. Quite apart from this, of course, the TUC had few sanctions to prevent unions from pressing excessive claims, and, given the political context of 1974, could not have used them. Effectively, this meant that the only restraint upon unions — apart, that is, from employer resistance — was the moral and political obligation to abide by the ground rules and support 'their' government.

Clearly, in the circumstances of 1974 this was quite inadequate. Indeed, with inflation accelerating, with rank-and-file pressure mounting, with widespread free-riding expected and with little to deter those who broke the guidelines (however interpreted), it was naturally the most rational strategy for union negotiators to demand substantial pay increases. To have done otherwise would have entailed a major conflict of interest. Not surprisingly, therefore, the 1974–75 wage round witnessed huge pay claims and some very large pay settlements. In response, the pace of wage inflation rose rapidly, to reach over 30 percent by the spring of 1975. Likewise, the annual rate of price inflation continued to accelerate and by July 1975 exceeded 25 percent.

The obvious failure of the TUC guidelines to restrict nominal and real-wage growth placed the government in an unenviable position. Somehow inflation had to be checked and real labour costs reduced, but there were few realistic or acceptable alternatives. A monetarist approach, which was favoured at the time by a growing number of Conservative politicians, was considered to be morally and politically untenable. The so-called 'alternative economic strategy', which involved an expansionary monetary and fiscal policy in the context of import controls and tough price controls, was thought unlikely to have much impact on wage bargaining or the rate of inflation, especially in the short term. And a statutory incomes policy, which was favoured by the Treasury and some on the right of the Labour Party, would present major political difficulties (see Castle, 1980; Haines, 1977; H. Wilson, 1979): Harold Wilson had campaigned vigorously during two elections (February and October 1974)

TABLE 1
Prices, wages and unemployment, 1970–79
(in percent)

	Retail price inflation (RPI)	Weekly earnings, all industries and services	Real earnings[a]	Basic weekly wage rates[b]	Unemployment rate seasonally adjusted[c]
1970–73 ave. p.a.	8.0	12.5	4.2	—	3.2
1974	16.1	17.8	1.5	19.7	2.6
1975	24.2	26.5	1.9	29.5	3.9
1976	16.5	15.8	−0.6	19.3	5.3
1977	15.8	10.2	−4.8	6.6	5.7
1978	8.2	14.4	5.7	14.1	5.7
1979	12.2	15.6	3.0	14.7	5.4

[a] Annual rate of change in real earnings equals the annual rate of change in average weekly earnings deflated by the annual rate of change in the RPI.
[b] Manual workers only; not seasonally adjusted.
[c] Excludes school-leavers.

Sources: OECD, *Economic Surveys: United Kingdom (various issues); Department of Employment Gazette*, 88 (June 1980): 701.

against legal controls on wages; the TUC was ardently opposed to a statutory pay policy; and it was very doubtful whether the required legislation could be carried in the House of Commons. Given this situation, the only remaining solution lay in a new, much tougher, pay deal with the unions. But would the necessary degree of support be forthcoming, and could powerful unions, such as the miners, be persuaded to comply?

Renegotiating the Social Contract
As matters transpired, the Labour government was greatly assisted, if not rescued, by two developments. In the first place, Jack Jones, probably the country's most influential and widely respected union leader, was persuaded of the need for the TUC to embark on a new initiative. Fearing the consequences for international competitiveness and unemployment if no action was taken, and deeply concerned to keep the Labour Party in power, Jones proposed in May 1975 that pay increases for the 1975–76 round be limited to a flat-rate figure. There were three main objectives behind this proposal: to check the rate of wage inflation and thus restore international confidence in the British economy, to redistribute incomes in favour of the lower paid, and to guarantee the real incomes of those earning less than the average wage. Not unexpectedly, the idea won immediate support from moderate trade union leaders, particularly those representing workers in low-paid occupations and public sector employment. The other catalyst which prompted a change in attitude on the part of many trade unionists was the dramatic fall in the value of sterling on foreign exchange markets on 30 June.[4] This highlighted the gravity of the economic predicament and led many of those traditionally hostile to incomes policies to moderate their stance. Indeed, within ten days of the sterling crisis a new pay deal had been negotiated with the government and ratified by the TUC General Council (see TUC, 1975: 346–64).

The new policy, or Phase I, as it became known, was very much stricter than the previous guidelines. There was a fixed limit on pay increases of £6, effective for 12 months. This represented a wage rise of just over 10 percent for those on average earnings of about £57 a week. Considering that price inflation was running at a rate more than double this and that there would be a significant time-lag before the rate declined, the majority of workers, most notably those on above-average incomes, could expect a fall in their real incomes in the year to August 1976. Moreover, there were few provisions for exceptions, and all improvements in fringe benefits and productivity deals had to be offset against the £6 limit. In addition, the Prime Minister threatened employers who violated the policy with the loss of government orders and contracts, the loss of assistance under the Industry Act, and penalties under the Price Code (*Hansard*, 11 July 1975, vol. 895, col. 902–4). He also indicated that the government would impose statutory wage controls if unions sought to press excessive claims.

In August 1976, Phase I, having proved remarkably successful, was replaced with a roughly similar policy. This time, however, the pay norm was set at 5 percent with a maximum of £4 and a minimum of £2.50, and the policy was combined with a small cut in direct taxes. Phase II expired in August 1977. As with Phase I, there were no major violations of the policy guidelines, and the level of wage drift in excess of the policy limits was surprisingly contained (Brown, 1979: 51–61; Daniel, 1976; Mayhew, 1981: 91–3; Saunders et al., 1977). Certainly, the growth of average earnings exceeded the target level by a few percentage points during both Phases I and II, but some of this drift was legitimate; for instance, the implementation of the Equal Pay Act was exempted from the policy requirements. How can this high level of compliance be explained?

Explaining the effectiveness of Phases I and II
Clearly, the conflict of interest experienced by bargaining groups during Phases I and II was very much lower than under the previous policy regime. This changed state of affairs was brought about by three factors. First, the economic recession, which began in 1974 and continued until early 1977, resulted in a sharp fall in company profitability and a doubling of the rate of unemployment (from 2.6 to 5.7 percent). Not unexpectedly, this brought about a marked rise in employer resistance to large pay claims and a relative decline in the bargaining power of labour. As a consequence, groups which sought to break the policy guidelines faced the prospect of higher strike costs and the threat of reduced employment. This meant, in effect, that the net payoff from any attempt to free-ride would probably be low or even negative. Such a situation applied in both the private and public sectors. Second, since the guidelines were clearly defined and permitted few exceptions, policy breaches could be more easily identified than during the 1974–75 wage round. The possibility of covert free-riding was thus much reduced. This of course lowered the expectation of there being widespread policy evasion and hence contributed to the willingness of negotiators to abide by the TUC–government agreements. Lastly, any union contemplating a strategy to break the policy limits had to reckon with the probable application of sanctions by the TUC and the government. This undoubtedly influenced the formulation and

pursuit of wage claims in a number of instances. In September 1976, for example, the National Union of Seamen called off its proposed strike action in pursuit of a pay settlement outside the Phase II guidelines when TUC leaders threatened it with expulsion.

But it was not merely the depressed state of the economy, the nature and clarity of the policy guidelines and the threat of private and public coercion which deterred groups from pressing excessive wage claims; also of vital importance was the high level of support for Phases I and II within the union movement. To put it differently, there was a much lower conflict of values than during the first year of the Social Contract.

Evidence to support this contention is available from a number of sources. Both the TUC General Council and the TUC annual conference voted by a wide margin to back the £6 and 5 percent policies. Opinion polls indicated massive public endorsement (*Guardian*, 8 June 1975; *Sunday Times*, 11 April 1976; *Daily Mirror*, 29 April 1976). Survey data (Willman, 1982: 127–9) reveals that plant negotiators, normally the group most hostile to incomes policies (whether voluntary or statutory), accepted the rationale for the pay limits. And the miners' union, unquestionably one of the most militant unions during the 1970s, endorsed both Phases I and II. A ballot of miners in August 1975 produced a vote of 60 percent in favour of Phase I, and a similar ballot the following year recorded a vote of 53 percent in support of Phase II.

Undoubtedly, the principal reason for the shift in union perceptions and attitudes between 1974 and 1975 was the mounting economic crisis. This had the effect of reducing the salience of narrow, sectional interests and fostering a commitment to broader goals and values — trade union solidarity, national unity, party loyalty and so forth. In these circumstances there were strong moral pressures on trade union leaders and members to sacrifice their immediate wants and demands in the national interest, and equally strong pressures for them to abide by nationally agreed policies. Such pressures were magnified in this instance by the realization that, unless they pursued a cooperative approach, the future of the Labour government could be imperilled. For instance, should there be an early election and a Conservative victory, the consequences for the labour movement would be very adverse indeed.

Thus a multitude of forces combined to ensure that Phases I and II received the formal endorsement of the TUC and the subsequent backing of union negotiators and rank-and-file members. Without the economic crisis there would have been no catalyst of sufficient strength to shift the balance of opinion within the TUC in favour of strict limitations on pay bargaining. Without the low level of company profitability, the steady rise in unemployment and the threat of sanctions there would have been greater difficulty in securing compliance. If a Labour government had not been in power, the ideological motivation necessary for union leaders to abandon, albeit temporarily, their commitment to free collective bargaining would have been absent. If the policies had not been so simple in form, or egalitarian in their distributional bias, they would not have received the same measure of union support and would have proved more difficult to monitor and enforce. Finally, if the economic and political circumstances had been different, union negotiators would have had less confidence that the pay guidelines would be observed. As a result, the rationale for compliance would have been undermined.

The collapse of consent

Yet if an economic crisis, by simultaneously reducing both the conflict of interest and the conflict of values experienced by bargaining groups, can assist in creating the necessary conditions for voluntary wage restraint, it is most unlikely to generate the prerequisites for lasting inter-class collaboration or a stable corporatist incomes policy. After all, once the immediate crisis is past and there is a return to economic growth and a greater measure of price stability, the consensus in favour of pay moderation is almost certain to disintegrate. This is all the more likely if the crisis has brought about a considerable fall in real incomes, if traditional patterns of income distribution have been significantly disturbed, or if the macroeconomic payoffs and governmental quid pro quos have fallen well behind expectations.

In the case of the Social Contract, the economic changes between 1975 and 1977 could hardly have been less favourable for sustaining union support for collective wage restraint. By the time of the union conference season in the spring of 1977, the short-term economic crisis had all but vanished: the rate of increase in unemployment had slackened; the pressure on the exchange rate had eased; price inflation, although still at 17 percent, was continuing to fall; and there were signs that the economy was beginning to emerge from the recession. In view of this, the need for further pay moderation was less evident, and there was growing shop-floor pressure for a return to free collective bargaining.

Such demands were intensified by virtue of the fact that many trade unionists, as a result of their experiences of the previous two years, felt that they had been cheated by the Labour government. There were numerous reasons for this. According to its original purposes, the Social Contract had been designed to secure full employment, enhance living conditions, improve social security benefits, reform industrial law and promote greater social justice. Yet the outcome had been radically different. Admittedly, the Labour government had passed legislation reforming aspects of the industrial relations system and had increased pensions as promised; but in virtually every other area progress had been minimal or negative. Unemployment had reached a postwar record; real pre-tax incomes had been cut by over 5 percent (on average);[5] and, at the direction of the IMF, the government had been forced in late 1976 to cut expenditure on social services. Although Labour ministers claimed that these macroeconomic outcomes were largely beyond their control, such assertions won little sympathy within significant sections of the union movement. Thus, maintaining that the government had reneged on its side of the Social Contract, the majority of union conferences during the spring and summer of 1977 voted against another pay deal with the government and pressed instead for a return to free collective bargaining. Effectively, this prevented the TUC from endorsing another wage norm, although it did support the retention of the 12-month rule prohibiting new pay settlements within a year of the preceding award.

The course of the remaining 20 months of Labour's counter-inflation policy (August 1977–May 1979) can be summarized roughly as follows. At the end of Phase II the Cabinet announced its intention of keeping pay rises to an average of 10 percent. The enforcement of this policy would depend on moral suasion and on a limited range of financial sanctions. In the event, the 10 percent target was not achieved: average earnings rose by 14.2 percent in the year to July 1978, and real incomes increased more rapidly than the government had hoped. Nevertheless, the outcome of Phase III was not as bad as some economic forecasters had feared.[6] The fact that nominal-wage growth did not accelerate more rapidly was no doubt due in large measure to market conditions: the economic recovery was still in its infancy, employer resistance to big pay claims was high, and the government was obviously determined to take a firm stand against free-riders, whether in the public or the private sector. But in addition to this, the trade union leadership was adamant that there would be no repetition of the disastrous free-for-all of 1974–75. Consequently, the TUC refused to give moral or financial support to those unions, such as the firemen, which sought to break the 10 percent limit. TUC leaders also tried to ensure that none of the key, trend-setting pay settlements, like those of the miners, the local authority manual workers and Ford workers, exceeded the government's target. In this they were largely, though not entirely, successful.

The outcome of the 1978–79 wage round, however, was very much different. In the middle of 1978 the government announced that the new pay limit would be 5 percent. This, it was hoped, would keep nominal-wage growth to below 8 percent and thus prevent a resurgence of price inflation before the next general election — which was originally expected to be in October 1978, but was delayed by Callaghan until mid-1979. However, the government's initial hopes were quickly dashed. Union leaders were angered by Callaghan's decision to postpone the election and considered that the 5 percent norm was too low. Hence, they were unwilling to exercise a restraining influence upon union negotiators, regardless of the consequences of this stance for Labour's electoral prospects. In any case, given the degree of militancy at the shop-floor level by the autumn of 1978, the union leadership could not have won rank-and-file endorsement for settlements under 8 percent, even if they had wanted to. Public sector workers, for example, were frustrated by the fall in relative pay which they had experienced since 1975, and many groups in the private sector were keen to take advantage of the improved level of company profitability to press large pay claims. This was highlighted when Ford workers went on a lengthy strike in September 1978 in pursuit of a 29 percent rise in earnings. They eventually settled in November for a package giving increases averaging 17 percent. From this point onwards everything went against the government (see Barnett, 1982; Dorfman, 1983): in December Parliament rejected the Cabinet's policy of imposing financial sanctions against companies which broke the pay guidelines; there was a massive upsurge in strike activity during the winter; and settlements above 10 percent became the rule rather than the exception. By the end of the wage round, average earnings were rising at a rate in excess of 16 percent, double the government's original target.

With the benefit of hindsight, such a result hardly seems surprising. The expansion of the economy during 1977 and 1978 led to a rise in the opportunity costs of compliance with the government's pay policy, especially for bargaining groups in high-growth sectors. Almost simultaneously, there was an upsurge in union hostility to the idea of collective wage restraint. Given this rise in both the conflict of interest and conflict of values, it was only to be expected that unions would press for big pay increases, and only to be expected that some of these claims would succeed. Once certain groups like the Ford workers and lorry drivers had settled well above the pay ceiling, it was undoubtedly in the short-term interests of virtually every other bargaining group to try and follow suit. In these circumstances, no amount of moral and political pressure for restraint could make much difference.

Conclusion

One question which arises from the above discussion is whether support for a corporatist incomes policy could ever be sustained for a period longer than two or three years in a country, such as Britain, with unfavourable structural and attitudinal conditions. In other words, could a Social Contract become effectively institutionalized? The answer here must be negative. The normative commitments of trade union leaders and negotiators in Britain are such that the necessary backing for voluntary wage restraint is likely to be forthcoming only during an economic crisis or war. Thus, any attempt to enforce mutual restraint in 'normal' conditions, or to enforce permanent or semi-permanent restrictions upon the bargaining autonomy of individual unions by either the government or the TUC (or both), seems doomed to failure. Only with a radical and sustained change in trade union attitudes towards pay bargaining, and probably also a change in institutional arrangements, could a longer-term corporatist strategy, say along the Austrian lines, be made to work effectively.

Yet how could such a transformation be brought about? One requirement would be for a sufficient number of trade union leaders to be convinced that it was in their interests (and also presumably the interests of their members) to coordinate their bargaining strategies at a national level, rather then pursue a strategy of independent short-term maximization (free collective bargaining). But for this condition to be fulfilled, the harmful consequences of free collective bargaining would have to be plainly evident, as would the advantages of a cooperative solution. While the 1980–83 recession in Britain appears to have persuaded at least some trade unionists of the pitfall of free collective bargaining under monetarist policies, it has not brought about any fundamental change of attitude. In fact, from all accounts, support for incomes policies within the union movement remains low. And yet, if the tragic impact of monetarism has proved insufficient to bring any major or lasting shifts in the perceptions and commitments of trade union leaders, it seems very difficult to know what could. For the Labour Party, committed as it is to an expansionary economic policy and an anti-inflation policy relying upon long-term trade union restraint, this state of affairs can only remain of grave concern.

Notes

1. Obviously, such 'defecting' or evasion of the policy guidelines will not necessarily be 'free'. A large money-wage increase, for example, may well reduce the amount of labour sought by employers. Whether or not such costs act as a constraint upon union negotiators will depend on the relative weight they attach to employment objectives and the extent to which they take the threatened loss of employment opportunities seriously.

2. The notion of a 'Social Contract' was drawn from the Social Contract theorists of the seventeenth and eighteenth centuries such as Hobbes, Locke and Rousseau. It appears that the term first entered Labour Party parlance in 1970 when Thomas (now Lord) Balogh, writing in a Fabian Tract after the June election (1970: 11), called for a new 'Contrat Social' between a future Labour government and the trade union movement.

3. Estimates of the number of workers fully or partially covered by the threshold system vary, but it probably amounted to over half the workforce. According to Mayhew (1983: 29) the number was in the region of 14 million.

4. During the course of the day, the pound depreciated from 27.6 to 28.9 percent against the 'currency basket' as measured by the Smithsonian parities, and from US\$2.2245–2.2255 to US\$2.1910–2.1930. This represented the largest fall ever recorded in a single day of trading, and clearly reflected the level of international anxiety over the state of the British economy.

5. Much of this cut in real pre-tax incomes was unintentional and was the product of the fact that sterling depreciated in value during 1976 by far more than had been originally projected. This increased import prices and hence slowed the pace at which the rate of price inflation declined during 1976–77.

6. For example, the stockbroking firm, Phillips and Drew, expected average earnings to increase by 15–20 percent.

5
Corporatism and Thatcherism: is there life after death?

Kevin Bonnett

Atavistic as it may seem, the neo-liberal approach to economic policy has by now enjoyed a lengthy resurrection.[1] It might appear obvious that corporatist intermediation was a 'fair-weather' phenomenon locked into the structure of the Keynesian welfare state (KWS), and that the rise to dominance of counter-inflationary strategy signalled the rapid (and largely unlamented) demise of tripartite compromises. The object of this paper is to evaluate this assumption and to explore the extent to which functional representation and bargaining really are incompatible with policies which displace Keynesian growth strategy.[2] It will be argued that neo-liberal policies embody a clear rejection of macro-corporatism; but, in line with the other contributions to this volume, one can identify a *variety* of modes and levels of corporatist intermediation, some of which might even facilitate the control of inflation and the stimulation of private-sector activity in the market place. In addition, monetarism and laissez-faire can be seen to have very severe limitations which may in themselves necessitate important departures in the direction of intervention and functional representation.

In analysing these contradictory consequences, it will be essential to employ the distinctions between macro-, meso- and micro-corporatism which Alan Cawson has spelt out in the introduction to this volume. In this chapter I will argue that neo-liberal policies will produce markedly different effects at each of these levels, and may indeed encourage the surprising emergence of new forms of corporatism. This will be especially evident at the micro-level, but in the particular guise of a *two-nation* diverse future for industrial relations. In contrast, the meso-level of sectoral policy contains such a complex diversity of representation linkages that no one model (such as corporatism or 'market freedom') can possibly encompass them all. The reality of industrial policy will be shown to be considerably more interventionist than neo-liberal ideology (or aspirations) might suggest.

This paper therefore argues that corporatism will live on in the wake of Thatcherism, but perhaps in distorted and divisive manifestations.

What is Thatcherism?
Thatcherism is much more than monetarism, but rather less than a whole new hegemonic common sense which redefines British political reality. In this brief section I cannot attempt to explain the origins of Thatcherism or trace in detail the troubled history of its application to the real world, but it is important to set out some of the key characteristics of the 'Thatcherite revolution'.

In terms of political, economic and moral ideology, the brand of Conservatism espoused by Margaret Thatcher owes most to liberal individualism in the sense of economic freedom in the market-place, allied to a strong but narrowly bounded state which guarantees a framework of legal contract and social ordering in order to facilitate economic activity and guarantee the secure possession of property and unequal reward. The roots of this may be sought either in the intellectual resurgence of the New Right or in the reaffirmation of narrow petty-bourgeois self-interest[3] — it hardly matters for our purposes here, since the outcome is the same. A broader stance, which was pro-market, anti-economic intervention and seriously ambivalent towards the welfare state, provided an underpinning of political commitment beneath economic policies which were initially regarded by many as purely technical instruments for disinflation. The neo-liberal approach to disinflation is not unitary: there are complex differences of belief about mechanisms, priorities and indeed on causal linkages among monetarist economists.[4] Despite this, the commitment to monetary control, to cuts in state expenditure (or at least borrowing) and to denationalization (or, as this pretends to be, 'competition policy') are all technical concerns which relate directly to political aspects of the neo-liberal or 'marketist' world view.

More controversial than this is the possible link to a growth strategy. Clearly, neo-liberals believe that both disinflation and diminishing state 'interference' create conducive conditions for unconstrained enterprise in the market. At the same time, there is a more general aspect of imposing restructuring from above. Weak management and the softness of firms which concede pay rises have always been targets for attack — this is one clear area where the government has sought to impose costs on some firms in order to strengthen the overall economy. Whether extreme squeeze is the best way to do this is far from clear, and a 20 percent loss in manufacturing capacity during the 1979–83 government is a high price to pay. Similarly, the Thatcher government never intended or expected deflation to be so heavily overlaid by recession that unemployment exceeded 3 million, but it certainly did seek to discipline and restructure the trade unions, both by legislation and by the fear of redundancy. Nothing could be further from the goals of social partnership or institutionalized corporatism as a means of regulating inflation and restructuring. Indeed, the distance between the Thatcher governments and the peak organizations of labour and industry stayed large; it is perhaps less so in the latter case, but consultation remains piecemeal — in no sense is there a bargaining of policy (Middlemas, 1983).

This distance between the Confederation of British Industry and the government highlights one aspect of the political character of Thatcherism: it is very hard to discern any real unification of political forces around the broader Thatcherite project. Fundamental differences of interest remain between different sectors of capital, whether they be bankers, multinational companies or producers for the domestic market. Quiescent acceptance is not the same thing as mobilized active support, and it is hard to argue that Mrs Thatcher has brought about a stable realignment of policy fully supported by different powerful economic interests.

It could equally be argued that the popular ideological success of Thatcherism is far less than is sometimes imagined. The proponents of the concept of 'authoritarian populism' (Hall and Jacques, 1983) seriously exaggerate the extent to which Thatcherism is a coherent alternative common sense which decisively breaks with existing political fundamentals (Jessop et al., 1984). The espousal of privatism and possessive individualism may be widespread in Britain, but so is acceptance of state-provided social benefits (particularly health and education). The electoral success of the Conservatives disguises a much more complex underlying reality, in which crisis and division among opponents interacts with the peculiarities of the British electoral system to provide a landslide and an apparent mandate for Thatcher.

It is true that the crises of industrial relations and stagflation seriously eroded the foundations of the postwar Keynesian welfare state political settlement. It is too sweeping to conclude from this that neo-liberalism now enjoys a broader hegemony over the British electorate; the question now is whether any alternative strategy can be constructed which could, in the changed political climate, be regarded as 'realistic' and 'credible' enough to seriously challenge neo-liberalism. Such a strategy not only would have to appeal to the electorate, but also would have to gain some degree of interest or compliance among powerful economic interests.

One way in which that question would be resolved is if Thatcherism defeats itself, either through internal failures (as with pure monetarism) or through political mistakes which finally meet the limits of what is feasible or politically survivable. By 1984 the indulgence of the City of London lapsed into a classic sterling panic, and the defensive weakness of the trade unions stiffened into the miners' strike. Whether these signal the advance of Britain's Napoleon-in-petticoats towards her Waterloo remains to be seen.

Macrocorporatism, disinflation and growth strategy

Despite the British experience since 1976, it must be emphasized that counter-inflation strategies need not take the form of simple deflation, nor need they be monetarist, pro-market and anti-corporatist. Indeed, one of the great achievements of successful corporatism (as, for example, in Austria) is that positive-sum outcomes can be secured, which give benefits to all parties to the corporatist bargain. A fully successful corporatism would thus be able to secure non-inflationary growth through elaborately institutionalized joint agreements on wages, productivity and possibly prices and distributed profits. Such a model has a number of implications.

First, this model implies a rejection of views such as Panitch's which regard corporatism as always producing zero-sum outcomes in the wage–profit share. For such authors, elaborate bargaining simply adds sophistication and collaboration to the process of exploitation. When the alternative of crude deflation with its unemployment effects is compared to this, the corporatist alternative suddenly appears much less 'zero-sum' — at least to this author. Unfortunately, the construction of positive-sum corporatism seems to depend precisely on the successful pursuit of growth, and in the British case growth has been notable only for its relative absence. As we shall see, however, this is in contrast to economies with a stronger legacy of corporatism, where important pressures for intermediation may remain even in the context of economic stagnation.

The second implication of our 'successful corporatism' model follows from this. If corporatist bargaining penetrates deeply enough into the process of setting wages and prices, and into labour market policy for training, mobility and flexibility, then macroeconomic management can take a variety of forms. Unlike countries adopting simple Keynesian fiscal management, or simple monetarist control of the rate of growth of the money supply, these macroeconomic levers are *not* expected to regulate the whole economy adequately in terms of growth, inflation and employment.

Whenever such purely macro-policies hold sway, the real economy is left to bear the brunt of adjustments 'from above' by the state, whether this is the stop–go phase of classic Keynesianism or the squeeze on production entailed in using high interest rates as a monetary control instrument.

As Fritz Scharpf (1982) has observed, some recipes for economic success are founded upon mixtures of policies which would seem contradictory and unworkable if it were assumed that monetary control must go together with neo-liberalism's free-for-all in the market and that corporatism has to be allied to fiscal policies to secure full employment and growth. West Germany in the 1970s, Scharpf argues, enjoyed inflation control through social partnership together with a 'Strukturpolitik', which implied intervention to pursue sectoral restructuring and labour market flexibility (even if this was not directive and fully selective). Although fiscal expansionism flowered briefly after 1967 in these characteristically corporatist strategies, the independent role of the Bundesbank in sustaining monetary 'rectitude' reasserted itself and became the predominant influence. The strains this imposed upon the trade unions' social partnership in the worsening world economic climate were real, of course; the recent outcomes will be taken up later. Similarly, Scharpf argues that in Austria, until recently, monetary stability was able to coexist with considerable fiscal expansionism, primarily because of the effectiveness of inflation control through institutionalized corporatism:

> The problem of cost–push inflation was delegated to the industrial relations system ... which managed to reduce unit labour costs.... With inflation under control, the Austrian government was free to use its second lever, fiscal and monetary policy, to pursue an aggressive expansionary policy to stimulate economic growth and to prevent unemployment. (Scharpf, 1982: 14)

There is thus no reason why disinflation need be deflationary if adequate mechanisms of inflation control can be sustained. In the British case, the later history of the Keynesian welfare state was marked by the repeated failure of voluntaristic corporatist regulation of wages (and sometimes prices); the response to this was occasionally laissez-faire in character, but more frequently it involved direct and obligatory intervention. The form this took varied from the simple coercion of an obligatory wage-freeze to the more innovative attempts to institutionalize equity and consensual outcomes, as in the National Board for Prices and Incomes or the Labour–TUC Social Contract of the mid-1970s.

All these efforts were directed towards inflation control, and none of them relied upon the response of the impersonal hand of the market to macroeconomic management (Booth, 1983; Tarling and Wilkinson, 1977). The proximate causes of the revival of British neo-liberalism lay not only in the rise of an ideology and in the broader economic crises of the 1970s, but also in the repeated failure of concertation and direct economic intervention. When the 1976 sterling crisis crippled the Social Contract, the foundations for monetarism and public expenditure cuts were laid by the Labour government. While the policy of that government was never based solely upon monetarist deflation, this element of the post-1976 policy mix helped to embalm the body of the postwar settlement, if not to finally lay it to rest (see Keegan and Pennant-Rea, 1979).

The distinctiveness of Thatcherism, therefore, lies not so much in its monetarism as in its apparently *unalloyed* monetarism, where broader neo-liberal policies (cuts, privatization, competition policy) are congruent with monetary control and seek to enhance the market freedom that monetarism both assumes to exist and seeks to enhance. One interesting question is whether the real conduct of monetarism and encouragement of markets and enterprise actually does imply and employ elements of corporatist intermediation, 'despite itself'. The fate of macro-corporatism (whether informal or institutionalized) is clear; the meso- and micro-levels show a more complex set of developments.

Disinflation by slump:
Thatcherism and macroeconomic corporatism

If the battle against inflation was won during the 1979–83 government (and that is by no means certain), it was a Pyrrhic victory,[5] achieved not through monetarist control of the money supply, but through generalized deflationary squeeze on real activity. That said, the broad stance on macroeconomic policy has remained consistent (critics would argue, perversely so) despite the onset of world recession which exacerbated the existing squeeze. This deflationary stance survived adverse world conditions in 1981 and a change of Chancellor in 1983; on the way, a wider range of targets and instruments have been employed, but the goal of policy remains the same: disinflation and restructuring through the discipline of economic hardship. It may be that the Minford school of monetarism, which assumes 'rational expectations', encouraged hopes for a rapid and relatively painless adjustment as economic actors altered their expectations about inflation rates; even when such faith was confounded, the response in the early years was to harden the policy rather than adapt it.

Other pieces of monetarist doctrine suggested that doubling VAT and pushing up prices of state-supplied commodities would have no real effect on inflation and wage demands; these factors, plus dearer borrowing and the payment of public sector pay increases, helped to fuel inflation through much of the first Thatcher government rather than reduce it.

In effect, the 'monetarist' pursuit of disinflation really took the form of an old-fashioned (only now pro-cyclical) squeeze through the instruments of very high interest rates and a tight fiscal policy which sought to cut government borrowing and spending. Of course this was not justified or motivated in terms of demand management, but rather in terms of controlling the rate of growth of the money supply by discouraging the demand for credit and diminishing the monetary base for credit created by government borrowing through the money markets. The fundamental problems of this strategy soon became apparent: despite clear evidence of squeeze, the monetary indicators showed excess money supply growth. Their role as surrogates for the Gold Standard, imposing monetary rectitude, was only too successful, however, as financial markets judged economic prospects and policy performance on these criteria. Not only were monetary indicators actively misleading[6] owing to disintermediation — the process where new modes of credit creation constantly evade regulation — but the authorities came to realize that effective control over monetary creation is incompatible with the freedom distinctive to the City of London (HMSO, 1980). If such direct control over the monetary base really had been sought, then detailed sectoral intervention would have been necessary with an enhanced role for the Bank of England as a regulatory agency of the State. This would have raised intriguing possibilities of corporatist intermediation in the Government-City relationship. At present that nexus is clearly not of a corporatist form despite elite associations such as the Accepting Houses amongst the merchant banks, or the Clearing Banks' collective Committee. If any mechanism embodies intermediation — influence on policy-formation together with responsibility for its implementation — it is the Bank of England which then cajoles the City institutions into line.

Certainly it is hard to find support for Jessop's (1982b) specula-tion that the pursuit of monetary control would necessitate interventionism, thus leading to a 'corporatizing' of monetarism. His argument went on, however, to suggest that the failure of 'technical' monetarism to reduce inflation would necessitate an engagement with the real causes of inflation. Such engagement could take the form of direct intervention to override market outcomes: wages and possibly prices would become a legitimate concern once more, as would bankruptcies, take-overs and invest-ment plans. All that would once more raise the questions of representation, negotiation and implementation. Corporatism might even be back on the agenda. Alternatively, Jessop argued, an approach more consistent with neo-liberalism would involve enhancing market disciplines through a toleration of unemployment, bankruptcies and uncontrolled capital movement and investment. Jessop at that time considered this alternative (dubbed 'recommodification') unlikely in view of its likely political costs in terms of protest and police repression.

Cursory observation would suggest that the second course has been pursued at further expense to corporatist structures. Despite occasional riots and strikes, the strategy of tolerating mass unemployment and strengthening the police appears to exert sufficient discipline to quell resistance. Meanwhile the policy of privatizing productive state assets continues apace (see *Observer*, 15 July 1984), despite political embarrassments about the conduct of the sell-offs and the irony of creating private monopolies in the name of competition. Can we conclude from this that neo-liberalism has evaded the contradictions within it, and if so how?

The reality of Thatcherist policy in practice reveals a diversity of measures and means and a range of compromises within the consistency of the macroeconomic stance. First of all, the failure of money supply control did not result in a direct attack on those real causes of inflation that lay within the domestic economy. The rate of inflation eventually fell during the 1979–83 administration largely because of reduced import prices and the transformed labour markets. High interest rates caused the pound to be 'overvalued', causing low import prices which helped consumers and squeezed the price increases of domestic firms as they competed for sales. The tight public spending constraints not only hit builders and manufacturers but also curtailed public sector pay rises; meanwhile the private sector labour market was disciplined by unemployment. In these ways the monetarist deflation succeeded, in effect if not by design, in changing the real conditions for inflation. A basic unresolved question concerns the extent to which underlying conflicts over the wage–profit share and over distribution and differentials have actually been suppressed in the long term. Whether neo-liberalism has really 'depoliticized' inequality and restored faith in market outcomes — a kind of new 'post-slump settlement' — remains in serious doubt.

In the field of macro-industrial policy, the evidence for neo-liberal transformation is even patchier. This is hardly surprising, since Thatcherism would dictate little more than an *absence* of industrial policy beyond privatization and competition policy. Even Sir Keith Joseph, when he was Industry Secretary, had to face the reality of nationalized loss-making industries and 'lame ducks' such as British Leyland which could not be allowed to hobble off to die. In so far as continued state funding of coal, steel and BL were defeats, the government retreated, but it must be acknowledged that drastic restructuring and eventual sales to private capital have been imposed. Privatization has not only sent money-spinners such as gas and oil assets into private hands, but has also imposed dramatic restructuring in enterprises such as British Airways. In basic industries such as iron, coal and vehicles, considerations of ever-shrinking current market demand have overridden concerns for national resources or social effects. Competition policy has had some effects on professional and state monopolies, particularly in transport and communications.

While all this is clear evidence of neo-liberalism at work, there are important qualifications to be made. First, privatization has had a significant role to play in reducing the Public Sector Borrowing Requirement and relieving some of the fiscal pressures caused by unemployment and tax-cut promises. This pragmatic benefit may be as significant as the ideological commitment to competition. Second, and more important, there is clear evidence for continued close relations between industry and government, even if this does not take an unambiguously corporatist form. Moreover, the importance of intervention for growth and investment subsidy has reasserted itself — nowhere clearer than in the field of microelectronics. These issues are taken up in detail in the section on sectoral corporatism. Third, by no means all tripartite institutions have been dismantled, even if those that remain have been subordinated (e.g. NEDC) or tranformed to limit union influence (e.g. Manpower Services Commission — see discussion below and chapter 3 above). Finally, it must be emphasized that the main force for restructuring has been the recession itself, deepened and sharpened by the high interest rates and the high exchange rates of the first Thatcher government. There is absolutely no guarantee that restructuring by slump will produce 'rational' outcomes, since the impact will vary not only by the inherent 'strength' or 'worthiness' of firms, but also by sheer size, extent of borrowings, degree of dependence upon particular state expenditures (for example, builders *v.* defence contractors), capacity for high risk investment in adverse market conditions, vulnerability to price competition in world markets and so on. For all those firms who had vulnerable characteristics, the monetarist deflation produced not restructuring but destructive de-industrialization. The absence of *effective* resistance to this inside or outside the governing party tells us much about the character of organized economic interests and their relation to the state in Britain.

Sectoral intervention, corporatist and neo-liberal

Nowhere is the gap between reality and rhetoric greater than in the field of industrial policy. This applies to all governments, but with particular force to the Thatcher years. The complex relationships between state agencies and various sectors of the economy may be affected only superficially, or only in certain cases, by political doctrines of governments. The sheer density and diversity of linkage defies any single analytical categorization (such as 'corporatism') and clearly poses immense difficulties for any neo-liberal withdrawal of the state from economic intervention. Even competition policy and de-nationalization is, in a narrow sense, intervention. But apart from this limiting case, even neo-liberal governments seem unable to rely entirely on 'free-enterprise' in 'liberated markets' to deliver the desired economic growth and recovery.

The most stringent neo-liberal approach sustains facilitative state functions — that is, functions sustaining the legal and social order as well as the material infrastructure which makes orderly market activity possible. Radical New Right proposals to allow railways to die and health to become a matter of private provision collide with this facilitative role (as well as with political boundaries), if, for example, they erode the availability of a healthy workforce with adequate transport to work. Beyond this, substantive intervention, which non-selectively subsidizes investment or other costs to a whole industry, has been expanded rather than contracted since 1979. Enterprise zones are only the visibly symbolic crest to a mountain of subsidies, incentives, tax write-offs and the rest. Much less in evidence, perhaps, has been directive control of individual firms' investment and employment decisions — though even here public sector companies have had restructuring imposed upon them, partly in preparation for selling off.

Given this pattern, our central question concerns the modes of representation which go together with these various dimensions of intervention; once again, they are diverse, but some authors have discerned emerging trends; among these are Grant (1984) and Streeck and Schmitter (1984).

Wyn Grant has speculated provocatively that 'the Thatcher Government is developing an "Ordnungspolitik" which emphasizes the importance of capitalist associability' in that the avoidance of directive controls produces 'a considerable willingness to delegate functions to interest associations' within capital (1984: 1). Indeed, Grant suggests that the whole focus of corporatist investigation must shift away from macro-level tripartism to sectoral representation through interest organization. The incorporation of labour representatives is made much less necessary by the impact of unemployment; therefore Grant regards bipartite state–industry contact as recognizably corporatist, so long as the relationship involves representative associations of some kind involved in full intermediation. In other words, those associations must implement policy as well as make representations during its formation. This is in direct contradiction to the 'parity' principle of equal rights to influence (if not equal in outcome) for both capital and labour — a criterion for identifying corporatism sustained by scholars such as Lehmbruch and Marin. Grant may be right to imply that this is too stringent when applied to Britain, with its much lower level of institutionalization of concertation than in Germany or Austria. As long as the key principles of associative representation and intermediation are retained, there probably is a case for retaining the corporatist model.

This identification is taken one step further by Streeck and Schmitter (1984) when they argue that the reaction against state direction characteristic of the 1980s (among both the New Right and the New Social movements) may signify a move not simply back to the market but instead towards elements of an associative order, in which organizational concertation is the key to representation and policy implementation. Like Grant, they emphasize the limiting conditions for genuine corporatism: the associations need to have a representational monopoly and to be sufficiently in control of their membership successfully to define their interests and implement policy bargains. The limit case of this (and one which is very close to Grant's new Ordnungspolitik) is 'Private Interest Government' (PIG) where monopolistic associations gain considerable autonomy for self-regulation together with public status and a tight grip on policy formation. Legal and medical professions are familiar examples; compulsory Austrian economic associations come just as close.

As it stands, this thesis may be less than plausible as an aspiration or active construction of neo-liberal governments, but the real test is whether such a new order is emerging by default despite attempts to move from state to market modes of organisation. Let us see if these do clarify the evidence.

First of all, the degree of continuity and diversity in state–industry relations remains impressive. The models already outlined as bilateral corporatism and private interest government are un-doubtedly applicable in some cases, but we must acknowledge the continuing importance of other forms of relationship between enterprises and governments. For example, a direct relationship might exist between a single firm and a particular state agency. Factors encouraging this include high levels of concentration in various sectors, and the extent to which various single-firm industries have been actually sponsored into existence by government subsidy of investment, public purchasing policy or merger policy. A key example is ICL, the sole British producer of mainframe computers, whose origins and survival have been totally dependent upon the state. Even when operations such as British Aerospace and British Airways become privatized, the scale of investment and the implications of purchasing decisions are such that state involvement is highly likely. Enterprises on the scale of ICL are hardly likely to be refused access to make direct representations to ministers and officials; associational representation may be less than crucial to such firms (see Grant, 1983b). (For a discussion of whether this relationship should be regarded as corporatist or not, see the Introduction to this volume.)

In other industries, the direct linkage may arise from a mutual dependence extending to the point of symbiosis. The clearest example here is the defence industry. Although many general manufacturers sell their products, the position of armament firms, ship and airplane builders and electronics manufacturers is obviously of a very special order. It is inconceivable that major items of research and development, or production itself, could take place without negotiation, agreement and effective subsidy. Similarly, the mutual dependence of the National Health Service and the pharmaceutical industry has been exposed to view in the debate over generic drugs and guaranteed profit levels to subsidize research (for a detailed account see Sargent, 1983).

In some instances such symbiotic relationships may display a distinctively corporatist dimension. Here one may observe that special relationship between mutually dependent bodies, one of which is a producers' association with the capacity to 'deliver' its members — a classic example is that between the National Farmers' Union and the Agriculture Ministry. The crucial difference here is that producers are sufficiently numerous and fragmented to necessitate corporatist representation, and so we might expect the pattern to be repeated where similar conditions apply. Agriculture, though, is always likely to be highly 'organized' — many have observed how Agriculture, with its 'wet' minister in charge, remained an island within Thatcherism isolated from the rest of the strategy.

Further variations in these relationships have appeared during the processes of industrial restructuring necessitated by the recession. Echoes of the 1930s are audible in some of the mechanisms employed, as trade associations and cartels collectively reduced manufacturing capacity. Whether spontaneous or externally initiated, the restructuring has to take a collective form. For example, the steel castings industry was induced to agree on rationalizing production by the merchant bankers Lazards (possibly with the encouragement of state authorities). The trade association eventually agreed to pool funds from survivor companies to buy out the capacity of weak ones.[7] How the bank's role relates to the apparent corporatism of such sectoral agreement is hard to categorize. A clearer case of sectoral agreement without corporatism is that of European chemical producers. A classic mode of top-level cartel bargaining seems to have been employed in the allocation of cuts in production capacity among the firms, with each specializing in certain products. Trade associations seem irrelevant to negotiations at such a level, even though sectoral concertation is being achieved. Indeed, Grant (1983b) has demonstrated the weakness of British chemical industry trade associations. In neither of these cases is the sectoral restructuring unambiguously mobilized on the basis of corporatism.

Further complexity attaches to the large-scale 'lifeboat' of clearing bank lending to private manufacturers during the crisis year of 1981 (*Sunday Times*, 6 March 1981: 15). This was mobilized by the Bank of England at the same time as that institution helped to create the firms' crisis by raising interest rates and squeezing credit creation. The banks were forced into the position of deciding the fate of major producers — and were forced to bear a mounting burden of 'bad debts' as the casualties succumbed.

This range of alternative modes of intervention-cum-representation means that governments who wish to impose regimes of either 'direction' or 'non-intervention' really only move towards some alternative modes in some sectors. Governments never cease intervention altogether (as the Right might wish), and they hardly need to depart from existing relationships to be 'directive' in various spheres (though the Left might wish to extend this, particularly in the realm of finance).

Complexities of intervention — the case of microelectronics

A key case for examining the possible variations in strategy and hence the strength of Grant's and Streeck and Schmitter's speculations is the microelectronics and information technology industry. Here I rely particularly on the detailed work of Strathclyde Research Project on 'New Technology and Employment Policies in Europe' (see Webber, Moon and Richardson, 1984; also Locksley, 1983; Grant, 1982).

Conservatives in charge of the Department of Trade and Industry emphasize a non-directive facilitative role for their actions. At the same time, however, their 1983 election manifesto was able to boast that state aid for the new technologies had risen from £100 to £350 million in 1979–83. In fact, all the previous programmes and interventions were continued in 1979, with a considerable expansion of new ones since. The American and Japanese domination of these lead industries has drawn European governments since the 1960s to protect and encourage their own domestic producers — but the political form of this intervention has varied quite widely.

Any over-hasty equation of intervention and subsidy with corporatism is quickly scotched by the importance of the American pattern, its economic predominance being founded on massive subsidies of general research and development — particularly in electronics — through defence and space expenditure. It is a complex of imperatives that move states towards subsidy — the goals of sustaining national independence in defence and technology, the desire for enhanced information technology to secure administrative savings (or increased capacity), the desire to safeguard the competitiveness of domestic producers, the perception of market failures in this high-cost, high-risk field.

The 'strategies' resulting, however, can vary from the symbiotic bilateralism of the American 'military–industrial complex' to the directive control exercised by the French state by virtue of Mitterrand's nationalizations. In general, where the problem is less one of fundamental innovation than of national production, states have sponsored large (even national monopoly) enterprises into existence to challenge the power of IBM or AT & T. Both France and Britain steadily merged and subsidized their computer firms throughout the 1960s to that end, developing direct bilateralism to the point of nationalization (Webber, Moon and Richardson, 1984: 10–16). The electronics industry more generally benefited more than other fields from the heavy subsidies to industrial research and development; even in the 1960s the proportion subsidized was 52 percent in the USA, 37 percent in Britain and 31 percent in France. Only West Germany, with 17 percent lagged behind in terms of general subsidies, particularly in electronics. Much of this still comes via military budgets; in 1981 52 percent of British state expenditure on research and development was in the military sector compared with 36 percent of French and 9 percent of West German funding. Moreover, the British Defence Ministry consumed almost one-fifth of electronics production in 1983–84 (Webber, Moon and Richardson, 1984: 19). One would expect this to be unevenly spread, as well. Marconi, for example, must enjoy a very close relationship with the Defence Ministry. Similarly, a very small number of telecommunications producers operated a cartel with the virtual monopsony consumer in Britain, British Telecom; however, this has been one area where competition policy has had a recent impact.

Not all of the new technology production is large-scale. The development of software and applications involves a greater number of innovators, and here industry-wide interventions have existed since the late 1970s. In addition, however, the Labour government extended large subsidies to three small firms created under the state aegis to develop components production and information applications. These arrangements were continued by the incoming Conservatives until 1984, when INMOS was sold off to the private sector.

Britain's pattern of intervention seems to lie midway between those of France and Germany, according to the Strathclyde research. French policy even before nationalization was rigidly selective, channelling large amounts to specific large enterprises. From the 1960s, the subsidy to investment has been planned and agreed in detail, which involves important elements of control.

West German funding has been general rather than selectively directive in intention, but industry-wide subsidies have still tended to accumulate in the hands of the largest producers, as a result of the degree of concentration of production. Where subsidy goes to applications and software, the effect is spread much more widely. It does not appear that the effective concentration of aid goes together with political selectivity, and it may be that a tension exists in the field of representation between (1) direct bipartism between the state and the biggest firms, and (2) bilateral or trilateral corporatism involving the industrial sector as a whole. Recent political shifts to a conservative coalition government have shifted the emphasis away from controlled selective subsidy towards more general subsidies without direct supervisory control. As in Britain, a shift towards rightist economic doctrine shifts the balance towards non-interventionist subsidy but does not abolish selectivity and direction. Competition policy remains tempered by the desire to prevent total loss of national involvement in new technology industries.

What can we conclude from this about modes of representation? First, it has to be said that there is little evidence available to confirm predictions of either 'private interest government' or devolved intervention in this field. The initial impression is of a mixture of direct bilateralism and non-organized industry-wide subsidy. There is little sign of devolution to producers' associations; rather, there are ad hoc bipartite relationships in particular fields. A current example of simple bilateralism is the renewed deal between Acorn and the BBC to supply computers for education — other

producers wished for a slice of the market, but they seemingly had
no representational means of securing it.

Perhaps the answer is that the industry is simply too young and
too competitive to have developed an 'associative order' — there is,
after all, significant evidence of producers' associations being used
as 'chosen instruments' by ministries in fields such as large-scale
construction (Grant, 1984; Grant and Streeck, chapter 8 below).
Whether this is bipartite corporatism or a state-colluded cartel is
open to debate, especially when the number of firms in key sectors
is so small.

One can only conclude that no single model can capture the
complexity of representation and intervention at sectoral level.
Radical governments of the Right (Britain) or the Left (France)
clearly do make significant inroads into the structure, but the
diversity and the inter-penetration of state–producer relations
remains. Let us now move down to the level of micro-corporatism
to assess the effects, once more contradictory, of the neo-liberal
experiment.

Micro-corporatism, deflationary discipline and industrial relations

It is easy to assume that neo-liberal policies will have a severe
impact on the general powers of trade unions and will transform the
character of industrial relations backwards towards coercive and
authoritarian management strategies. There is, of course, a substantial amount of truth in this picture when one considers the
disciplining effect of mass unemployment, or the management styles
accompanying forcible restructure in BL under Edwardes, or steel
and coal under MacGregor. There is clearly no question that the
balance of power in industrial relations has shifted sharply towards
redundancies and new working practices which place unions in a
weak defensive position. However, when the broader structure of
industrial relations is considered, together with the interests of
labour and employer associations, it is not so obvious that
'micro-corporatism' at enterprise or firm level will be destroyed by
deflation and slump. Especially in economies with more stably
institutionalized micro-corporatism (such as West Germany), there
may be powerful pressures to sustain the structure even if the
climate and balance of forces within has been transformed.

Most important of all, the lack of a uniform change in industrial
relations may become visible as a pattern of division: micro-
corporatism for a privileged sector accompanied by managerial
despotism and casualization of employment for a secondary sector.
These segmentations in the labour market have long been observed;
perhaps neo-liberalism is exacerbating this trend within a broader

context of 'two-nations' divisions between (in Britain) North and South, 'productive' *v.* 'unproductive', private welfare purchasers *v.* public users and so on. Such a two-nations effect thoroughly undermines the possibility of a consensual macro-corporatism, but it by no means precludes deals among the 'privileged' or organized at sectoral/meso-level and at micro-level.

Evidence on trends in British industrial relations under Thatcher is now beginning to emerge (Daniel and Millward, 1983; Jacobi et al., 1985), and arguments concerning the German developments have been forcibly presented by Wolfgang Streeck (1984). The evidence on Britain shows that formal structures of union representation remain extremely strong in both manufacturing and public sector employment. Most large establishments had union membership densities of 90 percent or more, formalized bargaining arrangements (71 percent of establishments with manual unions), and stable structures of shop steward representation involving both hierarchy and employer-provided practical facilities. This is reflected in the continued importance of multi-level pay bargaining for manual workers, hence focusing significance not only on central representation but also on the balance of power at enterprise and plant level (Daniel and Millward, 1983). Clearly, the effect of these patterns is that 'assaults' on worker strength need either to incorporate the shop stewards, and perhaps supplement them with other forms of cooperative representation (i.e. more micro-corporatism), or to engage in a confrontation with shop stewards in order to erode their power.

According to some current evidence, most firms appear to be avoiding confrontation in favour of increased micro-corporatism (within which the initiative and power is skewed heavily towards management, given the current economic climate). This is, on the face of it, a surprising aspect of the impact of neo-liberal policies; however, there is one important qualification: the very developments which strengthen micro-corporatism may also seriously weaken the solidarity and coherence of corporatist representation at sectoral and macro-levels. In other words, one response to recession may be a rise of sectionalism, instrumentalism and narrow definitions of 'realistic' strategies for survival. As Streeck emphasizes, this may lead further to a cooperative 'productivism' at enterprise level such that increased micro-corporatism facilitates voluntary redundancies, workforce flexibility and new working practices.

On the basis of survey evidence, Batstone (1983) suggests that only about a fifth of enterprises — though including some of the largest public-owned ones — are engaging in confrontationist assaults on industrial relations structures. In contrast, two-thirds of firms surveyed have since involved shop stewards more extensively and have consulted (not negotiated) on a much wider and deeper range of issues. This has been important in securing acceptance of the economic crisis faced by employers and the 'need for sacrifices'. Batstone also claims that, where unions are strongly entrenched in plants, firms have combined investment with major changes in skill flexibility and working practices. Parallel to this, over half the firms have extended employee involvement through consultation arrangements and/or quality circles; according to management, in about a fifth of firms, these moves have secured a diminution of the role and influence of shop stewards. Terry (1983) has emphasized the expansion of dialogue that 'consultation' has entailed — strategic matters are at last present in management and worker communication. But at present (whatever contradictory opportunities it may offer in the future) this is simply an alternative to actual bargaining, since it merely offers justification for unilateral management decisions.

Even so, the fact remains that most employers have secured manpower reductions and changed working practices through negotiation; it is the broader economic climate which has made these both necessary and achievable. Since negotiation still takes place, albeit on a different power basis, Batstone is at pains to stress that surviving shop steward organizations have not been fully 'incorporated' into a 'managerial perspective', and on this basis it is far too early to envisage the development of enterprise unionism — the 'Japanization' of British industrial relations.

It might be imagined that 'Japanization'[8] should be even more distant in the West German case, given the immense institutionalized importance of sectoral representation and negotiation through industry-wide unions and employers' associations with their binding contractual agreements. However, as Streeck argues, a productivist 'survival mentality' among workers at enterprise level can lead to a 'Betriebsegoismus', which gnaws at the roots of sectoral corporatism while creating fragmented forms of micro-corporatism.

From all the considerations made so far in this section, it can be seen that both macro-corporatist and neo-liberal 'systems' need means of ensuring order and productivism at the micro-level. The story of sectional strength at shop-floor level undermining macro-corporatist deals is a familiar one in Britain, but corporatist systems still need some means of coordinating intermediation. Of course, neo-liberal macro-policies may rely on market discipline backed by legislation to secure industrial order, but it is clear that productivist micro-corporatism could be a more effective underpinning when unions are not actually broken or banned. It may even be the case that trade unions have *more* of an interest in sustaining corporatist structures than the employers. The latter no longer *need* to compromise, but union confederations lose their rationale when they cannot negotiate or be consulted, and the whole basis of collectivist bargaining (at national or sectoral level) is undermined when members face widely diverging market conditions and employer strategies: 'From the perspective of labour organized as a class, erosion of the central bargaining level in the crisis amounts to a *de-capitation* of the workplace-based structures of interest-accommodation', which instead become controlled by market pressures (Streeck, 1984: 9).

Streeck argues from this that the main threat to corporatist structures during a crisis comes not from shop-floor militancy but from 'the emerging "wildcat cooperation" of individual workforces within workplace-based "productivity alliances"' (1984: 12). The scope for this seems considerably greater in Britain than in Germany, since there is no institutional basis for resistance from existing social partners. Streeck shows that sectoral representatives of both capital and labour are threatened by break-away enterprise deals which undermine the ordered nature of meso-corporatism. In addition, the legal backing to this structure provides ammunition to resist break-away developments. Most of this is absent in Britain, and the scope for division among workers, and for populist appeals to individual workers over the heads of representatives, is clearly evident when managements have moved on to the attack.

Broader collectivism in postwar economies has been founded on notions of job availability or of transferable skills. When these disappear (or never apply), the possibility of cooperative produc-tionist sectionalism is always present: 'a solidaristic, "class"-based union policy presupposes a labour market with high external mobility and, as a consequence, low identification of workers with the economic fate of their present employer' (Streeck, 1984: 25). Such trends are undermined not only by the economic crisis but also by the long-term growth of secure employment prospects, possibly through the development of an internal labour market in the enterprise. Even motor manufacturers (before 1945 the most cynical of employers) had effectively offered secure employment until the end of the long boom; now, as whole industries die off, defensive cooperativeness is one rational response.

When workers accept wage cuts, purges of shop stewards and substantial moves to 'flexibility' of skills and working practices, they are well on the road to a de facto enterprise unionism, even if (as Streeck argues for the German case) the formal structures of broader organization remain. Such nascent enterprise unionism deepens yet further the 'two-nations' implications of neo-liberalism: traditional unions are bad enough at representing the unemployed, but now a divided and sectionalist union movement could reproduce the splits between the 'haves' and the 'have-nots' — those in growth areas and those in de-industrializing sectors. Not only that, but Streeck points out that competing firms will carry with them competing workforces, and there will be no mechanisms for spreading the benefits won by the strong workers in profitable firms to the rest of the workforce. Workers in secure employment might even seek to keep out other workers by colluding in high overtime, closed internal labour markets and the like (Streeck, 1984: 39).

Such divisions make the chances for redistributive 'social con-tracts' at the macro-corporatist level more remote than ever, even if the neo-liberal macro-policies are finally replaced, and the chances for a class-solidaristic Alternative Economic Strategy look even weaker. Perhaps the only way forward in that case would be to offer an interventionist, productivist, programme for growth which stressed the need for conducive macroeconomic policies to back enterprise productivism. Whether the privatism and possessive individualism characteristic of the 'privileged nations' within Britain will permit such a strategy is a matter for speculation.

Conclusion
This discussion has stressed the complexity of relationships between macro-, meso- and micro-levels of intermediation in Britain today. It has been stressed that, while monetarist deflation is a purely macro- (and anti-corporatist) strategy, neo-liberalism has also involved action in the 'real economy' at sectoral and meso-levels. That action occurs in the context of highly complex and diverse relations between state and industry, such that neither 'corporatism' nor 'neo-liberal marketism' are models which capture the full reality of the policies, the instruments or their impact. Finally, it has been argued that the neo-liberal exacerbation of industrial crisis has further stimulated contradictory trends, increasing both market discipline and micro-corporatism. However, the particular form of this micro-corporatism is profoundly threatening to both meso- and macro-corporatism, even in countries with a much sounder institu-tional basis of corporatism than Britain.

Notes

The author wishes to acknowledge most warmly the intellectual stimulus, kindness and generosity he has received from all colleagues at the European University Institute. Their knowledge and their support has been invaluable.

1. The term 'neo-liberalism' here refers, of course, to the broad spectrum of New Right ideas in both economics and politics which are hostile to state intervention in the markets. In most respects this stress on economic freedom under the protection of a strong but narrowly bounded state is distinct from the British tradition of 'High Toryism' (see Bosanquet, 1983; Gamble, 1974).

2. The characterization of the postwar political settlement as the 'Keynesian welfare state' is not meant to imply that pure, unalloyed Keynesian theory was applied to the economy up until the mid-1970s. On the contrary, it can be argued that the internal problems of KWS generated powerful trends to intervention (Jessop, 1980; Martin, 1979).

3. The intellectual roots of monetarist doctrine in Britain were diverse, ranging across academic debates, analyses of financial institutions and journalists' campaigns. The third factor has been emphasized in many accounts (Ashford, 1984; Congdon, 1982; Keegan, 1984).

4. Significant divergences between 'international monetarists', Friedmanites, the Minford 'rational expectations' proponents and others mean that opinions about the Thatcherite 'experiment' have differed widely among the neo-liberals. The evidence given to the House of Commons Treasury and Civil Service Committee shows this clearly.

5. Pyrrhus' famous lament after the battle of Asculum that 'one more such victory and we are lost' could well be echoed by over three million British voices.

6. The important Bank of England economist, C.A.E. Goodhart, has noted that monetary indicators are self-invalidating because credit-creators will always seek to avoid that form of credit which is measured (see Goodhart, 1984).

7. Early notice of this plan was given in the *Guardian* (21 and 22 July 1981). It was reported that the chairman of the Steel Castings Trade and Research Association complained how 'the most modern plant has been closing down, because those who invested hard don't have the cash, while those with old plant and haven't invested are able to limp along. It has been a silly situation.'

8. 'Japanization' is a clumsy but expressive name for a process whereby industrial relations come to be characterized by enterprise unionism, extensive micro-corporatist incorporation within the enterprise, highly developed internal labour markets with job flexibility within the firm, plus a sharp division between 'privileged' long-term employees and casualized groups of workers excluded from these arrangements.

6
State corporatism as a sectoral phenomenon: the case of the Quebec construction industry

William D. Coleman

Theoretical discussions of the corporatist structures that develop out of the exchange between voluntary associations and state agencies in advanced industrial societies (what Schmitter, 1979a, has called 'societal corporatism' and we shall term 'liberal corporatism') differ in their assessment of the relative stability of these structures. These differences in point of view narrow, however, when it comes to considering what will happen once corporatist structures have begun to break down: most expect that the groups involved will revert to pluralist behaviour and it will again be pluralist politics as usual. Such assumptions reflect the tendency in the neo-corporatist literature to downplay and under-conceptualize the role and interests of the state (Birnbaum, 1982b; Cox, 1981; Diamant, 1981; F.L. Wilson, 1983). They also tend to ignore the systematic changes in organizational behaviour that occur in associations once they become engaged in corporatist practices. Once the interests of the state and the dynamics of associative action are given greater consideration, an alternative course to pluralism becomes evident. The state may decide, for whatever reason, that the corporatist framework should be retained even if it means coercing the social partners to participate. In legislating deliberately in order to ensure that pluralism does not return, the state may move towards the establishment of what Schmitter (1979a) has called 'state corporatism'.

This possibility may have been ignored by corporatist theorists because it touches on the politically sensitive issue of the possible tensions between the practice of corporatism and the principles of liberal democracy. There is perhaps a tendency to set aside the rather unpleasant possibility that the practice of liberal corporatism puts into place a structure that is as easily tranformed into a more authoritarian arrangement as into a more pluralist one. The question then that I wish to examine in this chapter is: If an established liberal corporatist network begins to break down, under what conditions might one expect the reconstitution of the network under a state corporatist form rather than its reversion to a pluralist form?

Although discussions of state corporatism have tended to be pitched at the level of the whole of society, just as it is possible that the development of liberal corporatism is restricted to particular sectors, so is it possible to find state corporatism at the meso- or sectoral level. This possibility will be demonstrated through an examination of group–state relations in a particular sector, the construction industry, in a single region, the province of Quebec in Canada. Within the Quebec construction industry, there has been a shift in the policy areas of collective bargaining and manpower training from a liberal corporatist mode of governance to one that is remarkably similar to what neo-corporatist theorists have described as state or authoritarian corporatism.

In order to develop the argument, this chapter begins with a brief recapitulation of the concept of state corporatism and the conditions under which it is expected to arise. A description of the change in the mode of governance from liberal to state corporatism follows, after which I shall suggest some socio-economic and political factors that may have precipitated the change. The conclusion of the chapter will then return to speak more generally of our core problem, the conditions under which state corporatism is likely to appear at the sectoral level.

State corporatism
On the surface, state and liberal corporatism look somewhat similar. A limited number of compulsory, non-competitive associations representing major socio-economic producer groups are recognized by the state, given a representational monopoly and then incorporated formally into the policy-making process. They join with the state in the formulation of (usually economic) policy, and themselves serve as policy instruments in the sense that they assume some responsibility for the administration of the policies in question. In assuming these administrative responsibilities, they undertake to exercise some control over the behaviour of their members, including often the administration of sanctions that are backed up by state authority.

However, these similarities in form mask important differences in the social and political processes that lead to the creation of each type and in the extent of state involvement in each case. In liberal corporatism, the structures arise out of an agreement between essentially voluntary interest associations to limit the conflict among their respective memberships and follow organizational developments in associational structures. In the case of state corporatism, not only are the structures imposed on conflicting socio-economic groups, but they are imposed through associations that are not voluntary but are themselves the creation of the state. The state creates an associational system of its own design by restricting the number of associations, defining their domains of representation, and making membership compulsory. The resulting associations are in a sense the opposite extreme to those found in a pluralist system. Whereas in pluralism, associations are tied closely to their members and are completely autonomous from the state, in state corporatism, associations are virtual adjuncts of the state and quite autonomous from their members. They serve as an extension of the state bureaucracy rather than of their members' political interests.

Liberal and state corporatism also flourish under quite different political conditions. Liberal corporatism, according to Schmitter (1979a: 22), is found in political systems in which there are relatively autonomous territorial units, open and competitive elections, and an ideologically polymorphous ruling coalition. In contrast, state corporatism is more likely in settings where territorial units are harnessed to a strong and central bureaucratic state, where elections are plebiscitory or non-existent, and where the ruling coalition is ideologically exclusive. In political systems amenable to state corporatism, the expression of economic and political interests is tightly controlled, freedom of association is weak, and generally the lines between civil society and the state are both blurred and formal rather than real. Unlike liberal corporatism, where the formulation of policy and also its implementation are tasks shared jointly by associations and the state, in state corporatism policy is strictly state-designed and is imposed through the particular instrument of the association.

Schmitter associates state corporatism with a particular, usually early, stage of capitalism. He sees it to be more likely when the transition is taking place to liberal democracy and associations are beginning to develop. Pluralism is at its most fragile stage. During this stage, the system may break down into social, usually class, conflict and the nascent bourgeoisie may lack the organizational cohesion and political strength to restore order. The state is forced to intervene. Schmitter writes that state corporatism

> seems closely associated with the necessity to enforce 'social peace' not by coopting and incorporating, but by repressing and excluding, the autonomous articulation of subordinate class demands in a situation where the bourgeoisie is too weak, internally divided, externally dependent and/or short of resources to respond effectively and legitimately to these demands within the framework of the liberal democratic state (Schmitter, 1979a: 25)

State corporatism is thus a means to force the bourgeoisie to get better organized. It provides the bourgeoisie with a political framework within which it can use the force of law to contain the demands of its class opponents.

As has often been the case with liberal corporatism, this presentation of state corporatism is one of a society-wide mode of governance. How might the concept be adapted for use at the meso- or sectoral level? We have already seen in other chapters that corporatist structures are to be found at the sectoral level. If these structures are state corporatist as opposed to liberal corporatist, they will have been imposed by the state on the associations in the sector without necessarily altering the overall values and principles of liberal democracy. However, within the sector itself, we can expect a breakdown in democratic norms to have occurred. Social conflict both between and within social classes will be sufficiently severe that a recourse to normal group representation becomes unavailable. The state is forced to intervene to restore social peace, an intervention made all the more necessary because of the weak and divided business class in the sector. If corporatist forms are imposed in a sector governed by a state that is essentially liberal democratic in character, then most likely a special state agency specific to the sector will be created and given extensive regulatory powers to effect the controls desired by political leaders.

As a final note, state corporatism at the sectoral level will be more likely in political systems that lack any society-wide liberal corporatist network. In such instances, the organization of business interests in specific sectors will be determined more by conditions within the sector and will be relatively unaffected by the structures of interest representation in other sectors. Where a more encompassing liberal corporatist network is in place, structures of interest representation in a given sector will be affected significantly by those elsewhere in society. The system of interest representation will be more likely itself to impose discipline on a specific sector in order to ward off state intervention.

The setting
The case to be studied here involves the construction industry in the Canadian province of Quebec during the period 1969–80. Quebec is the second largest province in Canada with a population of close to 8 million, that is, about the same size as Sweden. Slightly over 80 percent of this population is French-speaking, another 12–13 percent is English-speaking, with the remainder belonging to a series of immigrant communities. Unlike many industries in the province, the construction sector has been owned in the majority by

Quebec's francophones. Beginning in the late 1950s, the province underwent a 'Quiet Revolution' which saw among other things the transfer of control over education from the Catholic Church to the provincial government and increased intervention by that government into the provincial economy (Coleman, 1984a; McRoberts and Posgate, 1980). Perhaps the intervention of most importance to the construction industry was the nationalization in 1962 of most of the private electric power companies and their grouping under the provincial crown corporation, Hydro-Québec. During the period of study (1969–80), the province was the site for two massive construction projects, the building of the giant hydroelectric complex at James Bay by Hydro-Québec, and the construction of the site for the 1976 Olympic Games in Montreal.

Under the terms of Canada's federal constitution, the provincial governments have primary responsibility for the construction industry. Section 92(10) of the Constitution Act gives the provinces jurisdiction over matters of a local nature which include most construction projects. This power is reinforced by the judicial interpretation that has been given of the federal government's trade and commerce power (Section 91(2)), an interpretation which limits federal responsibility over trade and commerce to matters of an inter-provincial or international nature. Most construction activity falls into the class of intra-provincial trade and thus outside federal government jurisdiction. Finally, when these two constitutional rules are coupled with the assignment to the provinces of jurisdiction over property and civil rights, provincial governments come to assume primacy in the areas of industrial relations and collective bargaining for the construction industry. The focus, then, in this chapter will be solely on the provincial government in Quebec.

Regulation of construction, 1969
The system of collective bargaining, and particularly the administration and regulation of collective agreements as well as the system for manpower training in the construction industry, had a distinct liberal corporatist flavour in Quebec in 1969. The system that we will describe was that in place immediately following the passage of the Construction Industry Labour Relations Act in 1968. Hébert (1977: 5–8) suggests that this system had four major defining characteristics.[1] First, the agreement reached by the trade unions and employers' associations could by law be extended to bind employers who were not members of the associations. This principle of juridical extension had been in place in the province since passage of the Collective Labour Agreement Extension Act in 1934. Only those aspects of the agreement pertaining to pay and related

monetary issues, working hours and conditions of apprenticeship could be extended under the original act. The passage of the 1968 Act left room for further extension covering non-monetary items such as grievance procedures. This principle of juridical extension was supposed to prevent unfair competition by non-union labour, particularly in the area of monetary demands.

Second, collective bargaining was to be industry-wide: all trades were to be covered by a single agreement. This industry-wide agreement could take the form of one agreement for the whole province or a series of separate regional agreements but with only one agreement per region. Implementation of this principle had the effect of giving official recognition to several unions and employers' associations and hence of their acquiring a 'public status' (Offe, 1981). The Construction Industry Labour Relations Act of 1968 broke away completely from the usual North American practice of certification at the level of a plant, and hence the predominance of the union branch at the expense of central labour organizations. It did so by introducing the notion of 'representative associations'. Labour associations could obtain this status if they together represented 20 percent of the industry's labour force. Two trade union confederations were so designated in 1969: the Fédération des travailleurs du Québec (FTQ), which had as members all the locals of the major American building trades unions, and the Confédération des syndicats nationaux (CSN), which was almost exclusively Quebec-based and had originally been founded by the Catholic Church to counter the 'neutral' influence of the international (American) unions. The CSN was distinguished from the FTQ in that its affiliated federation for the construction industry was an industrial rather than a craft union.

On the employers' side, five associations were recognized and designated as bargaining agents in the Act. The existence of five employers' associations underlines to a degree the lack of cohesion on the employers' side. These were:

1. La Fédération de la construction du Québec (FCQ) (industrial, commercial and institutional building industry);
2. L'Association provinciale des constructeurs de l'habitation du Québec (APHQ);
3. L'Association des constructeurs de routes et grands travaux du Québec (ACRGTQ) (civil engineering industry);
4. La Corporation des maîtres éléctriciens du Québec (electrical contractors);
5. La Corporation des maîtres mécaniciens en tuyauterie du Québec (mechanical or plumbing contractors).

The existence of five distinct associations resulted from divisions between general contractors and trades contractors on the one side, and building and civil engineering on the other. Furthermore, the FCQ did not limit its domain to non-residential building but actively competed with the APHQ for residential building members. The FCQ was also plagued by internal conflicts among regions. Its largest affiliate, the Association de la construction de Montréal, which represented more output than its other 16 affiliates combined, finally pulled out in 1972. In short, the official recognition given to employers' associations in the Act sanctioned already deep divisions within the employer class.

These first two properties, when combined with the third and fourth, produced a liberal corporatist mode of governance in the industry. The third principle was the application and enforcement of the collective agreement by joint parity committees made up of equal numbers of employers and union representatives:

> In the interest of effective administration and supervision, the parity committees were vested by law with wide powers: they had the authority to prosecute those guilty of any infringement of the decree, to make claims and accept settlements, and to levy the amounts required for their administration. (Herbert, 1977: 7)

The committees set up their own extensive inspection networks for enforcing the agreement, and these were judged to be quite effective. The parity committees were justified by the argument that the contracting parties knew the industry best and that the natural competition in the industry could be harnessed as a tool of self-regulation.

The fourth principle involved the assumption of responsibility for vocational training and qualification of workers by the parity committees. The committees set up a system of compulsory tradesmen's certificates and specified the apprenticeship regime that was to be followed for each trade in order for trainees to qualify for a certificate. The parity committees were given the power to establish regional apprenticeship commissions whose task was to create regional training centres. These were financed by compulsory levies set by the committees. The whole system of training was thus run jointly by unions and management.

To conclude, the delegation of authority by the provincial government to 'recognized' workers and employers' associations so as to enforce and administer industry-wide collective agreements and to develop and implement manpower training involved the use of a liberal corporatist mode of governance in the construction industry. This system, put in place in early 1969, was to have been altered significantly by the time of our next date of reference, 1980.

Regulation of construction, 1980
In moving on to discuss the mode of governance in the Quebec construction industry in 1980, out of necessity I will not treat systematically the steps in the evolution from the system in place in 1969. The tale is a long and complicated one. Hébert (1977: 170) notes that, between passage of the Construction Industry Labour Relations Act in 1968 and the publication of his study in 1977, the Assemblée Nationale passed no less than 19 Acts related to the construction industry, six of which involved major reforms of the system. Supplementary to these Acts, the Cabinet passed over 100 orders-in-council to regulate various aspects of the industry, of which 40 were still in effect in 1977. For our purposes, the most important changes to the 1969 arrangements pertain to the operations and structures of the associations representing workers and the associations representing employers, and to the manner in which the collective agreement and vocational training and qualification were administered.

In order to understand the changes affecting labour associations, we must begin by noting the further fracturing of the labour movement during the 1970s. The divisions affected both the existing 'representative' associations, the CSN and the FTQ. In 1972 about 40,000 members, including several thousand in the construction industry, left the CSN for reasons to be noted below to form the Centrale des syndicats démocratiques (CSD). This split was followed eight years later by a schism within the rival FTQ. A number of Quebec branches broke away from the American building trades unions and formed their own organization, the Fédération des travailleurs du Québec—Construction. The remainder of the building trades then formed the Conseil provincial du Québec des métiers de la construction.

What is now characteristic of the system is that every construction worker must belong to one of these four organizations. In 1973, following the founding of the CSD, the definition of a 'representative association' was changed so that any labour union that was organized province-wide and included all trades could claim this public status. However, achieving this status did not automatically carry with it bargaining rights. The government added a majority rule provision which works today in the following manner. Six months before the end of a collective agreement, a secret ballot is held whereby each construction employee is given leave to select the union to which he will belong. Based on the number of votes received and the number of hours worked by each individual voter, each employee association is assigned a degree of representativeness. In order to negotiate a collective agreement, an association or coalition of associations must represent over 50 percent of the workers. If one union should obtain over 50 percent on its own, it alone can negotiate the agreement, which is then binding on all members of the other unions.

Compulsory membership in a trade union is matched now on the employers side by compulsory membership in an employers' association, both of which are rules to be expected in a state corporatist system. Every person in the construction industry in Quebec who employs at least one worker must by law belong to the Association des entrepreneurs en construction du Québec (AECQ). AECQ, then, is not a voluntary association arising out of civil society, as is characteristic of liberal corporatism, but a compulsory association imposed on its members by the provincial government. When the creation of the association was announced, the Assembliée nationale gave the existing associations the opportunity to write its constitution. Characteristically, they failed to agree, and so the constitution of the association was devised by the government. Under the terms of this constitution, AECQ has four divisions: residential building, industrial building, roads and civil engineering, and a 'general' category for employers who do not happen to fall into one of the three other categories. Its board of directors is composed of 21 members and is elected by the membership at an annual meeting. Each of the previous employers associations, which continue to exist as trades associations, nominates six candidates for the board, three of which are chosen by the assembled membership of AECQ. AECQ and the majority labour representative association(s) are then bound by law to negotiate a single collective agreement that covers all workers in all trades in the province. No other bargaining outcome is allowed.

The creation by the state of a compulsory employers' association and the establishment of compulsory membership in a trade union for workers change the mode of governance in the industry away from being liberal corporatist to being state corporatist. The system is no longer based on the incorporation into policy-making of voluntary associations that arose in civil society, but on the coerced involvement in the system of workers and employers' associations controlled by the state. Also consistent with state corporatism is the greater direct involvement of the state in administering the policy at the expense of the previous liberal corporatist parity committees. As we have seen, in the previous system the administration of the decree, the handling of grievances and the management of manpower training were the responsibility of the parity committees of workers and employers. After 1975 these tasks were transferred to a new state agency, the Office de la construction du Québec

(OCQ). The OCQ is run by three commissioners who are chosen by the government and who serve ten-year terms.

The creation of the OCQ has been complemented by an expansion of the regulation of qualifications for both workers and contractors. Workers must deal with a complex classification system of work types, work permits for each type, and more structured apprenticeship regimes. Contractors cannot engage in most construction tasks now unless they have obtained certificates of qualification for each task. The system for obtaining these qualification certificates is managed by another new state agency, the Régie des entreprises de la construction du Québec. Three of the members of the Régie are appointed by the government and are permanent employees; the remaining five are nominated from a list supplied by AECQ.

The only area in which associations have retained a role in administering industrial relations and manpower policy under the new system is through a parity Joint Committee attached to the OCQ. This committee is composed of 12 members, six nominated by AECQ and six by the representative labour associations. Its most important powers are the interpretation of the collective agreement and decree and the taking of decisions on the use of the unions' social security funds.

In summary, by 1980 both the basis for association in the construction industry and the manner of administration of policy had changed considerably. The concept of collective bargaining among voluntary associations of capital and labour had disappeared. Workers' associations had to meet stiff criteria, based on trades and geographical area covered, in order to enter the system. Workers themselves were required to join one of the associations that met these criteria. Employers were required to leave the associations they had founded and to join a new all-embracing association designed by the government. Both sides were told what kind of agreement must emerge from the bargaining. The state removed from the two parties their authority to administer the agreement and related policies such as manpower training. State agencies specific to the sector were created and given most of the administrative powers formerly held by the parity committees. Comprehensive schemes of qualification for both workers and employers were developed, facilitating state intervention and control of the industry. The new state-designed representative associations for capital and labour were given only limited administrative responsibilities under the watchful eye of the new state agencies and were systematically excluded from the policy formulation responsibilities which their voluntary predecessors had enjoyed. Hébert draws the following conclusion:

> The avalanche of Acts passed from 1968 to 1975 fits into the pattern
> Arnold Toynbee forecast: the emergence of autocratic governments
> regulating the living conditions and incomes of each trade or profession.
> When asked whether we were moving toward state-governed unionism,
> an old union leader pointedly replied: 'We are already there.' (Hébert,
> 1977: 7)

Factors precipitating the change

By abstracting from macro-level theories of state corporatism, I
postulated in the introduction to this chapter that state corporatism
may be introduced into a given sector if there is a breakdown in
social order whereby the usual norms of behaviour in a democratic
polity are no longer being observed, and conflict both between and
within classes is so intense that neither the associations of workers
nor those of capital are able to control their members; the state is
then forced to intervene to restore 'social peace'. Conditions close
to these did exist in the Quebec construction industry in the early
1970s, and appeared to precipitate the move towards state
corporatism.

In order to understand the intensity of the conflicts that occurred,
several background factors must first be noted. The general pattern
for the organization of business interests and workers in Quebec
hardly corresponded to the macro-societal mode of corporatism
found in such European countries as Austria. In the late 1960s, a
peak association of business, the Conseil du Patronat du Québec,
had been formed in the province, but it was too new to exercise any
control over those construction associations that belonged to it.
Accordingly, business was organized differently sector by sector in
Quebec, with no systematic integration of these sectoral organizations taking place. In addition, labour was divided, as we have seen,
and the dominant American unions in the construction sector were
highly decentralized. For most purposes, the key figure in these
unions until 1969 was the local business agent (Rose, 1980: 28). This
relatively pluralist system for the organization of business and
labour at the macro-level thus made it possible for changes in the
organization of social classes to take place in one sector in relative
isolation from other sectors.

The construction sector is one in which the potential for class
conflict is high. The industry is dominated by large numbers of very
small firms which generally fall into two groups: general contractors
and trades contractors. The general contractor takes overall
responsibility for the job and subcontracts with various craftsmen
for the completion of the particular tasks required. In Canada this

relationship is governed by the competitively bid, fixed-price contract (Keys and Caskie, 1975). General contractors compete for jobs by submitting sealed bids fixing a price for the whole job. The same type of bid competition exists among trades contractors in their relations with general contractors. A consequence of this system is that there is intense pressure on contractors to keep labour costs down in order to maximize their chances in the bidding process. When one adds to this system the irregularity of the building cycle and the employment insecurity it brings (Malles, 1975), and an industrial relations system that had been designed for manufacturing with its stable, identifiable place of employment, the chances for labour–management conflict in the construction sector become very high indeed.

The political situation in Quebec in the early 1970s was bound to add fire to any conflict that began. During the 1960s, the central labour organizations had become considerably radicalized (Coleman, 1984a: chapter 4). The CSN completed its transformation from a Catholic Church-based organization, with chaplains attached to each branch, to one that in 1971 and 1972 issued manifestoes which were heavily influenced by Marxist thinking. The Fédération des travailleurs du Québec (FTQ), which grouped the American building trades unions, in 1971 issued its own strongly socialist manifesto, *L'Etat, rouage de notre exploitation*. In 1972 the various labour organizations formed a Common Front, with socialist rhetoric much in evidence, and organized a strike in the public sector which paralysed the operations of the provincial government. Their leaders were eventually gaoled after they refused to end the strike.

During the same period, the movement in favour of the political independence of Quebec from Canada was gaining strength. It too tended to be politically on the left and formed a natural ally of labour in many of its struggles. Conflict in the workplace easily became transformed through socialist ideology into political conflict and then into nationalist conflict. Hence the strike by the Common Front in 1972 was not only a strike in favour of better wages for public sector workers; it was a strike against an exploitative provincial government, which was, in the eyes of the nationalists, part of a federal system unfair to the Québécois.

Because of the involvement of the provincial government in many construction projects, some strikes by construction workers had a similar impact. They were viewed by some as strikes against a federal state that was repressing the Québécois. The fact that at this time any strike against the provincial government was bound to find added sympathy among members of the nationalist movement

considerably heightened the intensity of some construction conflicts.

The breakdown in social order that took place in the construction
industry in Quebec in the early 1970s was not in itself the direct
result of disputes between labour and management. These, as we
have said, are endemic to the industry, and were just as prevalent in
some of the other provinces as they were in Quebec. What
distinguished Quebec were the intense struggles within classes and
the way these struggles were exacerbated by the corporatist system
already in place. The labour unions were required by law to
negotiate an agreement that covered all trades in a particular
region, and later in the whole province, and yet some of the trades
continued to desire special arrangements. The system forced the
unions to place all trades in the same framework, and each trade
with its own tradition and skills was reluctant to go along. The most
recalcitrant group was the elevator workers' union, which refused
repeatedly to accept the common agreement and eventually had to
be put into trusteeship in 1975.

After 1973, the system also accentuated the divisions among the
labour confederations. As we have noted, the Centrale des
syndicats démocratiques was formed in 1972 after breaking away
from the CSN. This new labour organization was viewed favourably
by government leaders because it rejected the socialism and the
political activism of the CSN. The government altered the definition
of a 'representative' labour association in 1973 partially in order to
afford this new organization a place in the system. However, in
attaching to this definition the notion that the workers' bargaining
agent(s) must represent a majority of the workers, the government
added fuel to the competition between the labour unions. From the
point of view of the FTQ, which had the largest number of workers,
if it could be shown to represent 50 percent of the workers, it alone
could negotiate the collective agreement on behalf of labour under
the new rules. The CSN and CSD, which had fewer workers, were
just as determined that the FTQ not achieve this majority.
Competition became so intense that violence broke out on many
construction sites. Unions began to hire goons in order to intimidate
workers. The violence culminated in a near riot at the James Bay
power project which resulted in $30 million of damage. When order
was restored, the government set up a commission of inquiry into
the violence which became known as the Cliche Commission after
its head, Judge Robert Cliche.

The intra-class conflict on the labour side was matched on the
employers' side, which was represented, as we have seen, by five
associations until 1972. In the centre of many of these conflicts was

the Fédération de la construction du Qúebec (FCQ). The FCQ was a federation of regional associations and its largest affiliate, the Montreal association, fretted over being under the governance of the other smaller affiliates. In 1972 it broke away, and in doing so lost its place at the bargaining table. It then attached itself to the road builders' association until 1973, when the government changed the definition for a 'representative' association. The Montreal association then appended the words 'du Québec' to the end of its name, claimed to seek members throughout the province (in competition with the FCQ) and took its place at the bargaining table as the sixth employers' association.

As we have noted, the FCQ also openly competed with the house builders' association, and the Cliche Commission (1974: 107) regretted its continuous feuding with the electrical contractors' association. These inter-associational tensions were accompanied by intra-associational ones. The thrust of bargaining since 1968 was more and more province-wide, and labour pushed specifically for the equalization of wage rates across the province. Employers outside Montreal in particular were reluctant to move in this direction, thereby adding to the tension between the Montreal contractors and those in other parts of the province. The Cliche Commission summarized the situation: 'Without a doubt the employers' side is represented at the bargaining table by six extremely different associations, often even opposed to one another because of their particular composition or their objectives.'

If class unity is a first prerequisite for the successful working of liberal corporatism, responsible autonomous action and a capacity to control members' behaviour are the second and third (Crouch, 1983a). The six employers' associations met neither of these latter prerequisites. They limited their range of vision to the short term and showed disdain for the workers. Hébert notes (1977: 51) that the employers sometimes colluded with the unions in their use of illegal pressure tactics, showed a lack of conscience in the areas of safety and accident prevention, and were manifestly ignorant in the area of human resources, particularly when it came to manpower planning, income stability and employment security. Placed in corporatist structures, the associations acted like pluralist pressure groups. The Cliche Commission (1974: 107) wrote: 'It is often regretted that the employers' associations had no means for imposing discipline on their members' (author's translation). Such a failure was critical, because discipline is at the heart of corporatism, as Crouch (1983a) has emphasized.

Once the natural conflict between labour and management is supplemented by this additional internal class conflict, and both occur within the structure of the parity committees, a mutually reinforcing destructive process is almost bound to follow. The conflicts were severe enough to ensure that the concertation both within and between classes needed for corporatist administration could not emerge. Trying to function within the committee structure simply magnified their intensity. The Cliche Commission noted that the corporatist administration system was constantly paralysed. One of the parties would refuse to attend, or discussions would quickly reach an impasse, or partial deals would be made on the side, and so on.

The provincial government had more than a passing interest in this failure. It had been elected in 1970 with a promise to create 100,000 new jobs, many of which were to come from the vast hydroelectric development at James Bay. It also saw its own prestige and that of the province threatened by a possible failure to have the Olympics site ready for the 1976 games. Strikes had constantly put the Olympics work behind schedule.

The failure, then, by business and labour to work the corporatist system led the government repeatedly to intervene in order to force the parties' hands. As long as the liberal corporatist structure endured, so too did the intervention until it became part of the system. Each intervention brought more compulsion and state direction into the system. Finally, in 1974 there was a complete breakdown of the social order in the industry. The employers' associations were unwilling and unable to unite in order to contain the conflict with labour and within labour. The state moved in to impose order on the employers and then to intervene much more extensively in the collective bargaining process, using what is close to a state corporatist model of governance. This new model has proven no more effective than the previous ones. Genuine collective bargaining appears to have disappeared from the Quebec construction industry. The formal state corporatist system, with its compulsory, universal participation, has spawned a black market in construction work estimated to account for one-third of the industry volume in 1984.

Conclusions

In the introduction to this chapter, the following question was posed: Under what conditions might one expect the reconstitution of a liberal corporatist policy network as a state corporatist network rather than its reversion to a pluralist arrangement? We have seen an example at the sectoral level of a shift from liberal to state corporatism. The issue, then, is whether general properties characteristic of such a process might be derived from this case study. To an important degree, this problem takes us back to the essence of corporatist governance and the conditions under which it arises. Corporatism at its roots is an arrangement that is designed to contain or prevent socio-political conflict among major producer groups (von Beyme, 1983; Panitch, 1979a, 1981). The state grants organizations representing these groups a formal role in policy-making provided they are willing and capable of binding their members to any policy that is agreed upon. The state may even delegate to them aspects of its own authority to facilitate the discipline and control of member behaviour. If for some reason, then, the arrangements were to be abandoned and the socio-economic producer groups were to be left to function on their own (a shift from corporatism to pluralism), the state would be leaving the resolution of that conflict to the groups themselves.

The question then to be posed is, Under what conditions is the state likely to be unwilling to tolerate this means for the resolution of the conflict and likely to coerce the groups to work together in a state corporatist structure? Four issues would appear to be relevant to such a decision:

1. How intense and potentially damaging to the sector is the conflict among the producer groups?

2. How politically salient are the conflicts involved?

3. How well-organized, in particular, is the employer class in the sector? Is it likely to be able to contain conflict with labour on its own over the long term?

4. What policy goals would the state sacrifice in seeing the corporatist arrangements dissolved, and how important to state authorities are such policy goals?

Looking then at each of these questions, we can begin to speculate on when state corporatism is more likely.

First, the more intense the conflict among producer groups in the sector is, particularly if it is conflict between employers and labour, and in a sector of importance to the economy, the less tolerant the state will be of a pluralist solution. The construction industry in Canada is of great economic importance and, at least traditionally, has been the scene of intense class conflict. Strike activity has been one-and-a-half times that found in manufacturing (Malles, 1975: 4). Although the industry accounted for only 7 percent of the non-agricultural labour force, it has been responsible for one-sixth of total strike activity since 1950 (Rose, 1980: 4). We have already alluded to why this is the case: the tension between labour and management that is built into the competitively bid, fixed-price contract; the irregularity of the building cycle and the employment insecurity produced thereby; the rather fluid relationship between employer and employee in construction; and an industrial relations system more appropriate to manufacturing with its identifiable place of employment, constant workforce in terms of size and mix of skills, and definable job descriptions (Malles, 1975). Hence one might expect state corporatism to occur more often in construction and in other highly conflictual sectors such as mining than in manufacturing.

However, it should be noted that the 'natural' conflicts between labour and management and within each group were exacerbated by their participation in a liberal corporatist structure. There would appear to be an additional lesson here. In his later discussion of corporatism, Schmitter (1982) has distinguished between corporatism$_1$ — the existence of a concentrated, centralized, monopolistic and vertically integrated associational system (we would add, within a sector) — and corporatism$_2$ — the formal incorporation of associations into the formulation and implementation of policy. He suggests that these two will usually occur together, and that a situation in which one obtains without the other will be unstable. In our case study, corporatism$_2$ was instituted in the absence of corporatism$_1$. Both the employers' and workers' organizations were fragmented and competitive; the associational systems were not sufficiently developed for liberal corporatism. By placing class organizations that were not centralized, concentrated, monopolistic and so on into a formal policy role, the conflict the system was designed to contain was made worse. The integration of the organization of economic interests in a sector appears to be crucial to the success or failure of liberal corporatism within that sector.

Second, it is likely that class struggles in some sectors are of greater political importance to the government than those in other sectors. Hence it will be more greatly tempted to repress the conflict directly. In the case discussed in this chapter, the conflict in the construction sector had high political salience. Important government projects such as the James Bay power project and the Olympic site were being constantly disrupted and even used by labour to hold employers to ransom. Organized crime became involved in the violence on the construction sites, a fact that was highly publicized through the hearings of the Cliche Commission. The conflict in the construction sector added to the public sense of a breakdown in the social order that had developed in Quebec in the early 1970s as a result of the strikes by the Common Front in the public sector and the radicalized, almost revolutionary, rhetoric of the trade unions. A panic developed in the ruling Liberal Party that investors would withdraw from the province, a panic apparently confirmed by secret studies of business attitudes carried out at the time. Politically, the government could not simply ignore the conflict and wait for some equilibrium to be reached. In the absence, then, of any prospect for the settlement of class conflict, and where that conflict remains highly salient politically, the state will be more tempted to use coercion and a state corporatist solution in a sector.

The third factor that comes into this decision is the strength and cohesiveness of the employer class in a sector. The example discussed in this chapter showed a rather weak employer class. The construction industry is one in which many obstacles are placed in the way of employer cohesion. There is the real tension between large and small firms (see Grant and Streeck, chapter 8 below), between general and trades contractors, among the different building trades, and between the building sector and the civil engineering sector. All of these tensions are reflected in a highly differentiated associational system, not only in Canada (Coleman, 1984b), but also in Britain (Grant, 1983a; Grant and Streeck, chapter 8 below), Switzerland (Kriesi, 1983) and other countries. Left to its own devices, the employer class in this sector is hard-pressed to unite and is weak in the face of organized labour at least relative to other sectors (Rose, 1980). In these situations, where employers are less able to draw upon their advantaged position in a capitalist system to contain labour, the state will be more likely to intercede on their behalf. Hence such situations are more favourable to state corporatism.

Finally, it must be remembered that the state plays a relatively strong role in any corporatist arrangement. It uses corporatist structures to reduce the incidence of class conflict. It will also have other objectives that it wishes to be realized through the corporatist arrangement. In our case study, three objectives of this sort can be identified.

1. The state wished to minimize the disruption caused by non-union labour and therefore to protect organized labour and the employers, whose unity suffers at the expense of free-riders when non-union labour is plentiful. This objective was pursued through the principle of juridical extension of collective agreements negotiated by 'representative' associations.

2. The state pushed for bargaining to become province-wide. It sought thereby to protect employers from whiplash negotiating tactics by unions where one locality was played off against another. It also sought to dampen labour unrest through the development of employee security plans and benefits which had to be administered province-wide to be truly effective.

3. The state insisted on multi-trade bargaining. It hoped to

minimize thereby the time lost to disruptions created by different trades striking at different times. It also hoped to minimize labour playing one trade off against another and the kind of sweetheart deals with crucial trades that then set a standard for all others.

If the labour relations system had been allowed to lapse to a pluralist arrangement, all three of these objectives would probably have been immediately undermined. Certainly, the system found in the neighbouring province of Ontario is a pluralist one; the only one of the above objectives that is achieved there is the second one, and even that is a recent and still tenuous accomplishment. The more the state wishes to retain its own additional policy objectives, accomplished through the working of corporatist arrangements, the more it will be tempted to increase its direct, usually coercive, intervention into the system.

In summary, then, if a liberal corporatist arrangement in a sector is breaking down, a state corporatist arrangement will be a more likely solution when the socio-political conflict among producer groups is very intense, when the level of organization of economic interests is low, when this conflict is highly salient politically, when the employer class in particular is weak and divided, and when the state cherishes highly the policy objectives that it has sought to achieve through the liberal corporatist framework.

Note

This research was supported by the Social Sciences and Humanities Research Council of Canada, Research Grants 410-78-0716 and 410-80-0280.

  1. My discussion of the labour relations system and the changes in it in Quebec will be largely drawn from the excellent and comprehensive study of this system done by Gérald Hébert (1977) for the Economic Council of Canada.

7
Neo-corporatist strategies in the British energy sector

Noelle Burgi

In Britain, the establishment of public corporations, from 1946 to the most recent example, the British National Oil Corporation in 1974, has been part of a reorganization project at the apex of the production apparatus. There is abundant information on the intentions of the economic, social and political actors — the way they conceived the redistribution of their respective roles on the national level and the resulting limits on the delegation of power. Through an analysis of the philosophical as well as the practical aspects of nationalization, it is possible to identify the existence of a strong neo-corporatist trend over a period extending well into the 1970s. Nevertheless, one cannot speak of a linear evolution, for experience has revealed counter-tendencies which must be taken into account in order to explain the fragility of neo-corporatism. These are the two questions I will treat in a detailed analysis of the state's role in the energy sector and more particularly in the coal-mining industry.

In so far as favourable tendencies go, Britain has experienced periods during which its political elite showed a strong receptivity to neo-corporatist projects, whether with respect to a bias towards a concerted industrial policy or an incomes policy. In the energy sector, these trends were most pronounced during the 1974–79 Labour administration. As part of his 'open government' policy, Tony Benn, then Secretary of State for Energy, set up tripartite institutions (for example, the National Energy Conference, the Energy Commission) designed to formulate an energy policy. In 1974 the new 'Plan for Coal' represented the first tripartite plan that had ever been worked out in a nationalized industry.

All these Labour Party initiatives do in fact express one of the most elaborate attempts to realize a concerted 'sectoral planning'. Thus, they may be considered as the outcome of a process which began before the war, but became manifest with the 1946–49 nationalizations, originally conceived as only part of a more comprehensive planning project (Parker, 1947). Even though national planning has been a failure in Britain (Leruez, 1972),

125

public corporations have largely served as an instrument for implementing various policies, including those for prices and incomes. For example, the average earnings of miners declined sharply in relative terms from 1947 to 1970 (Fine et al., 1983; Allen, 1981).

The unions' attitude, in particular that of the National Union of Mineworkers (NUM), had greatly favoured this situation. By the time of nationalization, the NUM represented more than 90 percent of the mineworkers. Despite its considerable strength, the NUM, on both a regional and national level, not only accepted the decline in the standard of living of its members, but also joined the government in pressing the miners to work on Saturdays. This occurred after the NUM had fought for, and obtained, the five-day week with great difficulty. Certain lodges even went so far as to help establish committees to fight absenteeism. Above all, the NUM set about to disrupt unofficial strikes, and refused to organize an official national strike until 1972.

Conversely, a series of resistances to neo-corporatism appeared, stemming from the business and finance milieux as well as from the working class. The 1972 and 1973–74 miners' strikes, for instance, challenged the Heath government's incomes policy and contributed very much to its electoral defeat in 1974. The same argument holds for the fate of the 'Social Contract', which resulted in the famous 'Winter of Discontent' of 1978–79 and the subsequent Labour Party defeat that year. Could one, then, interpret these events as a sign of working-class opposition to neo-corporatism? Such an interpretation, supported by authors like Panitch (1981), would lead us to believe that the strategies of the NUM, the NCB and the government are dependent in the long run upon cycles during which the workers are mobilized; or, as in the case of Tony Benn's strategy, that neo-corporatism can function only in the context of a particular regime, namely a Labour government. The latter hypothesis would be supported by the coincidence between the implementation of a nationalization policy and the taking of office by the Labour Party. Finally, we may consider that the instability of neo-corporatism is the result of private capital's opposition to it, a hypothesis which could be supported by the example of oil.

Although I do not disregard these arguments, they leave too many questions unanswered. First, they do not explain why the Conservatives themselves resorted to these policies, or why, as Panitch (1981) correctly points out, institutions such as the National Economic Development Office proved to be extremely resilient despite the inherent instability of neo-corporatism. Second, one notices that there is a considerable degree of convergence in the policies of successive governments, at least up to 1979, with the election of the Thatcher government. Yet, 'Thatchersim' itself rests upon a particular political culture. Apart from the 'innovative' forces the present government may claim to be offering, there are still constant factors shaping its policies. The latter seem to have much more effect on the fragility of neo-corporatism than does the mere will of a government in power. It may be added that there is within Thatcherism a large measure of symbolic politics. As far as the unions are concerned, the 'strength' attributed to them over the past 20 years or so has never been as 'gigantic' as has often been claimed. It is no secret that, as a result of its extreme decentraliza-tion, the structure of the union movement, as that of the employers' organizations, does not allow official representatives a tight control over their members. It is unjustified to find in the 'excessive' wage increases the determinant cause of British economic decline. Concomitantly, the unions had only a marginal influence on the conduct of public policies, as the case of the energy sector will reveal. Following the underlying logic of this argument, it could even be said that neo-corporatism has played only a minimal role in the conduct of the policies of various governments. This raises, therefore, the problem of the very nature of neo-corporatism in Britain. Beyond such socio-political factors as the cycles of workers' mobilization or the contradictions within capital, constant factors specific to the British polity will prove more helpful for a clear explanation of neo-corporatism in this country. In this perspective, state intervention can be seen as a key independent variable.

It is thus through the question of the state that I will conduct my investigation into the coal industry and the energy sector. First, I will briefly recall the historical, sociological and political factors circumscribing the limits and the fragility of neo-corporatism, not as a structure or a system, but as a composite of strategies integrated into informal British conciliation practices.

Limits and fragility of neo-corporatism

There is a strange coincidence surrounding the creation of a public sector and the factors underlying neo-corporatist developments in Britain. Nationalization set up the structural preconditions at the sectoral level — as defined by Schmitter (1979a) — for neo-corporatism to emerge. In the case of the coal industry, these preconditions included the centralization of its management and of the workers' representation through the establishment of the National Coal Board (NCB) and the National Union of Mineworkers (NUM); monopoly trade union representation; centralization of collective bargaining; and even union representation on the

NCB. This reorganization was partly a response to certain national and international constraints which are stressed in the literature on neo-corporatism. The 1946–49 nationalizations affected basic industries, the restructuring of which was generally seen as a precondition for the economic success of Britain in the postwar reconstruction period. Coal, for example, accounted for some 90 percent of UK energy needs at that time.

Political parties, business, and public opinion in general were all agreed on the principle of an extension of the role of the state (*The Economist*, 27 January 1945: 104–5). Even from the Conservative standpoint, its intervention in certain sectors appeared as an 'economic necessity'. The state could no longer let things follow their own course: it had to save some industries against their own will. Of course, the political parties remained divided on the specific issue of nationalization. Long awaited by both the Labour Party and the labour movement, nationalization met with open opposition from the right, especially the owners. Nevertheless, in Britain as in other countries, there was agreement concerning the need to extend the state's role — a development which was not self-evident in a country which historically and culturally has maintained a traditional distrust of public power (Solomos, 1980).

In the perceptions of the different actors, the extension of the state's role was to be of a limited nature, even for the Labour Party. Such an approach would introduce a separation of national responsibilities between the public authorities and the representatives of capital and labour. From a theoretical standpoint, this perspective fulfilled one of the fundamental conditions of neo-corporatism, which excludes the possibility of a total domination of the society by the state in contrast to authoritarian corporatism. On the eve of the 1945 elections, political parties, businessmen and even the coal owners were at least resigned to the view that the solution had to be found at the centre of the political system. A redistribution of the duties relating to the management of the economy and society had to take place at the national level in order to maximize profitability, which it was generally agreed would be a key part of postwar reconstruction.

Limits to the state's autonomy
In the wake of an overwhelming electoral victory, the Labour Party assumed the responsibility for outlining the duties of each actor. But as a result of their unpreparedness and inexperience, and of a multitude of pressing problems caused by reconstruction, the Labour government did not take the time to elaborate a new plan for the nationalizations. They drew their inspiration largely from a

few rare precedents, especially that of the London Passenger Transport Board of 1933 which bore the imprint of its creator Herbert Morrison (Morrison, 1933).

Morrison maintained that public corporations and the government should have a relationship 'at arm's length', each conceding the other's autonomy. This fundamental principle was based upon a somewhat utopian vision of the sharing of duties between the government and the corporation's managers. Naturally, the government was to represent the national interest while the managers, recruited on the basis of specific expertise, were to be concerned only with their own corporations' economic viability. Board members were expected to be untouched by the capitalist profit motive, because of the transfer of ownership to the state, and to see themselves as the guardians of the public interest. Morrison believed there would be an identity of interests between the board and the government which would guarantee the independence of the public corporations. According to his view, a disagreement over the definition of the national interest would rarely arise and, therefore, the sponsoring minister would have to intervene only in exceptional circumstances (Chester, 1975).

Morrison argued that this relationship would ensure the financial independence of the public corporation. Created by the law, it would be responsible to Parliament for political decisions of a general nature, through the intermediary of a sponsoring minister, but its day-to-day administration would be free from the tight control of the Treasury, or other ministry or Parliament. The requirement for independence is a condition of a second requirement: that of economic viability. The public corporation was seen as the instrument of a commercial and professional management. Although an organization without a profit motive, it has as its aims the commercial monopoly of goods and services, and the pursuit of efficiency and economic viability in the national interest.

The 1945–51 Labour government adopted this model with certain modifications which increased the Minister's powers by empowering him to issue directions of a general character (which the Board was obliged to follow) 'in relation to matters appearing to the Minister to affect the national interest'.

This approach presented a danger which the Labour government did not avoid. Since it did not specify the content and nature of the national interest, there was disagreement over the permitted extent of ministerial interference, and thus on the role which the state intended to assume in the nationalized sector. Whereas the restructuring of the industries affected by nationalization, and in particular the coal industry, necessitated radical reforms, the underestimation of the importance of this disagreement risked limiting the government to incremental action consisting of a series of marginal adjustments and limited reforms. There was a greater danger in that the entire concept of ministerial intervention and the corporations' independence relied implicitly on the Morrisonian vision of an identity of interests between the two parties. Moreover, it was generally believed that, in spite of his extended powers, the Minister would intervene only in exceptional circumstances, and this doctrine removed the necessity of outlining a hierarchy of priorities.

Thus, the contradictions which might arise from two contrasting forms of logic — one political and the other commercial — were greatly underestimated. In practice, the corporations' independence has been eroded by an increasing but ill-coordinated state interventionism, consisting of indirect action (e.g. pricing policy), ad hoc decisions and a 'wait-and-see' attitude. In the long run, this lack of coordination exacerbated these problems in the context of rising circumstantial factors, such as the progressive replacement of coal by oil as a primary energy source, and the oil crisis of 1974. Since the 'arms-length' principle remained deeply ingrained in the ideology and attitude of the actors, the government was easily able to deny its responsibility for any problems by invoking the principle of the all-powerful laws of the market, or the loyalty or disloyalty of the unions or firms.

In effect, this polarization towards the unions and the corporations suggested that the labour organizations, the administrators and the organizational structure of the corporations, as such, exercised a determining influence on the country's economic future. For this reason, certain political scientists began to argue that Britain was evolving towards a 'strong' neo-corporatist system. In actual fact, as we shall see, this polarization 'anaesthetized' the conflict only temporarily and displaced it from a 'macro-' to a 'meso-' level of interest intermediation (Wassenberg, 1982). This polarization could be exploited at different moments to provide either the justification for or an attack on neo-corporatist policies. The ambiguity hid a crucial factor: the deficiency of the political element ('la carence du politique') in the British tradition.

The deficiency of the political element in the British political tradition
Ironically, in the British coal industry the lack of an important political element is linked to the importance which the representatives of capital, labour and the state attached to the 'arm's-length' relationship, which was no more than symbolic in the context of a

growing interventionism, itself attracting significant consensual support. This is connected to the state's difficulty in seeing itself as a specific political structure, differentiated from civil society, and which is endowed with its own logic and imperatives (Badie and Birnbaum, 1983). Because they believed in an identity of interests between public corporations and the government, the architects of nationalization refrained from circumscribing the role of the state in the public sector, and this was to have a critical effect over policy choices in the energy sector.

Successive governments have attempted to use the nationalized coal industry, and more recently the British National Oil Corporation, as instruments of economic growth. However regardless of whether it concerned economic planning in general or a more modest energy policy, governmental action on the whole was characterized by limited control over, and an absence of coordination between, the individual corporations.

Initially, such a restricted role could be justified by the Morrisonian 'arm's-length' principle: 'Government was not required by statute to approve the corporations' plans and did not attempt to use them as a basis for monitoring their subsequent progress.' Even though, since the early 1970s, corporate plans have been submitted to government, they 'have not been used by government as a basis for developing an overall framework for planning and progressing' (NEDO, 1976: 91). The ambitious plans of the NCB, which had largely underestimated the impact of future oil imports as well as the consequences for coal production levels of the problems facing the gas and electricity industries, have been periodically scaled down by governments in response to national and international conjunctural pressures. Thus, ministerial intervention quickly confined the apparent independence of the public corporations within a sphere of symbolic politics.

These developments were not surprising, since it was considered well within the government's legitimate rights to ensure that the corporations' plans conformed to the national interest. In order to fulfil this requirement, the government employed three main methods. First, it attempted to readjust the imbalances caused by international competition in a series of Reports and White Papers. In order to facilitate the development of more 'economic' energy sources such as nuclear power, it downgraded what it saw as too-optimistic forecasts in other industries such as coal-mining (Select Committee on Energy, 1981). Second, from 1969 onwards the corporations' plans were submitted to the Public Expenditure Survey Committee (PESC), which reviewed public investment proposals on a rolling five-year basis (NEDO, 1976). Finally, under the Labour government of 1974–79, Tony Benn, who was appointed Secretary of State for Energy in 1975, adopted a policy of initiating a dialogue between government, unions and industry managers; by involving these different partners in the corporate planning process, he hoped that a coherent and sound sectoral policy would result.

These different policy initiatives, however, did not produce convincing results. None questioned the means of managing (as opposed to the utopian ideal of suppressing) the contradictions between the interests of the individual corporations and the global coordination of energy policy or of national planning. The industries were usually examined in isolation, and the White Papers appeared in large measure to be attempts to redefine a posteriori — if not to ratify — a new balance among the available domestic and foreign energy sources.

A further obstacle to the state's control over the energy sector arises from the very conception which the public authorities had of this control. With this question in mind, we will now study this aspect of the deficiency of the political element in the British policy-making process. It is notable that this outlook did not fundamentally change from the period of the first nationalizations of 1946–49 to the creation of the BNOC in 1974.

One might have been led to believe that, because of its deliberately limited nature, the state's control over the nationalized sector would not impose excessive constraints upon the industries concerned. For reasons relating both to the philosophy underlying British law and to the power relationships within the national and international arena, the state's role had been implicitly conceived in a utilitarian and systemic manner in 1946–49, as in 1974–79. It was utilitarian in the sense that its action was to be reduced essentially to the collection and redistribution of taxes or dues. It was systemic in the sense that the state would restrict its interventions to cases where it was necessary to re-establish a fundamental balance. This approach was, at the same time, to be a guarantee of efficiency. The state would be in a better position to defend the national interest if it let experts in the field administer particular sectors while retaining its ultimate control over resource allocation.

In practice, this vague definition of roles led to a confusion of responsibilities, and to growing state intervention which was disorganized and seen as meddlesome. This situation had three major consequences which are of interest. First, it indirectly limited the independence of public corporations and their overall management efficiency in the national interest. Second, it reduced considerably the span of political control. Finally, where the situation reflected the deficiency of the political element in the

British policy-making process, it displaced the conflict towards the industrial partners, so producing the contradiction of having recourse to neo-corporatist policies while at the same time placing an unavoidable obstacle to their actual development.

Neo-corporatist strategies

In a relatively recent article, Pierre Birnbaum tried to demonstrate the 'impossibility' of corporatism on the basis of this key argument: the state would seem to be either too weak (as is the case of Britain) or too strong (as is the case of France) to allow one to speak of a liberal type of neo-corporatist systems of structures (Birnbaum, 1982b). Other authors have also explained the fragility of neo-corporatism on the basis of this political variable (which has long been underestimated by the dominant theory). Andrew Cox and Jack Hayward in particular have pointed out in a comparative study that, in the case of Britain, not only is the self-regulation capacity of socio-economic organizations weak, but also, their hostile attitudes towards the government inhibits their participation. Moreover, given the weaknesses of the national economy, the state has little to offer its principal economic partners in exchange (Cox and Hayward, 1983). In the case of Italy, Marino Regini has shown how the trade unions have helped to legitimize the government's implementation of its policies through their influence at the shop-floor level and in the political system as a whole. Yet, according to Regini, their integration has remained precarious because of the weakness of the Italian state, which lacks sufficient legitimacy to confer on them a significant political status (Regini, 1982).

In highlighting the nature of the state, these three lines of inquiry point in the same direction, but Regini's analysis seems to take the subject a bit further. Not content with merely formulating a hypothesis about resistance to neo-corporatism, he implies that the shortcomings of the state could at the same time be the reason for the development of neo-corporatism and the cause of its instability. An understanding of this paradox is fundamental for the analysis of the nature of neo-corporatism. I will illustrate this point for the case of Britain by drawing out the implications of the previous discussion of the limits of state autonomy.

It appears, first and foremost, that neo-corporatism has taken the form of a conflict-displacement strategy. The shift occurs from the moment that the conflict is identified in terms of its consequences rather than in terms of a contradiction in its logical assumptions. Thus, in the case of the energy sector, the conflict between the logic of the state and that of public corporations has been displaced by problems of organization and finance and has therefore been dismissed as the principal source of instability. In much the same way, the responsibility for the poor performance of public corporations has been assigned to strikes, trade union activity, absenteeism, the 'idleness' of the miners and even communist influence, when it is evident that it flows instead from the manipulation of tariffs in the absence of effective counter-measures, and above all from the lack of clear priorities.

Thus, the displacement of the conflict has taken a neo-corporatist form in so far as the weakness of the state in Britain allowed the representatives of capital and labour to believe they were entitled, no less than government, to articulate the national interest. This phenomenon, which is linked to the conditions for the development of neo-corporatism, is readily visible in the initial process of nationalization. It has conferred a neo-corporatist configuration to postwar government policies in the public sector by polarizing public opinion on the responsibilities of interest groups, especially the unions. The reasoning was that, since these organizations had accepted a role in the national management of the economy and the society, they should also assume a share of the responsibilities.

These responsibilities were, however, relative. The consensus over the principle of an extension of the state's role, first in 1945 and then in 1974, offered a powerful source of legitimacy to the actions of the government, but did not necessarily lead to a marked political autonomy, at least not in the field of industrial relations. It is around the tension between these two paradoxical elements — the coexistence of growing state interventionism and a certain political deficiency — that neo-corporatism found its specific expression in Britain. The problematic 'autonomization' of the political element has made it easier for private interests to colonize the centre, but it should be stressed that the legitimation of political action does not imply the advent of a strong state. Ironically, as we shall see, collaboration strategies often flow from a position of deep mistrust of the state. The different partners have sought through costly compromises to preserve their independence as much as possible and to resist potentially irreversible constraints imposed by governments, so that these strategies have led to a relatively permanent fragmentation of the political system. In this sense neo-corporatism appears in Britain as one unifying mechanism (among others) which is specifically integrated into informal conciliation practices.

Autonomy and legitimacy

The legitimation of government policies has afforded a solid platform for anti-trade-union propaganda by Conservative governments, which ever since the end of the 1950s have denounced with increasing vehemence the 'gigantic strength' of the unions. It must be said that the latter have never displayed an open commitment to technological innovation for fear of the impact it could have on the structure of employment, or on their own bureaucratic power. Nevertheless, these hostile propaganda campaigns began with the premise that, because of their 'excessive' wage claims, trade unions were to be held chiefly, if not solely, responsible for the lack of competitiveness in British industry. These charges have undoubtedly grossly misrepresented the reality.

So far as the coal industry is concerned, the two main recent industrial conflicts of the 1970s — those of 1972 and 1973–4 — were concluded by an increase in wages of about 30 percent; and at the time of writing the 1984–85 strike remains unsettled. However, this figure should be seen in the context of the public authorities' 'contempt for production', which was a large contributing factor to the diminished purchasing power of the miners between 1947 and 1972. By dint of budgetary cuts and restrictions on credit and investment, government leaders, especially in the Treasury, did not allow wages to increase in line with productivity. Moreover, the poor performance of British industry in general can be accounted for to a large extent by ad hoc government policies and their lack of any medium- or long-term global perspectives (Fine et al., 1983; Pollard, 1982).

If, in the short run, the conflict over wages may have had an impact on the worsening conditions of the accumulation of capital, it cannot be argued that it constitutes the determining cause. Contrary to official statements, the trade unions did not possess enormous power. In the public sector, where their rights to negotiate at the national level were best recognized, they proved themselves unable to exert any influence over such vital issues as investment and credit, and thus indirectly over the total available wage levels. From this viewpoint, it cannot be said that these interest groups participated fully in the 'corporatist' formulation of national economic policies.

The attitude of the trade unions has its roots in a two-fold historical and cultural reality. Historically, the trade unions created the Labour Party in 1906, and hoped that it would act at their political arm in Parliament. This somewhat Utopian vision began to fade when the first Labour government was created in 1924, and all but disappeared after the electoral victory of 1929, when the Labour Party, under the influence of Ramsay MacDonald, 'began purposely to encourage its propensity towards "embourgeoisement", both through its appointments policy and through the cultivation of its image abroad. The idea was for it to appear as much as possible as a national party and less as the exclusive representative of working-class interests. The idea was also to assert its respectability vis-à-vis the Establishment' (Bedarida, 1977: 142–3; my translation). It was in the context of these developments that the trade unions abandoned their ideal of workers' control to devote their efforts to questions of 'profitability' and 'responsible' management of social and economic interests. Moreover, thanks to the privileged relation between the two wings of the Labour movement, and owing to the fact of political alternation which consequently allowed trade union representatives to be present in the state apparatus, trade unions have, so to speak, 'demystified' the state, have stripped it of its mysterious and charismatic nature and thus of its pretension to act as an arbiter.

To this historical factor one may add another cultural element which has often been emphasized. Shonfield, for example, shows how in Britain the left itself has not escaped 'the extraordinary tenacity of older attitudes towards the role of public power'. Obviously, the Labour Party does not go to the extent of condemning state action as such. 'There was, and is, a constant demand from the British left that the Government should intervene in more and more things. But the nature of this intervention is assumed to be of a strictly limited kind' (Shonfield, 1965: 88).

The distrust displayed as much by Conservatives as by Labour towards the role of the state, together with the state's difficulty in defining its own specific purview, have combined to favour the emergence of corporatist trends as well as to prevent their real accomplishment. Whichever government was in power, these tendencies were noticeable throughout the whole period in question. As far as the coal industry is concerned, in the wake of nationalization the NUM cooperated with the NCB and the government to limit the increase in wages and to control social unrest (A. Taylor, 1981), despite the internal tensions which this caused. Its active participation in the framing of various types of incomes policies, whether informal or formal, voluntary or imposed, showed proof of its committment to a 'responsible' and 'realistic' trade unionism.

In practice, this amounted to falling into the ideological trap of the national interest and its contradictions. It meant at the same time furnishing the government with the backing of the working-class movement and justifying the idea that inflation was chiefly the result of wage increases. In this sense, the NUM and the trade unions in general diffused the idea of a public good transcending sectoral interest. But this phenomenon could not have more than a limited span, for two reasons.

First, the trade unions gave a strictly provisional backing to the government, either because of electoral strategic reasons or more often because of their unwillingness to invest in it an absolute power over the conduct of social policies. Colin Crouch, who offers a particularly astute analysis of the development of 'voluntarism' in Britain, has pointed out that, rather than letting the state alone take the responsibility (through legal means) for implementing unpopular policies, the unions went to great lengths to put these policies into effect 'voluntarily', because they preferred to 'legislate themselves' (Crouch, 1977; see also Panitch, 1976). In this way, they could keep a tighter control over their rank-and-file. They could also, in principle, prevent these policies from becoming permanent, while at the same time avoiding their most negative aspects thanks to the highly decentralized structure of collective bargaining.

Second, *the development of these corporatist tendencies ran counter to the very nature of the policies they pretend to legitimize.* In the case of the coal industry these were essentially emergency measures, and neo-corporatism essentially took the form of a contingent strategy, sometimes but not exclusively determined by the electoral victories of the Labour Party. Beyond this, the recourse to neo-corporatist strategies resulted from the weak control of government over society as a whole.

The fragmentation of the political system
As we have seen in the case of nationalization and energy policy, the absence of priority goals, and the disarray existing among partners faced with the need to circumscribe the role of the state, constituted respectively a source of inertia and ad hoc interventionism. This situation of political deficiency resulted in a practical sense in the British government's weak control over the overall economy. In this perspective, the dichotomy between 'étatisme' and 'market forces', indicating the existence of two different types of management according to the party in power, seems rather artificial.

Beyond their ideological and strategic differences, successive governments have run into the same fundamental obstacle. Whether sectoral or national, the lack of coordination of the various policies was to a large extent the result of the public authorities' difficulty in thinking of the state as such. It was also one consequence of what may be described as the fragmentation of the political system.

This can best be defined as the coexistence of a great number of autonomous centres of power, all weakly linked to each other. In the context of the present inquiry, this phenomenon appears first at the level of the nationalized industries. Public corporations are in varying degrees accountable to a number of groups or people who each have their own ideas about the functioning of the public sector. Among the third parties which have a say in the control of these industries are the Civil Service, commercial auditors, members of Parliament, select committees of the House, the Public Accounts Committee of the House, consumer groups and, of course, ministers (Johnson, 1978: 27). The great majority of these have different and often opposed interests; but they consider that they have a 'constitutional' right to interfere in the affairs of these corporations, and to express their opinions over their running, on the grounds that they belong to the 'public' sphere. Several attempts have been made to design a more efficient, if not more coherent, system of control over these corporations, notably by reinforcing Parliament's right to inspect their accounts. But either because of the secrecy which surrounds public policies, or even more because of the opposition of the chairmen of nationalized industries, these attempts have not been effective.

Second, at the level of the energy sector, the supply and distribution of energy is controlled to a large extent by nine corporations, of which some also hold shares in private firms. In addition, there are various research bodies, of which Friends of the Earth is the most active. At the highest level, energy policy is influenced by European institutions, particularly the European Coal and Steel Community (ECSC).

The great majority of these organizations also have a particular and often conflicting point of view on energy policy and on their own role in its formulation and implementation. The positions they have adopted on this matter have generally gone well beyond their real responsibilities. With the gradual appearance of new problems, and the emergence of dominant sectoral interests, the alliances forged between these groups have been followed by counter-alliances. The Department of Energy, charged with reconciling these conflicting interests, is not only unable to impose its own views when it is deemed necessary, but may play different roles according to the organizations with which it has to deal. It may also change roles throughout the different stages of the decision-making process, as can the institutions concerned (Pearson, 1981: 69).

Finally, there is no single organized centre of power in the overall political system which can offset that of the Treasury. Obsessed by the problems of inflation and the balance of payments, the Treasury pushed the government to introduce budgetary cuts, restrain credit facilities, increase unemployment and thus sacrifice the production apparatus to fiscal and financial policies. The priority accorded to the market and the stability of the pound was instrumental in the poor competitiveness of British industry abroad. By the end of the

1970s, Britain had lost foreign markets partly as a result of an overvalued pound. Moreover, Britain's self-sufficiency in energy resources was counter-productive in that her American, French and Japanese competitors benefited from the efforts of their respective governments to pay for their oil imports from their exports of manufactured goods.

In comparison with the City and the financial interests it represents, the British government has proved relatively powerless. This can be accounted for on historical grounds, particularly by the fact that, very early on, the British Empire accorded a predominant position to financial capital and allowed some independence to industrial capital, particularly to develop an international dimension. In addition, unlike German, French and Japanese capitals, which coordinated their actions through developing ties with their respective governments and with their national banking systems, British banks are weakly regulated and remain reluctant to push their integration with industry any further (Pearson, 1981; Longstreth, 1979; Pollard, 1982). This fragmentation, which could not be overcome in the absence of a sufficiently strong central authority, encouraged the development of informal conciliation practices among the different actors.

The development of informal conciliation procedures

> The independence of public enterprises, and conversely the right of the government to intervene, have largely remained a matter of interpretation, subject to a *balance of forces* in which an 'intricate network of informal relations between Ministers and departments on the one hand and boards on the other ... [developed] ... towards an intimacy which, if not always cosy, nevertheless provided grounds for suspecting that the public corporations were becoming something like tenants in the great ramshackle mansion of central government administration'. (Johnson, 1978: 128)

This situation has no doubt allowed government leaders to exert a great influence over the activities of nationalized industries, but the latter have also influenced the options of the public authorities. As Johnson points out, 'it is remarkable how much confusion of responsibilities in British administration occurs simply because people like to be nice to each other....' In other words, compromise is often preferred for fear of the sanctions which can ensue from a less conciliatory attitude. He goes on to show that 'nowhere does the tendency operate more powerfully than in the relations between Ministers (together with their civil servants) and non-central government administrative bodies' (Johnson, 1978: 134).

We can therefore discern a kind of logic of political bargaining which is by now well established in Britain. Its multiple and complex ramifications are difficult to unravel, but without going into an exhaustive account of these, which is beyond the scope of this paper, one can draw a few important observations in respect of neo-corporatist theories.

It appears that concertation between the different interests often takes place within an informal framework. The negotiating partners are not necessarily the official representatives of capital, or labour, or a particular ministry. The fragmentation of the political system allows an unpredictable mechanism of alliances and counter-alliances to develop among the various groups concerned. On the other hand, the influence of the national democratic institutions and elected representatives (members of Parliament, select committees, local authorities, etc.) is reduced in the light of these informal practices. In particular, the role of the sponsoring minister, and the ambiguity attached to his powers, do not seem to indicate a tightening of the already slack parliamentary controls. As Professor Hanson emphasized in 1961 before a select committee, 'So long as the Minister is held by Parliament to be *generally* responsible for the performance of the nationalized industry under his supervision ... [he will continue] ... to try to ensure, by predominantly informal means, that its activities are such that he feels he can reasonably defend before the House of Commons' (quoted in Johnson, 1978: 134). Partly as a result of the secrecy surrounding governmental actions, it will always be possible to limit the control of industrial policies.

In the same way, there is a gap between the corporatist structures in which policies supposedly are formulated on the one hand, and the circles of informal negotiation on the other. This gap is widened by official neo-corporatist statements and by anti-union propaganda.

In the first case, there was the example of the 'Social Contract', which gave rise in the energy sector to tripartite institutions of 'concertation', which were to set the stage for an 'open government'. The analysis of the North Sea case demonstrates that, in practice, these policies played only a negligible role in spite of the presence of the oil companies themselves within the tripartite institutions. The power of the multinationals, coupled with government and its weak political control over the economy, have proved far more of a determinant in the development of energy policies, which largely mirrored the prevailing power structure.

In the second case, concerning anti-union propaganda, the official line seems rather removed from reality. The trade unions oriented their action at the centre on behalf of a vague and ill-defined ideology of the 'national interest' which they helped to diffuse. But they lacked any real influence over decisions affecting Britain's important economic choices (investments, the total available wages, employment factors, etc.).

This is why, rather than speaking of 'neo-corporatism', it seems to me wiser to emphasize the elements which develop more from a trend, or, according to Middlemas (1979), from a corporatist 'bias'. This bias finds expression in institutions or structures of a corporatist type, created through the will and the capacity of 'private' actors to act at the centre together with (if not against) the public authorities. But here we are speaking neither of a system (Lehmbruch, 1979), nor especially of a new state form (Panitch, 1979a). Indeed, neo-corporatism has not modified either the political system or the state. In Britain, it appeared to be nothing more than one conjunctural strategy (among others) which was assimilated into already well-established traditional conciliation procedures.

Specific neo-corporatist strategies
Within this context of multiple and relatively autonomous centres of power, neo-corporatism appears to be a strategy designed to enhance the role of the state, or to force into the political arena problems which otherwise would have remained at its periphery, or, temporarily, to 'anaesthetize' social conflict. We can briefly illustrate the first and the last eventualities through the examples of the 1972 and 1973 miners' strikes.

Edward Heath refused to compromise with the trade unions when he came to office in 1970. Faced with the discontent of the working classes, he tried from 1971 on to persuade them, initially informally, (through, for example, the NEDC), then later through more formal means. This strategy failed. The Conservative government then resorted to a typical conflict-displacement manoeuvre. It accused the miners and their organizations of carrying a heavy burden of responsibility for Britain's difficulties in overcoming the oil crisis. When a general election was eventually called in 1974, the campaign was dominated by the theme, 'Who governs? The trade unions or the government?' As will be recalled, the threat of energy shortages at the time did provoke an awareness and a consensus over the need to strengthen the role of the state in this particular sector. The hostile Tory propaganda against the trade unions added credibility to the possibility, implied in Labour Party policies, of managing the affairs of the nation from a neo-corporatist base. The logic was that, since the trade unions were so 'powerful', only their association with the government would avoid a confrontation. Thus, both parties made use of a neo-corporatist strategy but in a different manner.

The goal of the Conservatives was to 'anaesthetize' the conflict, while the Labour Party, acting partly from electoral considerations, supported a neo-corporatist approach in order to revalue the political role by claiming that in the future a 'national element' would be added to energy sector management.

Heath's failure, and the fate of the Social Contract policy, shows to what degree these strategies were ephemeral. This outcome was determined partly by the mobilization cycles of the working classes, but also by the fact that these strategies did not constitute a political project in any real sense of the word.

The politicization of previously peripheral issues can be illustrated by the recent example of pricing policy. The position of the government on this question was simple and clear: to allow market forces to operate unhindered. The leaders of British industry, especially of energy-intensive users, complained endlessly about the very high costs of energy in Britain compared with those of their main foreign competitors. In this light, the CBI met with government representatives and the TUC within the framework of the NEDC, which produced two reports in 1981 (NEDC, 1981a; 1981b). Their work did not lead to any tangible results, but as several of the participants to these meetings admitted in personal interviews, at least one fundamental objective had been achieved: through the intermediary of the NEDC, they had succeeded in pushing the key issues to the forefront of the political arena. Subsequently the CBI conducted its own inquiry and used various other channels to press its case. Thus we can see that, once again, the NEDC restricted itself simply to the role of a forum for pressure group activity of variable effectiveness. The NEDC does not fulfil its neo-corporatist 'mission' any more over economic issues than over social issues, but it does at least permit the different partners to express themselves at variance with official policies.

Conclusion

When analyzing this particular sector, neo-corporatism emerges in a rather different manner from the prevailing ideal types. This is why it seems to me unwise to propose a new definition of this phenomenon. I have rather chosen to examine a series of key elements which are present in the various definitions: the interdependence of interests; the delegation of powers; the preliminary structural conditions; the modes of policy formulation, the patterns of interest representation outside the context of the parliamentary institutions; the questions of a functional requirement in relation to the accumulation of capital, the integration of the working classes and of their representatives, and so on — all factors which are indicators of neo-corporatist trends. I have chosen to focus my inquiry on the state partly because I consider it impossible to isolate neo-corporatism from the public policies for which it is said to be conceived.

To conclude this paper, I will summarize the implications of my research on nationalization and the energy sector for the fragile nature of neo-corporatism.

Since neo-corporatism in Britain constituted a strategy rather than a system or a political structure, it developed alongside more traditional pressure group practices. In this sense, it is a response to the fragmentation of the political system and a result of the constraints on the autonomy of the state. In times of crisis, neo-corporatist strategies help to displace conflict, to reduce its intensity, and/or to enhance the role of the state. In periods of relative social quiet, it often serves as one means of bringing particular issues into the political sphere.

Neo-corporatism does not constitute a transformation of the form of the state. On the contrary, the historical conditions of the development of the state in Britain — which have played a part in the difficult process of its autonomization — appear as a source as well as an obstacle to corporatist practices.

At the macroeconomic level, it seems that this organizational pattern produces only temporary effects, and cannot be seen as a historical necessity for systematically ensuring the accumulation of capital. The poor integration of the state and of industrial and financial capital in Britain has removed any possibility of a corporatist management of different interests. Governments have remained prisoners of the conflicts of interest between the various fractions of capital. Neo-corporatist strategies have, in particular, permitted Britain to defer or to cushion social and economic crises but not to overcome them.

The failure of corporatism as a means for a deep transformation of the state does not necessarily imply the conditions for the development of a 'strong state'. It is possible to envisage a reinforcement of the police, military and judicial apparatuses, coupled with appeals for national unity, so that the government can keep the different social partners 'on a short leash' during periods of serious crisis. But there is always the risk that the problem of the legitimacy and sovereignty of the state will recur again, particularly in the field of industrial relations. These reflections, if pushed a bit further, lead us to question the appropriateness of the 'strong state' alternative to neo-corporatism in the British case.

These conclusions do not necessarily contradict the general theoretical hypotheses of neo-corporatism which remain highly useful. They do, however, permit a more precise formulation in order to improve their explanatory cogency. But there is no evidence that the alternative of a more directive state would be any more effective in resolving the obstacles which frustrate the successful adoption of neo-corporatist strategies in Britain.

Notes

This chapter is based on a wider research project on the British energy sector, and I would like to thank the British Council for financial support.

8

Large firms and the representation of business interests in the UK and West German construction industry

Wyn Grant and Wolfgang Streeck

Introduction: large and small firms and the problem of 'political design'

One of the most persistent divisions of interest among business is that between large and small firms. Conflicts between large and small firms may arise from competition both in the product and in the labour market. In the former, large firms are interested in a stable and predictable environment, enabling them to protect their large-scale, longer-term investments. Measures that large firms can take to limit competition to this effect include take-overs of smaller firms; efforts to raise barriers to market entry; support for more demanding product and safety standards, which smaller firms cannot meet; cartelization between the small number of large firms; economic or institutional market segmentation, closing off large firms' market segment from smaller-scale competitors; etc. Large firms may also, of course, simply out-compete smaller firms, making use of their superior access to credit facilities and of risk-reducing diversification in different sub-markets. In addition, there may be customer-supplier or subcontracting relationships between large and small firms in a given industry, and this may give rise to dependence of the latter on the former. In the labour market, large firms tend to be able and willing to pay higher wages and grant better conditions than small firms, thus gaining competitive advantages in local labour markets, and their large size makes it possible for them to develop internal labour market strategies not open to smaller organizations.

Coming to terms with the division of interests between large and small firms is one of the fundamental problems in the organizational design of business interest associations. The most obvious choice here is between separate or common organization of firms of different size. Separate organization has the advantage that it creates (relatively) homogeneous groups having (relatively) homogeneous interests that can be expressed without being 'watered down' by internal compromise. On the other hand, as conflicts of interest between firms in the same industry always coexist with interest communalities, there still remains a need for interest accommodation and coordination, which, in 'associational systems' with separate organizations for different categories of firms, has to be satisfied through inter-organizational contacts and linkages. Moreover, political prudence may advise 'big business' not to have its interests represented separately, but wherever possible to join forces with 'small business' — even at the expense of having to make internal concessions on individual issues. Interest representation through a common, comprehensive association may enable large firms to 'hide behind the backs' of their smaller competitors and to avail themselves of the political 'pull' that small business has with many political parties and government agencies. At the same time, small firms may be prepared to forego the 'unmediated' expression of their special interests if this gives them a share in the superior organizational resources that associations can mobilize from large firms, and if they can in this way win some control over the political articulation of large firms' interests.

This is not to say that the second possibility, comprehensive organization, is any more self-evident than the first. A unitary pattern of interest representation does not by itself do away with existing divisions of interest. Just as a fragmented associational system has to build up inter-organizational structures to cope with interest differences, comprehensive associations with a heterogeneous membership have to develop intra-organizational institutions for the same purpose. Organizational devices to manage interest heterogeneity arising from differences in firm size include special committees or working parties for large firms, formal or informal rules of representation of large and small firms on the executive board, a right for 'minority groups' to dissent and not to be bound by the association's decisions, ceilings on individual members' dues payments, de facto subsidization of small by large firms arising from the different financial contributions to, and utilization of, the association's selective goods, etc. However, while these and other organizational mechanisms may go some way towards reconciling divergent member interests, the result is likely to remain precarious, and members' commitment to associational policies may be low because the policies are merely the result of intraorganizational compromise. Not least, on issues that are highly controversial, comprehensive associations may not be able to develop a policy at all, and this may lead to the parallel separate organization, formal or informal, of categories of their members. More generally, while large firms in comprehensive organizations may feel that they do not get adequate political returns on their high financial and manpower investment in associational activities, small firms may find that their political capital is used primarily to advance the interests of their large competitors. As a consequence, the internal politics of comprehensive associations organizing both large and small firms are often dominated by tacit or open threats of secession by one group or the other, and preventing such secessions may become one of the major preoccupations of the professional staff of such associations.

Nevertheless, joint organization of large and small firms is frequent, if not the rule, and it is the objective of this chapter to point out some of the factors that may account for this fact. As its empirical reference, the chapter looks at business associational systems in an economic sector — the construction industry — that is characterized by a particularly strong division between large and small firms. The typical pattern in the construction industry of advanced industrialized countries is one of coexistence of a small number of large, technologically advanced companies on the one hand, with a large number of small, artisan-type firms on the other, holding a substantial share of the market. The assumption is that the differences between the two categories of firms are so significant that, as far as the economic structure of the industry is concerned, separate organization is the most likely pattern of associability. To the extent that, empirically, one does find forms of comprehensive organization in the sector, the hypothesis would be that these must be due to factors outside its economic structure, in particular to political factors in the widest sense. The general notion behind this is that associational systems, of business as well as of other social categories, are affected not only by a 'logic of membership' — the composition and the perspectives of their social constituencies — but also by a 'logic of influence', i.e. the structural dynamics of, and expectations held by, their organized interlocutors such as the state and the interest associations of other classes with which they interact (Schmitter and Streeck, 1981).

To assess the importance of political factors in the shaping of business interest organizations, the chapter compares the associational systems in the construction industries of West Germany and the UK. While there are some significant differences in the economic structure of the two industries (see below), it will be argued that these do not satisfactorily account for the existing variations in patterns of associability, in particular with regard to the relations between large and small firms. As a further and primary explanatory factor, the chapter will turn to differences in the political and institutional environment of the two associational systems. This causal relationship is of more general theoretical interest because of the crucial role the structure of organized social groups plays for 'corporatist' interest intermediation. The devolution of state authority and state functions to organized interests is facilitated by the existence of encompassing interest aggregates grouping together heterogeneous sub-interests — including those of large and small firms — and holding a monopoly of representation for their respective organizational domain. Comprehensive interest associations that undertake to represent the same interests are in a position to work out binding compromises between the diverse interests they contain, and to make their members comply with agreements negotiated on their behalf with external interlocators. Thus, they may make an important contribution to 'governability' on both the 'input' and the 'output' side of the political process (Schmitter, 1974, 1977). This is why the formation of comprehensive interest organizations is frequently encouraged by government agencies. However, the potential and the limitations of 'political design' (Anderson, 1977) of social interest representation by the state are little explored and are therefore the subject of considerable controversy. The following analysis of the impact of different economic and political environments on the associational representation and integration of large firms may help to clarify some of the institutional preconditions of effective corporatist interest intermediation.

The construction industry in the UK and West Germany: basic economic characteristics

In both the UK and West Germany, the construction industry in 1980 employed about 1.7 million people. This represented a share in the two countries' total employment of 7.0 percent in the UK and 6.8 percent in West Germany. While in nominal terms the output of the British construction industry in 1980 was about 27 percent lower than the German output, compared with their countries' gross domestic products the two industries were of almost equal size (9.8 percent in the UK, 9.5 percent in West Germany).

Another characteristic that the two industries have in common is their dependence on public sector contracts in particular and on the state's economic policy in general. In 1982, 33 percent of the industry's output in the UK, and 37 percent in West Germany, were produced on direct central and local government contracts. Largely as a result of cutbacks in government spending and of government efforts to curb inflation by raising interest rates, the two industries during the 1970s and early 1980s suffered their worst economic crisis in recent history. In West Germany the average rate of real growth per year in the 1970s was 4.2 percent, while in the UK, there was on average a decline of output by 1.7 percent.

Of particular importance in the context of the present paper is the role of large and small firms in the two industries and the relationship between them. In both countries, the construction industry 'constitutes an environment that encourages employees to start their own businesses because the required level of initial capital outlay is low' (Scase and Goffee, 1982: 65). Accordingly, average firm size is small compared with other industries, firm turnover — to a considerable extent arising from bankruptcies — is high, and the size distribution of firms is relatively constant over time. The vast majority of firms operate in small, local markets, frequently acting as specialized subcontractors on larger projects. While their technology is traditional, their overheads are low and their operational flexibility is high. At the other end of the scale, there is a limited number of large firms with advanced technology — especially in civil engineering — and high capital intensity that operate on a national and even international basis. Compared with other industries, however, their share in the market is small, and for logistical reasons even they operate mostly out of local subsidiaries.

The following observations on the structural differences and similarities between the UK and German construction industry seem to be possible on the basis of the existing data.

1. The number and importance of very small firms is higher in the UK than in West Germany. Including firms with an employment of only one person, there was a total of 113,632 private contractors in the UK construction industry in 1980 (Housing and Construction Statistics). Of these, 91,657 (81 percent) had less than eight employees. Not counting one-man firms, this figure was still as high as 55,108 (48 percent). Given that less than 15 percent of the German construction workforce in 1980 was employed in establishments with less than *ten* employees, it is safe to conclude that the share of small firms in total sectoral employment is higher in the UK than in Germany.

2. Private medium-sized construction firms are a rare species in the UK as compared with West Germany. In 1980 there were 1914 private construction firms in the UK that employed between 60 and 599 employees; their share in the total employment of the industry amounted to 17 percent (289,500 employees). In Germany, by contrast, there were 5133 private contractors with a workforce between 50 and 499; together they employed 653,700, i.e. 38 percent of the total employment.

National differences notwithstanding, what is apparent in both countries is that it is the medium-sized firms which have been most adversely affected by the decline in demand in recent years. Such firms are not large enough to enter the overseas market. At the same time, they lack the operational flexibility of the small enterprise. Their overheads are generally higher and they are often committed to a skilled labour force which, once dispersed, is difficult to reassemble.

3. Like UK industry in general, the UK construction industry is relatively highly concentrated. The 140 private firms with 600 or more employees that existed in 1980 employed 229,000 workers, i.e. 13.5 percent of the industry's workforce. In Germany in the same year there were 197 firms with more than 500 employees; their share in the workforce was a mere 6.6 percent.

4. Large UK construction firms are more vertically integrated than their German counterparts, and some of them are conglomerates extending into very different sectors of the economy. Large construction firms in Germany concentrate their activities almost exclusively on the construction industry proper, especially on civil engineering. Where they branch out into other areas, this tends to be confined to the production of building materials, in particular concrete (backward integration). In the UK, on the other hand, there is also considerable forward integration into housebuilding. Housebuilding accounts for 25 percent of the turnover of the largest UK company (George Wimpey), and the sixth largest UK company, Barratt Developments, specializes in housebuilding.

There are a number of reasons why similar developments have not taken place in Germany. Forward integration into housebuilding is difficult for German construction firms because large housing projects are often carried out by cooperative housing associations or non-profit development firms that are supported and frequently controlled by state or local government. Moreover, the market for individual family houses in Germany is still primarily in the hands of small- and medium-sized local building firms. Finally, diversification is generally less frequent in German industry than in the UK. Also, since the crisis in the German construction industry was somewhat less severe than in the UK, economic pressures to diversify were lower; and they were further reduced when firms found other, more conventional, ways of responding to the contraction of the domestic construction market.

5. The 1970s were a period of rapidly rising 'export' activities of large construction firms both in the UK and West Germany. The increase in purchasing power in the OPEC countries after 1973 created an international market, especially in civil engineering, that offered opportunities for UK and German firms with advanced technology to find compensation for declining domestic demand.

There was also increased activity in non-OPEC countries, in particular the USA. By the end of the decade, foreign earnings of the construction industry, previously regarded as a purely domestic industry, contributed 2.8 percent to the export earnings of both the UK and the German economy.

In West Germany as well as the UK, it was only a small number of firms that benefited from the increase in overseas contracts in the 1970s. The 303 foreign orders received by the German construction industry in 1980 went to no more than 47 firms, some of which are subsidiaries of other firms in this category. In the UK, where 93 percent of all overseas work is carried out by 20 firms, the number of firms active in foreign markets appears to be even smaller.

Patterns of competition and market segmentation
The product market of the construction industry is known to be fiercely competitive. One factor contributing to this is the system of price formation through competitive bidding for individual projects. Unlike in other industries, construction firms competing for a specific contract ideally do not know the price offered by their competitors; in principle, they do not even know who their competitors are. This results in considerable uncertainty. The situation is made still more difficult by the fact that construction firms are normally engaged in only a small number of projects at the same time. If one of those projects runs out, they are in urgent need to win a new contract in order to cover their fixed costs; otherwise, they have to cut their capacity. As a consequence, there is a good chance that, among the firms submitting tenders for a given project, there will be at least one that needs to win the contract at any price and therefore is prepared to offer below costs. If contracts are as a rule awarded to the lowest bidder, unlimited competition may thus in fact jeopardize firms' economic viability.

Further complications are added by the possibility for construction firms to form consortiums and to engage in subcontracting arrangements. Consortiums are groups of firms that join together to bid for and carry out a given project. By forming a consortium, small firms may challenge large firms in their traditional markets. Large firms, for their part, may decide to cooperate on a particular project to share risks, diversify their project portfolios and avoid bidding against each other. They may also, for various reasons, admit small- or medium-sized local firms as consortium members. Alternatively, a firm that wins a contract may subcontract part of the work to other firms. Unlike in a consortium, where the partner firms are of equal status, subcontracting tends to create an asymmetrical relationship of dominance and dependence, and it leads to conflicts of interest between main contractors and subcontractors and between different subcontractors. About a third of all work in the UK is subcontracted, the proportion being higher in new building and particularly in the big and complex projects in which large firms are involved. Subcontractors on the whole tend to be smaller firms, although some subcontracting is done by very large firms; equally, not all smaller firms engage in subcontracting. Nevertheless, complaints by small subcontractors against large main contractors imposing on them unfair prices and conditions can be heard in the UK, and the widespread practice of 'squeezing the subby' adds to the risks and uncertainties, especially of small- and medium-sized construction firms.

In both the UK and West Germany, the high insecurity for firms created by the basic pattern of competition in the construction industry has given rise to successful demands for some form of institutionalized market regulation. The arrangements that have been devised in the two countries are similar in that they stabilize existing lines of market segmentation — by speciality, locality, etc. — and thus protect specific groups of firms from competition of other firms and/or new entrants to the market. However, they differ considerably both in their legal status and in the lines of segmentation they reinforce.

The main institutional mechanism regulating the German construction market is the 'Handwerksrecht' (law of artisan firms). It has a long tradition that dates back to the nineteenth century, and it applies not only to the construction industry but to a number of other sectors of the economy as well. In its present form as re-enacted after the establishment of the Federal Republic, Handwerksrecht specifies a list of 125 trades that can be legally engaged in only by firms owned by, or employing, an artisan certified in this particular trade. Of the 125 Handwerke in the list, 23 belong to the construction industry; they include almost all finishing trades as well as, for example, carpenters and bricklayers. To become a certified artisan, one has to undergo a three years' apprenticeship and, after several years of working as a journeyman, a two-year 'master' course. Certified artisans are assisted in setting up their own businesses by special government-subsidized credit programmes. Artisan firms are by law members of regional 'Chambers of Artisans'; these are public law bodies that offer their members, among other things, training programmes and consulting services. They also enforce the Handwerksrecht by bringing legal proceedings against non-artisan firms or uncertified individuals engaging in one of the 125 Handwerk trades.

Handwerksrecht segments the market and limits competition in the construction industry in several ways. For one thing, it restricts market access at the lower end of the scale and thus protects especially smaller firms. It also places restrictions on the 'black economy', and it largely explains the relative absence in the German construction industry of the UK 'one-man firm'. Second, it impedes horizontal integration of small firms trying to combine different specialist trades; by granting certified specialists a legal monopoly on the performance of particular jobs, it preserves the distinction between different specialities. Third, Handwerksrecht makes it difficult for non-artisan firms to enter specialist markets; for example, a producer of roofing materials could not undertake to apply the materials himself — thus competing with traditional roofing firms — unless he managed to be entered on the register of artisan firms kept by the Chamber of Artisans.

In assessing the structural consequences of the German Handwerksrecht, it is important to note two points. One is that the law does not entirely prohibit non-artisan firms competing with artisan firms; they may do so if they use distinctively non-artisanal ('industrielle') production methods and forms of organization. In other words, road-building being a Handwerk, a non-artisan road-building firm may carry out large motorway projects; it might however encounter legal difficulties if it competed for a contract for a pedestrian zone in an inner city. Second, unlike for example in France, there is no general size limit in Germany for artisan firms. In the construction industry, an artisan road-building firm may employ as many as 500 workers without losing its legal status, and, unlike a non-artisan firm, it can engage in whatever kind of road-building work it finds profitable. The result is that there is considerable overlap in the size distributions of artisan and non-artisan construction firms.

The main mechanism in the UK providing for institutionalized segmentation of the construction market is the extensive use of selective tendering for public sector contracts. In the mid-1970s, 77 percent of public sector contracts in civil engineering and 65 percent of public sector contracts in building were issued on the basis of select competition (NEDO, 1975: 42). The method of selective tendering used differs to some extent from one public sector client to another. In many cases an ad hoc list is compiled for a particular project, although where the construction activity requires the purchase of expensive specialized plant, a single, short list of tenderers who have entered the field may be used. In general, lists do not change very often.

These arrangements assist larger firms as they are protected against smaller competitors trying to break into their traditional markets by offering 'unfair' prices, although the system also provides, for example, medium-sized civil engineering contractors with a slice of the market in which they can operate without direct competition from larger firms. It is significant that this kind of market regulation has been demanded again and again without success by large firms in the German construction industry; one reason why no classification system was introduced in Germany was strong resistance by small- and medium-sized firms, especially within the Handwerk.

Another market-regulating arrangement that large German firms have been refused is institutionalized exchange of information between construction firms on bids and contracts. Many UK construction firms are members of regional 'builders' conferences', to which they have to provide information on any building work that they apply for or accept. It is characteristic that a similar monitoring arrangement in Germany that was operated by regional business associations was declared illegal in 1973 by the Federal Cartel Office on the grounds that it enabled firms to identify their competitors and, perhaps, work out price agreements with them. Subsequent attempts to have this or a modified form of collectively organized 'market observation' reinstated were fruitless.

German construction firms have to operate in a legal environment that subjects them to the same rules of 'fair trading' as any other industrial sector, regardless of whatever special conditions may exist in the construction market. As most of the smaller construction firms are to an important extent protected by their Handwerk status, it is the large firms that are primarily affected by this. Ever since the passage into law of the Fair Competition Act of 1959, large construction firms have demanded legal and institutional changes by which the construction industry, just like (for example) banking and agriculture, would in effect have been exempted from central elements of postwar competition legislation. None of these various initiatives was successful — partly because of the indifference of small firms in the sector and partly because the other industries, most of which are clients of the construction industry, were not willing to lend their political support. As a substitute for legalized ways of reducing competitive pressures and insecurity, large construction firms have resorted to large-scale illegal collusion and price-fixing, and this has made them an easy and favourite target of law enforcement agencies. More spectacular actions include the 1973 and 1982 police 'razzias' on the offices of all large firms in the industry which resulted in fines of up to several million Deutschmarks.

Summing up, the relative position of large and small firms in the UK and West German construction industry differs in some important respects. In the UK, the industry is more polarized between the large and the small end of the scale, and competition rules are more responsive to the needs of large firms. Moreover, UK large firms have significant interests outside the construction sector proper, and this further improves their situation in comparison to their smaller-scale competitors. In fact, differences in size and status of large and small firms are so pronounced that competition between the two groups has to a large extent given way to (frequently unequal) exchange through subcontracting. In West Germany, by comparison, the size distribution of firms is more continuous, market-regulating arrangements are more in favour of small- and medium-sized firms, and large firms are exposed to strong competition both between themselves and by a large number of ambitious medium-sized firms. On the other hand, in recent years large firms have found a new area of activity in foreign markets that up to now has been inaccessible to their medium-sized competitors.

As a substitute for diversification and vertical integration, increased 'exports' have made it possible for large German construction firms to prosper at a time when the rest of the industry was in its worst crisis for more than three decades. The different effects of the crisis on different categories of firms have led to complaints by smaller firms about large companies using their profits from foreign projects to subsidize their domestic capacity, or about the privileged relationship of large construction firms to the leading banks (each of which holds substantial shares in at least one of the largest construction firms). An important factor that helps contain tensions is that large German construction firms, more than their UK counterparts, concentrate on civil engineering work and leave most of the private housing market to smaller firms. While this creates somewhat different interests with regard to government economic policy, it reduces competition without generating new conflicts over the terms of subcontracts between large and small firms in housebuilding.

Patterns of associative action: associational systems in the UK and German construction industry

The associational systems of the UK and West German construction industry differ in important respects. Among other things, boundaries between associations run along different lines, associations group together different categories of firms, and the relations between associations exhibit differing degrees of overlap, duplication and competition. In this part of the chapter, we will briefly describe the systems of interest associability in the two industries, giving special attention to the position of large firms in the two systems.

United Kingdom

The system of construction industry interest associations in the UK is characterized by extensive overlap between the domains of associations and overt competition between some of them for members. Hence, a large firm is likely to find itself in membership of a considerable number of associations. The likelihood of multiple membership is increased by the tendency of many large firms to organize themselves on a product division basis, with each product division being involved in the work of the appropriate association.

There is one 'catchall' association in the system, the Building Employers Confederation (BEC), which has a complex internal structure based on territorial and functional divisions. The BEC plays a leading role in industry-wide wage negotiations, and for this reason, if no other, large firms are likely to be active in it. However, some of the specialist aspects of the BEC's work are also likely to be of interest to large firms. For example, because building houses for sale is an important activity for many large British construction companies, the BEC runs the House-Builders' Federation, membership of which is open only to BEC members.

Almost all large firms engage in civil engineering activity and thus belong to the other principal organization in the industry, the Federation of Civil Engineering Contractors (FCEC). This organization operates a 'reputation test' to screen prospective members; whereas the BEC has a large number of small- and medium-sized firms in membership, the FCEC is entirely composed of medium-sized and large firms. The bulk of civil engineering work in the UK emanates from the public sector, and this gives the FCEC a special concern with the level of government capital expenditure. The FCEC has a close working relationship with the BEC; together they form the employers' side in national wage negotiations, and they have joint committees on a number of subjects ranging from taxation to computers. Traditional divisions between the building and civil engineering industries have eroded in the period since the war, and the possibility of a merger between the BEC and FCEC has been discussed. However, the larger firms in the industry tend to see the FCEC as very much 'their' organization in a way that the BEC, which often has smaller builders as presidents, is not.

The small number of large firms engaged in overseas work have their own specialist organization in the form of the Export Group for the Construction Industries (EGCI). This organization has a close working relationship with the Department of Trade.

Large-scale projects for the oil and chemical industries are of considerable importance to the largest firms in the UK construction industry, and firms such as Wimpey, Taylor Woodrow and John Laing are actively involved in them. Large UK construction sites are prone to serious industrial disputes, and the Oil and Chemical Plant Contractors' Association (OCPCA) was formed as an employers' organization in 1969 to tackle this problem.

Smaller builders, particularly those undertaking general building and small-scale housebuilding work, may join the Federation of Master Builders (FMB) as an alternative to BEC's Smaller Builders Section. There is a long history of bad relations between the BEC and FMB, dating back to the formation of the FMB in the second world war as a government initiative to mobilize building industry resources to cope with war damage. This rivalry has been intensified in recent years by the FMB's negotiation of its own industrial relations agreement with one of the main construction industry unions, the Transport and General Workers' Union. (The TGWU's involvement in this rival bargaining agreement is explained by its competition for members with the other main union in the industry, the Union of Construction, Allied Trades and Technicians, UCATT.)

While not all small firms are subcontractors, the bulk of subcontracting work is done by smaller firms. The BEC has its own Federation of Building Sub-Contractors, but there are two rival organizations in the form of the Federation of Associations of Specialist Subcontractors (FASS) and the Committee of Associations of Specialists and Sub-Contractors (CASEC). Both FASS and CASEC are associations of associations, and are relatively weak bodies in terms of the resources and authority they command; but their separate existence is evidence of the importance of the division of interest in the industry between main contractors and subcontractors.

West Germany
The associational system in the West German construction industry is both more comprehensive and more decentralized than in the UK, and there is less overlap and almost no duplication and competition. The main division is between artisan and non-artisan firms. Large and very large firms, which as a rule are not Handwerk, are organized in 16 regional 'Bauindustrie' associations that are affiliated to the Hauptverband der Deutschen Bauindustrie (HDB). Affiliates have a high degree of autonomy; for example, they determine their dues independently, and they can resign from HDB membership (which four of them did for a short time in 1975).

Membership in HDB affiliates is not limited to large firms; in principle, almost all of the about 10,000 non-artisan firms in the West German construction industry are eligible to join. Most of the 3700 members, however, are considerably larger than average. Moreover, owing to the regionalized structure of the HDB, local subsidiaries of large national building firms are organized individually and each is counted as one member.[1] As a result, the ten leading construction firms which together have roughly 300 subsidiaries account for about 8 percent of the HDB's total membership.

The largest organization of artisan firms in the German construction industry, and indeed one of the largest business associations anywhere, is the Zentralverband des Deutschen Baugewerbes (ZDB). It represents 43,000 firms from the 'Bauhauptgewerbe' as well as from some of the finishing trades (such as tilers and floor layers). Statistics on the size structure of ZDB firms are not available. There were, however, 29 artisan construction firms in 1980 with more than 500 employees, and the number of Handwerk firms in the same year with more than 100 employees was higher than the number of non-Handwerk firms in the same size category (1142 as compared to 878). All of these firms can be assumed to be members of their respective associations.

Firms represented by the ZDB are organized in 687 local guilds; 684 of these are affiliated to 25 regional associations which, in turn, are affiliated to the ZDB. Another four regional associations have direct firm membership. Guilds and regional associations have a high degree of autonomy. Some of them are specialized by trade while others include the entire range of firms covered by the ZDB. The basic structure of Handwerk business associations is prescribed in law and is the same in all sectors of the economy. Most importantly, local guilds are public-law bodies which are serviced by the respective Chamber of Artisans. Although membership in guilds is not compulsory, about 90 percent of the firms in the ZDB's domain are members of its local and regional affiliates.

There are different kinds of tensions inside the two main associations. In the ZDB, most of the conflicts between members are related to problems of demarcation between the different artisanal trades. Normally, demarcation disputes are sparked off by the appearance on the market of new building materials or the invention of new processes of which it is not immediately clear which of the various Handwerke is legally entitled to apply them.

Conflicts within the HDB centre around the division between large- and medium-sized firms. Many of its members believe that the HDB is leaning too much towards the large building concerns, the 'Twelve Apostles'. The main object of such suspicions is the HDB's largest and most powerful regional affiliate, the Wirtschafts- vereinigung Bauindustrie Nordrhein-Westfalen. However, the final disintegration of the HDB was always avoided, and while both small and large firms have for years been wondering whether separate organization of the 'twelve apostles' was not better for everybody, up to now no serious attempt to set up such an organization has been made.

Cooperation between the two main associations in the German construction industry is close, and there are a number of institu- tionalized bonds between them. Four regional construction associa- tions organize both artisan and non-artisan firms; they are affiliated to the HDB and the ZDB at the same time. The two federations negotiate joint agreements on wages and conditions with the Industrial Union of Construction and Building Materials Workers (IGBSE). This is facilitated, among other things, by the overlap in the size distribution of the two associations' firms, which makes for the existence of a joint labour market, and by similar industrial relations problems. Conflicts between HDB and ZDB exist in the areas of economic policy — where the HDB tends to favour government spending on civil engineering projects while the ZDB prefers measures to stimulate private housebuilding — and of competition law, with the ZDB refusing to share the strong feelings of the HDB on the need for better protection of large firms.

Comparing the associational system of the German to that of the British construction industry, the following characteristics would appear to be of particular importance.

1. There is a high degree of internalization of cleavages in West Germany between categories of firms within associational bound- aries. Large firms are grouped together with medium-sized firms in the HDB, and medium-sized firms are organized in the ZDB together with small firms. Both HDB and ZDB represent main contractors as well as subcontractors. Exporting firms have no separate association but form a committee inside the HDB. There is, however, a separate association for medium-sized firms (the Bundesvereinigung Mittelständischer Bauunternehmen, BVMB) which has no counterpart in the UK. The BVMB was founded in the mid-1960s by an official of the largest regional HDB affiliate, who felt that the special interests of middle-sized firms willing and able to compete with the large firms were not adequately catered for. While the existence of the BVMB shows that there are limits to the capacity of German associations to internalize conflicts, it should be noted that the BVMB is a small association and that all of its

members are also members of one of the large associations, the majority belonging to the HDB.

Although there is one comprehensive association in the UK — the BEC — which undertakes to represent the entire construction industry, there is an overriding tendency for different categories of firms to organize in separate, economically homogeneous associations. For all major groups of firms, there exist specialist organizations, some of which are in outright competition with the BEC. Large civil engineering firms have the FCEC to represent their special interests, and large firms that operate on foreign markets have a separate association as well. The cleavage between subcontractors and main contractors is reflected in the existence of two federations of subcontractors competing with the BEC, and in the division between these two federations and the FMB. The low capacity of associations in the system to bridge economic cleavages is also illustrated by the fact that the FMB and the two federations of subcontractors represent far more firms in their respective categories than the BEC.

2. In West Germany there is a high degree of interorganizational coordination. There is virtually no competition for members between the German construction associations. In the UK, by comparison, the vast majority of firms have a choice between BEC on the one hand and the FMB or FASS and CASEC on the other. Coordination of policies is further facilitated in West Germany by the presence of only two major associations (HDB and ZDB), while in the UK this number is as high as six (BEC, FCEC, EGCI, FMB, FASS, CASEC). Furthermore, the fact that association boundaries tend to cross-cut economic divisions in West Germany leads to similar interest definitions and policies on the part of the major associations. While it is true that HDB firms tend to be large main contractors in civil engineering, the association also represents medium-sized firms that work frequently under subcontract and primarily build houses. As a consequence, it has to take into account the interests of this second group as well. Similarly, while the ZDB organizes mainly small firms that are often subcontractors and specialize in single-family houses, it also has among its members road-building firms with 500 employees which are almost always main contractors. Each of the two large associations has to reconcile internal conflicts of interest that arise from such differences, and the resulting policy compromises are likely to be similar enough to permit close cooperation and concertation. This is different in the UK, where the divergent interests of the various groups of construction firms are reflected in inter-associational boundaries permitting their unmediated expression and thus heightening the

level of inter-associational conflict. The result is a clear division of the UK associational system into three distinct subsystems: an alliance of the two federations of subcontractors (FASS, CASEC), an alliance between the FCEC and the BEC (reflecting probably the strong position of the leading FCEC firms in the BEC), and the FMB.

The most obvious differences between the two systems in terms of inter-associational coordination exist in the area of collective bargaining. Apart from minor exceptions, there is only one collective agreement for the construction industry in West Germany, and this is jointly negotiated by the two main associations. In the UK, by comparison, BEC and FCEC have different industrial agreements even though they operate through the same collective bargaining machinery. Also, there is, in the form of the OCPCA, a special employers association for large building sites. Most importantly, the FMB negotiates its own agreement for the building subsector rivalling the BEC agreement. Finally, FASS and now CCS believe that the interests of subcontractors are not sufficiently taken into account by the BEC.

3. In West Germany there is a higher degree of decentralization by territory, and a lower degree of differentiation by specialties. There is no specialized civil engineering association in West Germany, nor is there a special association of 'master builders'; HDB and ZDB comprise firms from both categories. Moreover, none of the federations in the German system has affiliates that are differentiated by specialties, as is the case for BEC, FASS and CASEC; affiliates are defined almost exclusively on a regional basis, and the ZDB even has a three-layered regional affiliation structure. While UK associations do have regional and local groupings, these are not nearly as independent and autonomous as the respective German groupings (with the exception of the Scottish Building Employers' Federation). In the UK autonomy clearly lies with the product groupings. The important point here is that, for associations of firms with regionally segmented markets, conflicts of interest arising from different location are easier to manage than conflicts of interest related to different functions, and organizations that are structured around territorial divisions can therefore be expected to be more cohesive than organizations whose structure follows functional divisions.

4. Excluding double memberships, the number of firms that are organized in the West German construction industry associations exceeds the respective number in the UK by one-third (an estimated 60,000 as compared with about 45,000). Given that the total number of firms is higher in the UK, this makes for a clearly higher density of membership in the German system.

The organization of large firm interests: economic, organizational and political–institutional determinants

In neither associational system under study are large and small firms completely separately organized, nor are they always and for all purposes organized together. Each system strikes a peculiar balance between comprehensive and specialized organization which is the result of an interaction of its specific forces of cohesion and fragmentation. The difference between the two systems is not one in kind but one of degree: while in West Germany the balance is closer to a comprehensive pattern of organization, in the UK it is more inclined towards fragmentation.

The following discussion will look successively at three categories of factors that may account for the different degrees of comprehensiveness and specialization of the two systems: characteristics of the economic structure of the two industries; the inherent logic of interest associations as organizations; and the properties of the political–institutional environments of the system. At each step, the aim is to identify on a comparative basis both the forces of system cohesion that work against separate organization of large and small firms, and the forces of system fragmentation that inhibit a merger of existing associations into one comprehensive interest organization.

Economic factors

In Germany, both an internalization of cleavages in comprehensive associations and a coordination between them seem to be facilitated by the existence of a strong 'middle class' of medium-sized firms. In the UK, where the size distribution of firms is more discontinuous, different size is more likely than in Germany to give rise to divergent definitions of collective identities. While a continuous size distribution is associated with more intense competition, it lends less support to categoric distinctions between 'large' and 'small'. A discontinuous distribution, on the other hand, provides a basis for the formation of distinctive groups that, while competition between them is limited, view themselves as being different in kind. Comparison between the two associational systems suggests that, for business just as for other social groups, solidarity depends less on the absence of competition than on the presence of a common sense of identity — the latter being compatible with, and even requiring, structural conditions that may engender strong competition.

Another important economic factor is the organizational structure of large firms. A characteristic feature of large UK construction firms is that they are organized internally into separate product divisions. For example, apart from its building materials divisions, Tarmac has construction (civil engineering), international, and housing divisions (as well as industrial and properties divisions looking after its interests outside the industry). Product divisions participate in the appropriate trade associations; for example, the housing division in the House Builders Federation within the BEC, the civil engineering division in the FCEC and the international division in the EGCI. The relative independence of product divisions helps explain why large firms in the UK are organized in a number of associations specialized by product or market segment and why they do not press for a merger of these organizations. In West Germany, by contrast, large companies are more organizationally centralized in terms of product lines, and thus differentiation of associational structures by products would make it necessary for their leading staff to be involved in a number of associations at the same time. Internal differentiation in large German construction firms is mainly along territorial lines, and the territorial decentralization of the otherwise comprehensively organized HDB corresponds to this.[1]

The fact that the conglomerate structure of large UK firms often extends beyond the construction industry also contributes to associational fragmentation. Firms that operate in different industries are used to belonging to different trade associations, and their interest in any one of their industries is limited. On the other hand, firms that, like the large German construction firms, are confined to one particular industry are more dependent on that industry's economic fate and are bound to identify more closely with it. The higher degree of identification of German large construction firms with the industry seems to generate a stronger interest in this sector being effectively represented; to the extent that this requires close coordination with smaller firms, comprehensive organization is preferred over specialized, particularistic organization.

Third, different rules of competition also have an influence on associational systems. A crucial factor seems to be the extent to which associations, either formally or informally, are themselves involved in the regulation of competition; where they do not have to, since this function is performed by other agencies, firms can afford to tolerate a more fragmented, 'pluralist' pattern of associability.[2] Thus, in the UK the existence of the builders' conferences and the practice of selective tendering relieve associations of the need to contribute to a more orderly pattern of competition. Moreover, with the exception of the EGCI, there is no explicit or implicit devolution of competition-regulating functions to associations. This is different in Germany, where the ZDB plays an important part in adjudicating conflicts between different specialties over Handwerk privileges. In addition, among the most important reasons for the involvement of large firms in the HDB was that, up to 1973, most of its regional associations operated the above-mentioned 'market observation' schemes. It is significant that, after this practice had been outlawed by the Federal Cartel Office, the HDB went through the most difficult crisis in its history, with its large member firms accusing it of ineffectiveness and even temporarily withdrawing from it.

There are other ways as well in which German competition rules contribute to cohesion of the associational system. As has been said, the Handwerk system offers a legal framework to deal with conflicts of interest between different specialties, and it defuses the potentially explosive conflict between contractors and subcontractors. UK competition rules, by comparison, reinforce distinctions between size categories — through the system of selective tendering — and afford only limited assistance and protection to small firms, thus in effect stabilizing the positions of large firms and making them less dependent on joint action with the rest of the industry.

Organizational factors

Comprehensive organization of large and small firms can come about only if small firms find it advantageous to align their interests with those of large firms. One reason why they should do so is that, for them, joint organization is less expensive. Where small and large firms are jointly organized, subscriptions are normally based on turnover or total wages paid. Thus, the inclusion of large firms brings about a considerable increase in the available resources for collective action and reduces the demands the association has to make on its small members. Moreover, large firms, having specialist staff of their own, tend to use the services offered by associations to a lesser extent than the small members although they contribute more to their costs. Joint organization of large and small firms thus implies a redistribution of resources from the former to the latter, and this may be an incentive for small firms not to set up independent associations.

Intra-organizational redistribution contributes to system cohesion in both the UK and West Germany. For example, the BEC offers a wide range of generous selective incentives to attract small builders, and this seems to be a major reason why it is able to compete with the respective specialist associations, in particular the FMB. In West Germany, internal redistribution takes place in particular in the HDB, whose smaller members would find it difficult if not impossible to keep up the present level of services if the large firms were to resign. Association services are particularly important for small firms in Germany as a result of the high formalization of labour law and the ensuing frequent litigation in the Labour Courts. Advice and legal representation provided by associations in this area have been found to be a major reason for smaller firms to join (Streeck and Rampelt, 1982). The need to provide selective incentives comparable to those that can be offered by a comprehensive organization makes it extremely difficult for specialist associations of small firms to emerge. This is demonstrated by the history of the Mittelstand break-away from the HDB, the BVMB, whose members have to remain simultaneously in the HDB to have access to its vastly superior services. It is mainly this factor which has prevented the BVMB becoming a serious competitor to the HDB.

Buying the allegiance of small firms by internally subsidized selective incentives is a device frequently used in building comprehensive business associations. Small firms are often prepared to compromise on the 'public goods' produced by their association if they get attractive selective goods in exchange. Nevertheless, the UK case shows that, where there is a deep structural cleavage between large and small business, the resulting fears of small firms being 'submerged' in a joint organization cannot easily be overcome even by a highly elaborate system of selective benefits. It is significant that, in spite of the BEC's considerable investment in selective incentives, both the FMB on the one hand and FASS and CASEC on the other organize more firms in their respective categories than BEC.

Political–institutional factors
The way collective interests are organized depends in part on the constraints and opportunities offered for collective action by the institutional environment. Different institutional environments create different 'logics of influence' for collective actors to which these must adapt if they want to be successful (Schmitter and Streeck, 1981). For business associations, the two most important such environments are the system of collective bargaining and industrial relations, and the machinery of government. The impact of the state on business associability can be unintended, or the result of deliberate regulatory intervention. Finally, the political environment at large may impose on collective actors strategic imperatives that influence their definition of common interest, their choice of common enemies and the rules of political prudence that they have to follow. In the following, each of the four dimensions — industrial relations, state structure, state intervention and strategic imperatives — will be discussed in turn.

Collective bargaining and trade unions. In no area is there a greater difference in the environment of the two associational systems than in this, and in fact the impact of the different structures of industrial relations goes a long way in explaining the variation between the systems. In West Germany, there is only one trade union in the industry, which organizes both blue-collar and white-collar workers. Also, the legal framework encourages and facilitates industry-wide collective bargaining, restricting supplementary bargaining at the individual firm level and giving associations the power to make industrial agreements legally binding even on firms that are not their members. While the high degree of trade union unity makes it imperative for the two large associations to coordinate their collective bargaining, the legal framework enables them to make members and non-members comply with agreements and to prevent them from negotiating on their own.

In part, the successful coordination between the large German associations in collective bargaining may be due to the structural similarities between the leading firms in the ZDB and the majority of the members of the HDB. But this does not explain why the special interests especially of the very large firms do not find expression in separate bargaining arrangements. In fact, large construction firms in Germany do have their own 'social policy' resembling the respective policies of large firms in other branches of industry. As a result, they are much less interested than the small firms in the various social funds set up by the 'social partners' for the industry as a whole, and they have lately been pressing for these funds to be reduced or dissolved. Smaller construction firms, in turn, tend to complain that the HDB, under the influence of its larger members, is too easily prepared to make concessions on wages. However, neither the large nor the small firms would find a union to negotiate with if they broke away from existing arrangements. Moreover, the system of works council co-determination provides large firms with sufficient flexibility to regulate their specific labour problems by works agreements ('Betriebsvereinbarungen') outside collective bargaining proper, and this makes industry-wide bargaining more acceptable to them (Streeck, 1981).

In the UK, on the other hand, an essentially 'voluntary' system of industrial relations and a highly fragmented trade union structure reinforce divisions within the associational system of business and engender considerable inter-associational competition. Both countries have industry-wide negotiating agreements, but whereas the construction union in Germany (IGBSE) accounts for at least 98 percent of unionized workers, the UK has five principal unions in the construction sector, two of which (UCATT and TGWU) are in competition with one another. The TGWU has concluded a separate negotiating agreement with the FMB (although it is also involved in the main industry agreement with the FCEC and BEC) and the FMB's reluctance to surrender this agreement is a major obstacle to any attempt to merge the BEC and FMB. Thus, in the UK tensions between the trade unions have intensified rivalries between two of the main industry associations. In addition, the voluntary character of the collective bargaining system facilitates the creation of different bargaining arrangements for different categories of firms and projects, and this explains the presence of several specialized agreements even for the homogeneous group of large firms (through the BEC, the FCEC and the OCPCA).

The structure of the state. There is a close correspondence between the lines of differentiation in the two associational systems and the organization of the state with which they interact. West Germany is a federal state with considerable decentralization of authority along territorial lines; at the same time, authority over economic policy at the national level is concentrated in one key ministry, the Ministry of Economics. As a result, business associations have strong regional subunits at the Länder level while there is very little differentiation and high inter-associational coordination at the national level. The UK, by comparison, is a unitary state; however, authority within the national government, at least with regard to the construction industry, is distributed over a number of departments. This is reflected in low vertical differentiation of associational structures in territorial terms, and in considerable horizontal differentiation at the national level in terms of different specialties and functions.

An important factor influencing associational structures in the UK is the existence of 'sponsoring departments' for each industry (Grant, 1982: 30–1). Sponsorship divisions act to some extent as spokesmen for their industries inside government, and they explain government policies to the industries. The sponsor for the construction industry is the Department of the Environment, which is a major government department; its minister is a senior member of the Cabinet. In West Germany, which does not have a sponsoring department system as such, the Federal Building Ministry is a relatively weak department, and economic and industrial policy concerning the construction industry is made primarily by the Ministry of Economics. The very weakness of the Building Ministry provides a powerful incentive for the German construction industry to make sure it has effective associations to press its case with the Economics Ministry — which is the main target agency for most of the other industries as well. The UK associations, by comparison, can to a certain extent rely on the Department of the Environment to aggregate the interests of the industry and represent them within government.

In both the UK and West Germany, there is a separate Ministry of Transport which has close links with the civil engineering side of the industry. In the UK this helps perpetuate the distinctive sense of identity of civil engineering interests reflected in the separate existence of the FCEC. (Another reinforcing factor is the existence of an Energy Department interested in specialized construction work for the energy sector.) When for a time the highways programme was the responsibility of an enlarged Department of the Environment, this was resented by the civil engineering firms, which preferred to have a separate department (Dudley, 1983) and in 1976 the old Ministry of Transport was re-created as a Department of Transport. The German Ministry of Transport, by comparison, does not induce specialized organization of civil engineering interests because of the devolution of much of the responsibility for road-building to the Länder and the local communities and, again, the centralization of responsibilities for economic and industrial policy in the Ministry of Economics.

An example of how division of authority and responsibility among different governmental departments leads to horizontal differentiation within associational systems is the EGCI. In the UK, responsibility for the export activities of the construction industry rests with the Department of Trade rather than with the Department of the Environment. One important reason why the EGCI exists as a separate organization is that it is a 'chosen instrument' of the Department of Trade to promote UK construction exports. Since in Germany .foreign trade is under the jurisdiction of the Ministry of Economics, there is no support in the structure of government for a special organization of construction export interests. It is interesting to note that, when German firms began to enter foreign markets in the early 1970s, they did form an informal group for 'exchange of information' and 'discussion of matters of common interests'. But rather than developing into a full-fledged organization, the group was incorporated in 1975 as a subcommittee in the formal organizational structure of the HDB. The case shows that, in Germany as well as in the UK, firms exporting construction services do have special interests in need of collective organization, but in order for these interests to become separately organized, some degree of external institutional support is essential.

An important channel of access for organized interests to government are formal or informal 'forums of functional representation' (Schmitter and Streeck, 1981). In West Germany in the 1970s, the Building Ministry set up a 'Discussion Group of the Construction Industry' including, in addition to the Minister, the two main industry associations and the union. Basically, this was part of an effort by the Ministry to improve its position at the expense of the Ministry of Economics. Since this was rightly seen as hopeless by the associations, they did not take their participation very seriously, and the 'Discussion Group' soon died away. UK construction associations, by comparison, participate actively in the 'Group of Eight', which was created to provide representation for the industry at prime ministerial level, a function it continues to perform. However, in 1979 the new Environment Secretary recognized the Group of Eight as the industry's main channel of access to him, as well as to the Prime Minister, at the same time abolishing formal consultative machinery which had involved the smaller builders and subcontractors. Unlike the 'Discussion Group', the Group of Eight provides access to an important target agency, and the fact that it includes, along with the trade unions and the design professions, representatives of only the FCEC and the BEC had important consequences for the associational system. Exclusion from this special representative device is deeply resented by the FMB and the subcontractor organizations, and government action in putting together the Group of Eight has clearly intensified rivalries between the various associations.

Finally, channels of access to government may or may not provide for direct contacts by individual large firms with government agencies, and this too has an effect on associations. In the UK, large firms can choose to contact government directly rather than working through industry associations. For example, Tarmac has proposed a scheme to build a privately funded road as a way of meeting the government's ideological reservations about public road-building. Direct contacts between their most important members and government undermine the position of associations as intermediaries, and by admitting such contacts government agencies impede the development of strong associations. German ministries tend to refuse to talk to individual firms and refer them instead to their associations; this enhances the latter's power and status (Streeck, 1983). The greater willingness of UK civil servants to deal with individual firms may be related to the generally higher degree of concentration of the UK economy and to the conglomerate structure of many of the largest firms; it also seems to reflect a more individualistic view of business interests than is commonly held by West German civil servants.

State intervention in associational structures. An important source of cohesion in associational systems is state intervention aimed at making interest representation more comprehensive. However, there are differences between societies in the extent to which the state may engage in such intervention. In the UK, the Department of the Environment is concerned about the lack of coherence in the system of construction industry representation. But the Department is constrained in what it can do about this by the general acceptance by UK civil servants of a paradigm of business interest associations as voluntary bodies whose organization is a matter for firms to decide among themselves. The Department would welcome a reconciliation of the differences between the BEC and the FMB to create a single voice for the industry, and it would support any move in that direction agreed upon by the associations concerned. Its own role, however, it sees as being limited to responding to initiatives taken by the associations themselves.

There is much less reluctance on the part of the German state with regard to 'political design'. The central structural parameter in the associational system of the German construction industry is the distinction between Handwerk and Industrie which is legally based. In addition, and as an organizational complement to the legal privileges of artisan firms, the Handwerksordnung establishes an elaborate system of public law associations to look after the interests of the Handwerk. (The HDB, as has been said, is a national peak association of local building guilds that are public law bodies.) Handwerk associations receive considerable legal and financial assistance from the state which, among other things, makes membership in them almost inevitable for artisan firms even where it is not, as it is in the Chambers, compulsory. This explains why the ZDB can have a density ratio of about 80 percent in an industry as fragmented and unwieldy as construction. (The HDB, which does not have state organizational assistance, organizes only about 40 percent of its potential members.)

In the UK, the proliferation of specialist associations and product groupings can be seen in part as a response to the absence of Handwerk status. Many of these associations try to establish craftsmen status for their members and are sometimes able to persuade local authorities that they should only deal with the 'craftsmen' in their membership. Thus, for example, the Institute of Roofing set up by the National Federation of Roofing Contractors has as one of its objectives 'to confer a recognized status on individuals in the industry'. Unlike the situation in West Germany, these activities are undertaken by associations on their private, 'voluntary' initiative without public support and regulation, and this both limits their effectiveness and increases rather than reduces inter-associational competition and fragmentation.

Legal Handwerk privileges and the existence of strong, established Handwerk interest associations seem to give small and middle-sized construction entrepreneurs in West Germany a somewhat greater sense of security than is characteristic of their counterparts in the UK. (This is also a reflection of, and is justified by, the size structure of firms in the industry.) The relatively well established position of small business in the German construction industry seems to reduce the fear of small builders that their interests may be submerged in collective action coordinated with the large firms. There is certainly more 'Angst' in this respect in the UK, where many small builders hold an ideological outlook which is opposed simultaneously to state and trade union collectivism and to big business, in short to the modern corporate economy (Scase and Goffee, 1980; 1982). (It is not surprising that the FMB was one of the industry associations to affiliate to a Private Enterprise Consultative Council set up by the Conservative Party under Mrs Thatcher's leadership.) The reflection of this attitude in the structure of the associational system is the division, accompanied by intense competition, between the BEC and the FCEC on the one hand and the FMB and the subcontractors' associations on the other.

Strategic imperatives: common interests, common enemies, rules of political prudence. Large and small construction firms have common as well as divergent interests, and they also have common enemies. In both countries, this contributes to making associational systems more cohesive. For example, firms of all sizes derive some benefit from public expenditure on construction, with small firms undertaking finishing work or repair and maintenance. Large and small firms are both interested not only in securing a higher workload for the industry but also in getting government to smooth out fluctuations in workload. Common interests encourage common organization, or at least the coordination of political action, and this effect is strong enough in both systems to prevent large as well as small firms organizing completely separately.

For business as well as for other groups, common enemies are also important in forging political coalitions. In the UK, both large and small firms in the construction sector have been threatened by nationalization under successive Labour governments. Another common enemy is the institution of 'direct labour', which all private firms in the industry would like to see abolished. No such political challenges exist in West Germany; here, their place is taken by persistent tensions between the construction industry and other economic sectors. Construction, as a low-technology, labour-intensive sector, does not enjoy the prestige accorded to other industries, which many construction contractors think is due to them. This seems to make itself felt particularly within the national peak associations of industry like the BDI and the BDA, where the influence of the construction industry is low. Moreover, the other industries are often clients of construction firms, and this seems to be in part responsible for their refusal to support the construction industry's demands for exemption from the Fair Trading Act. Finally, both large construction associations have often been criticized by associations of other industries for their close relationship and their pioneering agreements with the industry's trade union, and this has undoubtedly strengthened the two associations' mutual alliance.

Rules of political prudence result from a realistic assessment of one's own political power and opportunities. For large construction firms in West Germany, they dictate close political cooperation with middle-sized and small firms. The poor public image of the construction industry and the overriding concern of the German government and the German public with 'Mittelstand' make it politically advisable and profitable for large construction firms to present their interests as those of an industry dominated by small business. Moreover, unlike chemicals or motor cars, construction as such is not considered a 'key industry' by the government, and to the extent that it is at all given political attention, this is almost exclusively on account of its Mittelstand character. A separate association of the 'Twelve Apostles' would be politically extremely weak in this environment, not least because it would stand little chance of winning reliable allies in other quarters of industry.

Large firms in the UK face a different situation, which offers more opportunities for independent political action. Mittelstand is not an issue for government in the same way as it is in Germany, and there is more direct access of individual firms to government agencies. Together with the high perceived need of smaller firms for independent representation of their special interests, this accounts for the higher fragmentation of the UK associational system. In Germany, by comparison, while the political weakness of large firms constrains them to take cover behind their smaller competitors, the latter are legally and organizationally so well established that they can afford to cooperate closely with the large firms. The result is a relatively high degree of cohesion in the associational system.

The general conclusion that may be drawn from this chapter is that, in order to understand the organization of business interests on a comparative basis, it is important to look at economic conditions in the sector being studied, but it is even more important to take account of 'logic of influence' variables such as the pattern of union organization, the state structure and the ways in which state action shapes the market. The way in which the state structures the market has a particularly important influence on the ability of large and small firms to attain their goals without coming into serious and recurrent conflict with one another, and hence on the extent to which large and small firms are organized into separate and competitive associations.

Notes

This paper arises from our participation in a nine-country project on business interest associations, coordinated from the International Institute of Management in West Berlin by Philippe Schmitter and Wolfgang Streeck. The objectives of, and methodology used, in the project are extensively described in the research design (Schmitter and Streeck, 1981). One of the four industrial sectors studied in the project was construction; the others were chemicals, food processing and machine tools. The present paper, which was presented at the 1983 Annual Meeting of the American Political Science Association in Chicago, Illinois, benefited from the assistance of Irmgard Müller, who helped with the compilation of the statistical data. The German research was funded by the Stiftung Volkswagen.

1. It is important to note, however, that the independence of large firms' local subsidiaries is limited and also differs between firms. This injects an element of tension in the HDB in that the head offices of large firms tend to find it awkward that they should not have more direct access to the HDB's federal bodies.

2. This idea has been suggested to us by Frans van Waarden on the basis of comparison with the Dutch case.

9

Corporatist and pluralist patterns of policy-making for chemicals control: a comparison between West Germany and the USA

Volker Schneider

The background

The issue of the control of chemicals results from a major deficiency in environmental laws and regulations. Whereas chemicals in their role as food additives, drugs, cosmetics, pharmaceuticals and pesticides were regulated relatively early in the 'environmental decade', decisions with regard to chemicals used in industrial processes (as solvents, adhesives and paints, insulation and carpets, etc.) still rested with the chemicals industry itself. Subsequently, since the mid-1970s there has been an increasing effort to introduce more comprehensive and preventive measures in the control of potentially hazardous chemicals. Influenced by some alarming reports on the deleterious effects of chemicals on human health and environment (cancer, birth defects, bio-accumulation in the environment), some countries produced legislation which prescribe the testing and examination of new chemicals before allowing their use. Since Switzerland in 1969 and Japan in 1973 enacted the first laws requiring pre-marketing notification of new chemicals, more than a dozen other countries have followed. The USA enacted the Toxic Substances Control Act (TSCA) in 1976, and in West Germany, the Chemical Act (Chemikaliengesetz) was passed by parliament in 1980 and entered into force in 1982. In both countries, these laws in effect converted the chemical sector as a whole into a regulated industry.

It is interesting that, although the two regulatory policies deal with exactly the same policy problem, they differ significantly in the way they handle it. Whereas the US policy is to give the regulatory agency a broad discretionary power to require testing of almost every chemical substance, the West German approach is to restrict the scope of the law to certain categories of chemicals, and to define within the law precisely and in detail the testing obligations of the industry. This suggests that these different regulatory approaches cannot be dictated by the nature of the policy problem itself, created *ex nihilo* to tackle this problem, as some functionalists believe. Rather, they grow out of specific structural configurations of political actor-sets, conditioned by pre-existing political arrangements and institutions. Such a concept of policy-making derives from propositions developed within the debate on neo-corporatism, although it also draws on 'structuralist' positions which emphasize relationships between different state apparatuses as well as legal and constitutional orders. It is interesting to study the differences between the two policies within this analytical framework. From this perspective, the diverging policy outcomes could be conceived as effects of different structural patterns of political arenas in these countries: the main political actors seem to be tied in with the policy-generating network in a very different way. Therefore explanations could be found in:

1. the specific systems of interest intermediation, in particular on the level of government–business relations;
2. the different systems of government, in particular the relationships between the legislative and executive branches of government;
3. the administrative systems, that is the different legal and institutional frameworks determining the manner of enforcement (implementation).

In rather simplified terms, the specificity of a policy outcome is explained within such an approach by the specific structures of the political arenas in which a policy is 'generated'. Political arenas differ in the number of involved actors and in the particular allocation of power among them. Pluralist arenas are characterized by a multiplicity of competing, independent and voluntarily organized actors. Political power is relatively dispersed and groups are overlapping. In such a competitive and turbulent environment, the actors have to exploit favourable positions. Following the logic of pluralist situations, offence, or at least 'active resistance', is the best defence. The political process is, therefore, dynamic and constantly changing. As Latham put it, 'Groups combine, break, federate and form coalitions and constellations of power in a flux of restless alternation' (1964: 55). The state merely registers the overall group pressures, and executes the inter-group compromise: 'what may be called public policy is actually the equilibrium reached in the group struggle at any given moment, and it represents a balance, which the contending factions or groups constantly strive to weight in their favour' (Latham, 1964: 49).

Corporatist political arenas, ideal-typically, show a diametrically opposite picture. According to P.C. Schmitter's (1974) definition, the number of actors is limited and their interrelationship is non-competitive and hierarchically ordered. The state is neither one power beneath another nor a mere passive responder to group pressure, but the 'force organisatrice' of the political game itself. In recognizing, licensing and subsidizing specific organized interests, and in determining who should have access, when and how in the process of public policy-making, the state can exploit a very subtle arsenal of resources to channel interest group activity for its purposes. In such a corporatist setting, where powerful organizations represent and control entire sectors, the government can reduce implementation problems in public policy by giving these organizations routinized access to governmental policy-making in exchange for securing policy-conformist behaviour in their domains (cf. Mayntz 1983; Streeck 1983; Streeck and Schmitter 1984). For interest groups, this may be a rational strategy for promoting and realizing their long-term interests to reduce or at least to co-determine state regulatory activity in their respective domains. Public policy in these arrangements therefore tends to be more a bargained outcome between the state and a stable set of a limited and select number of organized interests, than the result of pluralist group pressure impinging upon the state. The comparison of the German and US pattern in chemical control policy-making provides a clear example of the importance of these differences.

The German Chemicals Law and the American Toxic Substance Control Act: convergences and differences in regulatory policy
The rationale of both the German Chemicals Act (ChemG) and the Toxic Substance Control Act (TSCA) in the USA was that a merely reactive stance would give insufficient control over toxic chemicals. In contrast to the cases of DDT and PCB, which were used for several decades without toxicological testing, marketing of chemicals would be allowed only after testing. Thus, both laws provide procedures for reviewing chemicals before they appear on the market and give an agency or the government the ultimate power to apply regulatory measures ranging from simple labelling requirements to the veto of production or marketing. But, as already mentioned, the two acts prescribe quite different ways of carrying out this task (see table 1).

The most apparent difference between the USA and Germany lies in the information-gathering requirements and notification imposed on industry. TSCA requires manufacturers to notify the Environmental Protection Agency (EPA) as much as 90 days before a chemical is produced (pre-manufacture notification). If the EPA does not take regulatory action within this period, manufacturing of the new substance may begin. With respect to a 'veto power' (Rehbinder, 1981), the agency has a very broad mandate. If it believes that the information supplied is inadequate, the EPA can require the manufacturer to provide additional data from tests on the substance. The absence of established testing limitations turns the TSCA into a 'quasi-licensing' approach: for instance, when a company has sent pre-manufacturing notice to the EPA and the latter considers the toxicological data as rudimentary, it can tell the manufacturers that production will not be permitted until the company provides data proving that the chemical does not harm people and the environment. If the tests reveal that the chemical substance 'may present an unreasonable risk to health or the environment', the Agency must act. The regulatory options and procedures available range from labelling requirements and further testing to the restriction of a particular use or the banning of products. In addition, EPA is empowered to place this burden of developing testing data on *any chemical substance (new or existing)* that 'may', in the view of the Agency, present 'an unreasonable risk to health or environment'.

The West German law, in this respect, is less extensive and less burdensome for both industry and government. Whereas the US approach requires notification before manufacturing, the chemical industry in Germany has to notify the relevant agency (Bundesanstalt für Arbeitsschutz und Unfallforschung) of a new substance only 45 days before marketing (pre-marketing notification). Moreover, not all new chemicals are subject to such procedure. The Chemicals Act does not include substances which are produced in quantities of less than 1 ton per year and does not cover polymers (plastics). Long-term effects have to be tested only when a substance is produced in quantities exceeding 100 tons a year. In addition, the German Act pays almost no attention to chemicals which are already on the market. At best, it authorizes the German federal government to identify particular existing substances for which there are indications of a hazard, and to demand their examination with a minimum base set of tests. Thus, the actual number of regulated chemicals is much smaller and the 'depth of the regulations' much shallower in German law. But on the other hand, in defining when and how a chemical has to be tested, the ChemG is very specific. Where as TSCA contains few direct and concrete regulations, and therefore grants the EPA a high discretionary power to set rules for enforcement, the German legislators have written detailed testing requirements into the Act. By being as precise as possible, the German Act provides industry with a high degree of security in its decision-making environment. Obligations and rights for both industry and administration are narrowly defined.

For instance, according to thresholds defined by the volume of chemicals marketed, the German Act prescribes for each 'step' required tests and testing methods. In addition, with respect to confidential data, it ensures for the industry a high level of discretion and protection. The contrast to TSCA is striking: most of the provisions of the TSCA are triggered only by the EPA's promulgation of rules. Hence, the final burden on industry is determined largely by administrative rule-making, which, however, is potentially great, so that EPA has considerable scope in making its judgements. Industry leaders complain about the 'absolute power' and the 'dictatorial competences' of this agency (Blair, 1976). As chemical company officials explained in 1976, 'The EPA would have extensive power to restrict production and marketing of existing materials — far more extensive than any US governmental agency has today' (Blair and Hoerger, 1976: 86). The surrounding uncertainty and unpredictability, particularly the impact on innovation and competitiveness associated with the Act, remains the greatest source of fear for the industry. A further important difference between TSCA and ChemG is that US law, combined with the provisions of the Freedom of Information Act (FOIA), provides that technological information gathered by the agency is accessible to the general public. The chemical industry fears that the protection of industrial and trade secrets will no longer be safeguarded.

Since the TSCA leaves the EPA considerable scope in deciding the manner in which the law will be applied, the US chemical industry finds itself in a highly insecure and unpredictable situation. This is further increased by the openness of the US implementation process. In US regulatory proceedings, even peripheral groups have the opportunity to voice their interests, and TSCA itself provides organized groups and individuals with several 'avenues' for direct participation in the making of rules. First, the general public is informed through public notices about any proposed rule-making (time, place and content), which offers any interested persons an opportunity to comment. Second, by means of the Freedom of Information Act, the public can gain access to the data collected by the EPA. Finally, through citizen action, groups or individuals can present petitions and sue for the application of the law. This way is not only open to interested persons (as for instance in the US Clean Air Act), but, according to TSCA, 'any person is authorized to sue for enforcement of the Act or to seek review of agency actions.'

TABLE 1
Basic differences between TSCA and ChemG

	TSCA	ChemG
Basic concept	Pre-manufacturing notification; 'quasi-licensing approach'	Pre-marketing notification
Categorical scope	All chemicals, new and existing	Only new chemicals, with many exceptions
Temporal scope	Notification 90 or 180 days before production	Notification 45 days before marketing
Testing requirements	Undefined and principally 'open-ended'	Narrowly defined; dependent on volume of chemicals marketed
Confidentiality	Calls for public disclosure; only limited protection	Offers broad protection

TSCA goes even so far as to provide that the EPA would have to award 'reasonable attorney fees and costs'.

This extremely open implementation process is therefore totally exposed to potential short-term shifts in the existing constellation of political power. For instance, changes at the 'commanding heights' of the state apparatus (for example, election outcomes), politically motivated turnovers in the personnel of the adminstrative agencies or shifts in public opinion caused by accidental event such as disasters can result in dramatic swings in goals and priorities of regulatory action. Of course, this could be advantageous for industry, but it can also damage it. For example, since the Reagan administration came to power, TSCA has been implemented in its weakest possible version (c.f. Gusman, 1982). But equally, a change in the other direction might have serious consequences for the industry and could generate a considerable climate of uncertainty. In this respect, the West German case offers a significant contrast. In combination with the common practice of institutionalized participation by concerned organized interests through the creation of multi-partite expert committees, the Chemicals Act is enforced by a closed circle of professionals. Since participation is usually channelled through recognized associations, which have a long tradition in cooperation with government in policy-making, as a rule no dramatic changes can affect existing alignments and the process is thereby effectively insulated from electoral pressures. In addition, in West Germany the continuity and the 'state-of-law principle' of

German administration breeds predictability. This is further backed by stable coalitions in participatory institutions (boards, councils, committees and advisory bodies). Thus, regulations can be determined in detail through bargained compromises occurring during the formulation phase of the law.

The overlapping of the formulation and the implementation phase in the West German policy process is the basic feature which distinguishes it from the US policy process. In the German chemical control policy, political and technical issues concerning the application of the law have been resolved as far as possible early in the phase of policy design, through consultation and bargaining between the regulators and the regulated. Public officials and representatives of the industry cooperated from the initial stage of the policy process. This provided government with indispensable information and political support for effective implementation. Industry, in exchange, got the chance to co-determine the way in which it will be regulated.

How the necessity of a cooperative relationship in policy-making between industry and government was felt within the German government is shown from the statements of two former officials from the German Federal Ministry of Interior:

> Chemicals control policy, because of its particular problem situation depends to a large degree on the cooperation between government, industry, trade unions and science. Thus, the environmental assessment of chemicals ... requires a good deal of scientific, technological and economic information, which the administration does not have, and can only get from those concerned. Since the provision of appropriate reliable information from industry and science can be secured only to a limited extent through compulsion, cooperative relations between government, industry and science are necessary conditions for the guarantee of a sufficient supply of information. (Hartkopf/Bohne, 1983: 304; my translation)

In the US case, formulation and implementation are almost totally separated. A victory in the legislative process does not prevent defeat in the implementation stage. Industry, therefore, has to struggle time and time again against potential regulations, which could be imposed or enforced at any time. Unlike the situation in West Germany, where the main battle is generally over after the formulation phase, in the US context any organized interest must be willing to devote considerable time and energy at all stages of the policy process if it expects to realize its interest. 'Until we get the regulations from the EPA, we really won't know what we have', commented the president of the Manufacturers Chemists Association in the final phase of TSCA's legislative process. 'Implementing the regulations can now be just as critical as passing the Act' (*New York Times*, 7 September 1976: 49ff).

There is another important dimension: the US approach to the control of chemical substances places a much heavier burden on the regulatory agency than does the West German approach. The far-ranging competences and obligations associated with participatory openness of the implementation process make the administration more vulnerable, and the regulatory rule-making more cumbersome and resource-intensive. As Gusman et al. (1980: 19) explains, 'The requirement that each regulatory control action regarding a specific chemical or category of chemicals take the form of an administrative rule, places a heavy burden on the US Environmental Protection Agency to choose its action carefully.' The procedure of rule-making under TSCA follows the informal notice-and-comment rule-making process of the US Administrative Procedure Act (APA). This means that the agency has to publish a general notice of the proposed rule-making in the Federal Register, setting forth a statement concerned with the time, place and nature of public rule-making proceedings, in order to give interested persons opportunity to participate in this procedure through submission of written data, views or arguments (Riegert, 1967: 72f).

In addition to APA, TSCA provides for oral hearings (Gaynor, 1977: 1176). It is therefore understandable that TSCA's implementation has been very slow. EPA has missed almost every important deadline that was established by the Act in 1976. As early as one year after TSCA enactment, Kevin Gaynor (1977) called TSCA a 'regulatory morass' and predicted many of the difficulties in the application of the law which have subsequently occurred. Environmentalists, chemical industry executives and even officials of the EPA agree that confusion and ineffectiveness have hampered application. The West German Chemicals Act, by contrast, has been implemented rather quickly. The five most important regulations concerning implementation had been promulgated before the Act came into force in January 1982. As far as it can be assessed at present, the way in which the Chemicals Act works appears to be very simple: the producer submits the data, which are prescribed in detail by the law, to the competent authority 45 days before marketing a given chemical. Since this agency does not undertake its own testing, and since assessment of a chemical is based on data provided by industry, this approach places a great deal of emphasis on the 'collective self-responsibility' of the chemical industry. However, there is still some suspicion, especially from environmentalists, that these data lack credibility. Nevertheless, for the government this seems to be an 'economic' and very pragmatic solution which does not require the same administrative resources as the US approach. Of course, this does not mean that the system performs 'better' in controlling chemicals. Brickman *et al.* (1982: 34f) suggest that, despite the fact that the Americans spend more resources than the Germans, there is no significant difference between the regulatory outcome between these two countries. But such a judgement is not very convincing. The actual number of chemicals covered by TSCA and the potential extent and depth of regulations, combined with the participatory openness, might suggest a tighter control, but how this potential is realized depends, in the pluralist US system, totally upon the actual constellation of power. Thus, an ultimate judgement about comparative performance will be possible only on the basis of a longer-term comparison.

From the point of view of effective policy implementation, the US approach to chemical control is much less attractive for government and industry than the German one. But how does this difference arise? Why did the US legislators disregard these aspects? The basic premise of this paper is that the different structures of politics of the two countries provide the answer. Put more succinctly, different government–interest group relationships on the one hand, and different relationships between governmental branches on the other, produce different 'rules of the game' in politics, and hence different patterns of public policy-making.

Pluralist and corporatist patterns of policy-making: different 'mechanics' of public policy

The German Chemicals Act is a textbook example of a 'co-operative' solution to a policy problem. Both industry and government have been involved in bargaining in order to find the 'best' solution which has lightened the regulative burden placed upon industry and saved scarce resources for the administration. This has been possible because of pre-existing cooperative arrangements between government and industry, backed by a political infrastructure, which enable institutionalized consultation and bargaining. In other words, West Germany maintains a network of 'integrated participation in public policy-making' (Olsen, 1981), which offers major organized interests access to decision-making in exchange for responsible and cooperative behaviour during the enforcement stage of the Act. It is interesting that such an arrangement is even formulated as the 'cooperation principle' in the German environmental programme of 1971: 'The cooperation principle is a recognition that effective environmental policy relies on the co-responsibility and involvement of those concerned — be they industry, science or the individual' (Bundesminister des Inneren (unt Umweltbundesamt) 1982: 11f.).

In West Germany, fundamental decisions about the structure and the scope of the Chemicals Act had been made at an early and relatively secret state prior to the bill being presented to parliament. During this period there was an intensive process of information exchange, review and consultation between the Chemicals Producers Association (Verband der Chemischen Industrie e.V., VCI) and different executive branches of the federal government. In the German political context this is not seen as illegal, as it would be in the USA (cf. Sunshine Act), but as a legitimate practice based on the 'cooperation principle'. The VCI, which has the de facto monopoly of representation within the chemical sector and speaks, in its own words, 'with one voice for the whole German chemical industry', was consulted from the very moment that the legislative initiative came from within the German Ministry of the Interior. This association had representatives and experts on all national and international commissions, committees and working groups which were relevant for this legislative project (in particular, at OECD and EEC level). The organization's annual report for 1980 states: 'With the beginning of the German legislative activities in autumn 1977, the work of the association focused on bargaining with five federal ministries and their dependent agencies. Until 1980, the VCI had commented in all on twelve bills, and had proposed its own formulations.' This did not happen without conflict, however, but only in 1979 was the issue drawn into the visible arena of public discussion. After this, the policy process acquired a more 'open' profile. The bargaining compromise between government and industry with its three key elements (the 'step sequence approach', the pre-marketing notification requirement and the restriction to new chemicals) was presented to a wide range of interest groups and independent experts in the following fields: industry, the environment, consumerism, trade unions and science. In the autumn, the bill was submitted to the Bundesrat, the House of Representatives of the constituent states of the Federal Republic, which reviewed the bill and proposed amendments only in minor details. In November 1979, the bill was introduced into the lower house of the German parliament, the Bundestag. Since all major issues and potential interest conflicts had been resolved and intermediated by preceding consultations, only one independent deputy voted against the proposal.

Meanwhile the issue had also been dealt with by a working group on environmental matters, the 'Arbeitsgemeinschaft für Umweltfragen', which conceives itself as the 'clearing instance' and 'early coordination system' for these issues. This body is another important element of the institutional expression of the West German 'cooperation principle' with regard to environmental policy. It had been set up by the government in the mid-1970s 'to ensure a constant exchange of information and views between the state and all those affected by its actions' (Bundesminister für Inneres, 1982: 12). In this working group both interest groups and parliamentarians are brought together with the government. This seems to be an important aspect which has the effect of guaranteeing coordination between the legislative and the administrative branches. Inasmuch as the bargained bill between state and industry becomes law, it is expected that parliamentary legislators will not 'interfere' in these matters. This can be guaranteed on the one hand by strong party discipline, and on the other by the involvement of the relevant parliamentary experts in the bargaining process.

Hearings in the relevant subcommittee of parliament did not change the key elements of the act, although there had been much criticism, especially from 'independent' scientists and environmentalists. Essentially, it was the version that was discussed and jointly drafted with the VCI that was enacted.

The policy formulation process of TSCA was strikingly different. Unlike West German law, the US chemicals act (TSCA) was actually elaborated within Congress, although the idea for a new approach toward chemicals control started with the Council for Environmental Quality (CEQ). In 1970 this council collected information on hazardous chemicals not controlled under the air and water pollution statutes. Meetings with federal agencies followed and a proposal was worked out, which was submitted to Congress. Already in this phase, there appeared some important interest conflicts between the pro-industry Office of Commerce and the 'professional environmentalists' of the CEQ and EPA. In the spring of 1971 the administration's bill arrived in the House of Representatives and the Senate. The Senate rewrote the bill completely and introduced some stronger provisions concerning the regulation of both new and existing chemicals. After intensive discussion and negotiation in committees, plus some review and modification, the bill was approved in senate by a vote of 77 to 0. Four months later, the House Commerce Committee reported out its own bill, which was approved by a vote of 240 to 61. Despite this overwhelming majority, the bill later died in conflicts between the two chambers. In October 1972 the Congress came to a close, with the TSCA still not enacted.

With the opening of the Ninety-third Congress, the process started over again. Several bills passed the House and Senate, but all died in conference. At this stage, the US chemicals industry attempted to block every bill on chemical control by playing-off the two legislative chambers against each other. Chemical industry officials explained their tactic as follows:

> Industry's tack had been to support the less-restrictive House measure in opposition to the Senate version, which placed such heavy emphasis on pre-marketing testing that many thought it would destroy industry. With the help of the generally more conservative House forces, this approach had worked for some years. But by the end of 1975, times had changed. (Schwartz and Marion, 1977: 52)

Changes in the members of congressional committees and increased publicity about toxic chemicals triggered by the Kepone disaster (where workers were poisoned in a chemical plant in Virginia) suggested to industry that a toxic substances act was inevitable. The major part of the US chemical industry changed its tactic and moved from principled objection and active resistance to a more coopera-tive posture.

The chemical industry's most influential business association, the Manufacturing Chemists Association (MCA), appointed a special committee which had the authority to bargain directly and immediately without having to go through the internal machinery of the MCA. Within the US context this seems to be a very unusual occurrence. This ability to make decisions 'on the spot' seems to have been the key to the committee's success in bargaining with congressmen and environmentalists for the 'tough but workable compromise bill' (*Business Week*, 25 October 1976) that was finally enacted in October 1976. Unlike the situation in West Germany, within the US chemical industry there was still opposition to this new stance. In the smaller companies, which would be hit harder by the new law, there was a marked preference to try to block the passage of any bill whatsoever. Among the big companies there was dissent: while Dupont, Union Carbide and Monsanto took a moderate stance, Dow Chemical fought against regulation at every opportunity and with all the resources it could muster. This company employed 'direct strategies' in the political arena, which would be out of the question in West Germany. A striking illustration gives a letter, signed by Dow's President Earle B. Barnes:

> Before long we will want to encourage the broadest and strongest possible grass roots political action campaign in opposition to Toxic Substances legislation. Hopefully, it will be based on mail to and calls on Senators and Representatives from employees, relatives, friends, distributors, vendors, customers, state organizations, etc. The objectives are to kill the bills or to register a minority vote sufficient to sustain a

> hoped-for veto or, as a last resort, to get the bills moderated significantly through floor amendments in the House. Now the time is near for a big push .... (quoted in Reynolds, 1977: 51)

In this respect, the strategic diversity of the chemical industry seems to reflect its politico-organizational structure. Constrasting sharply with the German case, where one association speaks for the whole sector, in the USA there are at least 60 competing US trade associations representing manufacturers of 'downstream' chemical products, such as paints, pesticides, soaps and so on. The four most important associations are the CMA, the CSMA, the SOCMA and the PMA. The oldest of them is MCA, the Manufacturing Chemists Association, which has existed since the late 1800s, has 190 members and represents only manufacturers of industrial chemicals. Unlike the situation in Germany, the smaller companies are organized in separate organizations, the Chemical Specialities Manufacturer's Organization (CSMA) and the Synthetic Organic Chemical Manufacturers Association (SOCMA). CSMA was set up in 1914 and has 412 members. SOCMA, the smallest of the 'Big Four', has 88 members, and these are mainly small companies. The Pharmaceutical Manufacturer's Association, which was formed in 1958 through a merger of two other trade assocations, has 129 members and the largest budget of the four. Many companies belong to more than one association. Union Carbide, for instance, belongs to as many as 100 trade associations (*Chemical and Engineering News*, 20 December 1976). Even if one does not take into account overlapping membership within these four organizations, it is striking that they amount to less than 70 percent of the firms organized in the German VCI. It is therefore not surprising that these associations are not considered by the US government to be very representative of the interests of the entire chemical industry. Thus, their intermediary role is very different from the function of the VCI in Germany. Says the head of SOCMA, Roland Lang:

> our philosophy is that members of Congress are not especially interested in what SOCMA has to say. They are concerned with what their constituents think of this or that, so that when an issue comes up and it's necessary to talk to members of Congress about it, we get the word out to member companies and encourage them to come down to Washington and talk with their Congressmen. We give them the background, we keep them informed of the timing and the issue. (*Chemical and Engineering News*, 20 December 1976)

Many companies act through 'governmental relations units' directly in the political arena, or support 'friendly' congressmen through the device of 'political action committees'. Almost 80 percent of chemical and drug companies have set up a governmental relations unit (*Chemical and Engineering News*, 2 July 1979: 18). Thus, the economic diversity of the US chemical industry, which is not significantly different in terms of size of firms from its German counterpart, is not sufficiently 'bundled' on the political level. By contrast, the chemical industry in West Germany operates politically in a strategically coherent manner and is therefore a predictable opponent or potential partner of government. Owing to the competitive context and the absence of an overall coordinating structure for concerted action, the US chemical industry behaves less consistently and predictably. In this setting, cooperation between government and industry would seem to be a very difficult matter — even if it were desired by all interests concerned. Even if the administration today were ready to relieve the industry from some heavy regulatory charges in exchange for cooperation and conformist behaviour in the implementation stage, there is no single organization which could be held responsible for industry's part of such a 'gentleman's agreement'. But the same is true for the administration. The relative openness, and the unlimited numbers of actors involved in the regulatory proceedings, make it impossible for industry to 'trust' the EPA. The consequence of this is a necessarily adversarial relationship between agency and business. What Gaynor said in 1977 seems to be a warning to industry: 'whatever course he follows, the Administrator will be forced by citizens' petition to adopt an aggressive regulatory posture' (Gaynor, 1977: 1178). In such a setting the strategy of 'pre-emptive aggression' is rational. A less aggressive stance would permit regulatory proponents to seize the initiative and make an unfavourable swing in policy more likely (Brickman et al., 1982: 274). The same authors therefore conclude: 'The knowledge that government can do unpredictable and significant damage and that loud protest and persistent challenge can make a difference leads to an industrial strategy of active resistance in regulatory affairs' (Brickman et al., 1982: 271).

In contrast to many studies of corporatist politics, this example suggests that the likelihood of corporatist arrangements occurring in public policy-making is not only based on the structures of intermediation between government and organized interests (as Schmitter suggested in 1974), but also depends upon a certain type of relationship between the legislative and the executive, and on a specific legal framework which sets the procedural rules for policy implementation. If government settles interest conflicts between state and industry by informal bargaining and consultation mechanisms, and if the prerogative for the ultimate decision in the legislative process still rests with the parliament, there must exist some kind of control or coordinating structure which guarantees that no parliamentary instance would interfere in the 'corporatist game' between industry and government. Strong party discipline and the control of parliament by strong party apparatuses on the one hand, and the system of parliamentary government on the other hand, seem to fulfil these prerequisites in West Germany. In addition, the fact that parliamentarians are also tied in to the consultation and bargaining network between government and the major interest groups leads to some coordination between the executive and the legislature.

A further condition of corporatist arrangements is that agreements made in the formulation phase of the law are not distorted within the arena of implementation. In this respect the German administration shows with its state-of-law principle, and its continuity at the level of agency personnel, a high degree of certainty and predictability. Although in the German case, too, the law enforcement process is ineluctably compounded with law-interpreting, the discretionary power of the German administrative agencies is incomparably smaller than the power of corresponding US regulatory agencies (Scharpf, 1970; Dolzer, 1982).

The presidential system of government in the USA, and its particular administrative system, distributes power and institutional domains quite differently. In Germany, the system of parliamentary party government ensures a close relationship between executive and legislature. In such a system the executive leadership is usually recruited from the majority party or party coalition in parliament, and it is that party leadership which controls both the executive and the legislative branch of government. It is therefore not surprising that, of all bills which have been introduced in the Bundestag, on average as many as 70 percent have been enacted. Contrasting sharply with that, Congress enacts only 10 percent of all bills introduced (Schindler, 1979: 268; Polsby, 1971: 90). Scholars generally agree that Congress plays a more important role in shaping legislation than the Bundestag has done. For Levine (1980: 4), the 'Congress is a major maker of American policy, sometimes substantially outweighing the president himself.' In the US policy process the decisive political 'engagements' take place in the parliamentarian arena, which is the focus of lobbying efforts for all US interest groups. In contrast, the decisive battles of the German law-making process take place in the institutional network between the executive branches and the major interest groups. Decisions established in these pre-parliamentarian bargaining systems are difficult to change in the subsequent sequences of the policy process. The fact that about 70 percent of the German industry's influence is addressed to the executive branch and only slightly more than 10 percent to parliament indicates where industry presumes the power centre to be in the German system of government (Weber, 1977: 248f).

Another important feature of the US system is the particularity of its administrative structure. Since the burgeoning literature about implementation and the 'crisis of regulation', the broad discretionary power and the high degree of independence of US regulatory agencies are well known. Legislative delegation and quasi-judicial functions make them far more powerful than their German counterparts. This is especially true for the EPA, which is the largest regulatory agency in the executive, is not part of a Cabinet department, and reports directly to the president. But this high degree of independence is, on the other hand, 'checked' by far-ranging control power of presidency and Congress. The influence of the president begins with his power to designate the chairman and to appoint members of administrative agencies. Congress is empowered to oversee, to supervise and to control agency action. Each standing committee of Congress is authorized to exercise continuing review of the performance of administrative agencies enforcing laws that fall within the jurisdiction of each committee. In addition, Congress can enact legislation nullifying or overriding administrative rules (Freedman, 1978: 62ff). This high degree of independence, combined with effective 'checks and balances', gives the relationship between the different branches and agencies of government a competitive character. Such a configuration of constitutional arrangements, combined with the absence of party discipline, magnifies and institutionalizes pluralism. As Prewitt and Verba describe it very succinctly;

> Any bill introduced must get over a series of hurdles. If a piece of legislation stumbles at any point along the way, it is very likely out of the running: you can clear the first tests, fail on the sixth, and then lose the entire effort. The result of such a system is that interest groups and political opponents have numerous points of access to the legislative process. They can tie up, rewrite, or defeat a bill at many points along the way, adapting their strategies and shifting their forces accordingly. As a result the kind of power required to manoeuvre a bill through Congress is the power to shape formulas acceptable to the majorities in subcommittee, full committee, on the floor, and in conference. (Prewitt and Verba, 1977: 297)

As a result, a piece of legislation is often an inconsistent amalgam of compromise items with total disregard for administrative problems of implementation, something which would hardly be thinkable in the West German context. In the USA, the quantity and the complexity of regulatory measures on the one hand, and the pluralist arena with a multiplicity of power centres on the other, leads to the strategy of conflict postponement through a high degree of legislative delegation. Especially with TSCA, the Congress enacted a skeleton, and restricted itself to the formulation of general principles and guidelines; it would say to the EPA: 'Here is the problem: deal with it.' In similar fashion, a European chemical official compared the TSCA with an EEC directive which as a measure of European policy harmonization is almost identical to the German Chemicals Act: 'The difference between TSCA and the ... [EEC Directive] ... is that TSCA calls for an adequate study without indicating what that is. But the European law is based on Roman law; it lays out what must be done: A, B, C' (*Chemical Week*, 1981).

The lack of coordination between the government and industry on the one hand, and between the legislature and the agencies charged with implementation on the other, reflects the absence of an institutional infrastructure for these purposes. Although for decades US government has usually consulted affected interests in regulatory policy-making (Schwartz, 1962: 55ff), and relies on a large number of advisory bodies, the structure of organized interests is too dispersed for associations to be used as 'private interest governments' (Streeck and Schmitter, 1984) in order to ensure the policy implementation at the firm level. In addition, the pluralist openness and its characteristic dynamic in the policy process makes it very difficult to engage in cooperative agreements which hold over time.

Conclusion

By way of conclusion, it should be kept in mind that the different structures of politics in these two countries generate quite different approaches to regulatory policy-making. In other words, these specific patterns of public policy depend on the institutional and organizational conditions within which they are embedded. Each structural configuration seems to create its own 'logic' and dynamic. A pluralist arena which responds to short-term political forces makes it very difficult to sustain cooperative agreements over time. As constellation of power change, political actors exploit advantageous opportunities.

Adversarial relationships in the USA and formal cooperation in West Germany are, therefore, rational strategies which follow logically from the different structures of the political arenas. The variety of institutional arrangements in West Germany, designed to facilitate cooperation among federal departments and legislators, as well as cooperation between government and interest groups, allows the consideration of implementation issues within the Act's formulation phase. The effective implementation of a regulatory policy is unmistakably dependent on the cooperation of those being regulated. This cannot be achieved merely by coercion. But on the other hand, cooperation between autonomous actors seems to be based on the expectation of mutual gain from this relationship. Although these benefits can be distributed unequally, there has to be some kind of positive inducement for the regulated to cooperate with the state in designing and implementing an effective regulative policy. This is at least an opportunity to co-determine the way it will be regulated.

TABLE 2
Policy-making patterns in TSCA and the Chemicals Act

	W. Germany	USA
Political arena		
Actors	Limited	Unlimited
Inter-organizational relations	Less competitive	Highly competitive
Group alignments	Stable	Unstable
Executive–legislative relations	Hierarchical	Competitive
Government–business relations	Cooperative	Adversarial
Independence of admin. agencies	Low	High
Policy process		
Foci of policy formulation	Pre-parliamentarian arena	Parliamentarian arena
Participatory openness	Low	High
Mode of implementation	By cooperation	By 'command and control'

10
Organized interests and industrial crisis management: restructuring the steel industry in West Germany, Italy and France

Martin Rhodes

Introduction

The modes of crisis management adopted in response to the recession of the European steel industries have displayed a considerable degree of diversity even if the principal objective — a slimmer, more competitive industry — has been a common one. The aim of this paper is to examine three quite distinct experiences of crisis management in steel in the 1970s and 1980s — West Germany, Italy and France — and to consider, in particular, the following question: if, as seems clear, the different approaches to crisis management adopted by these countries have been shaped by existing institutional structures and relations between capital, labour and the state, how have these structures and social relations withstood, in turn, the impact of persistent stagnation and economic decline? More precisely, how has the pressure of continued crisis conditions altered both the internal constitution of interest organizations and the balance of power between them? Has there been a convergence or a divergence in the nature of crisis management across these countries and in the consequences of the crisis for patterns of interest organization and articulation? In order to answer these questions, the nature of the steel crisis and the concept of crisis management itself require some brief introductory comments.

The crisis of the steel industry has been dramatic in its proportions and far-reaching in its consequences. It can be attributed to a number of convergent factors: the general recession of the Western economies since the 1974 energy crisis; the parallel decline or stagnation of many of its traditional customers (construction, cars, shipbuilding); the displacement of European producers from foreign markets by more competitive steel-makers (the Japanese) and by the rise of new steel-producing nations in South East Asia and South America; the loss of home market shares to these low cost competitors; and a secular decline in consumption owing to product substitution in the manufacture of previously high-steel-content commodities. The technical industrial response to this crisis has taken a variety of forms, involving various combinations of retrenchment, rationalization and diversification across the steel sector and accelerated product and process innovation at the level of individual companies and plants. Since the end of the 1970s, the attempt of the European steel producers to conform with international 'best practice' in terms of plant and process organization has been accompanied by efforts to align Western managerial practices and labour relations with those of their fiercest and most successful competitor, Japan. The adjustment of the European steel industry to new market conditions has therefore had both an industry-wide impact, requiring reorganization and mass reductions in employment, and important consequences within the firm itself, especially as far as plant-level politics are concerned. Thus, while there are a number of levels at which crisis management can occur (adjustment in steel is conditioned by the macroeconomic policies of national governments, as well as by the supranational crisis régime of the European Community) our attention in this paper is drawn to the two distinct but interrelated levels of the industry itself: the meso-level of the sector, where concentration, mergers and large-scale job loss require a political–social response from the state (in providing public funds and helping alleviate or avoid social conflict), and the micro-level of the company or plant, where closures and modernization have permitted modifications in managerial strategies and pose the greatest challenge to union influence and strength.

In actual examples of industrial restructuring, crisis management strategies will proceed simultaneously at both levels, since conflicts of interest will be generated across the sector as a whole as well as within particular firms. But the level at which these conflicts are primarily resolved will be of critical importance for the actors involved (capitalists and business associations, workers and unions) and will constitute an object of struggle as crucial as the issues at stake. It has been suggested that meso-corporatist crisis management (in other words, a collaborative strategy bargained and implemented by business, unions and the state) offers a number of advantages over alternative forms and may increasingly be adopted (Wassenberg, 1982). Others, such as Goldthorpe (1984), have predicted a divergence between inclusionary strategies of industrial adjustment (corporatism) and exclusionary strategies (dualism), depending on the balance of power in social relations and on the role and ideological complexion of particular governments. Neither of these interpretations is sufficiently nuanced, however, to account for the complex reality of development tendencies in Western capitalist societies. While Wassenberg minimizes the costs to capitalists of bargained, sectoral solutions, Goldthorpe neglects the importance of levels of conflict resolution and considers only fleetingly the possibility that inclusionary and exclusionary strategies may co-exist in economies with differentiated industrial structures and segmented labour markets.

In the following analysis of crisis management in the steel industry, close attention is given both to the forms of crisis management (in ideal-type terms, they may range between the hegemonic and the collaborative) and to the levels (meso- and micro-) at which they occur. As the three case studies reveal, collective bargaining and collaboration at the meso-level of the sector are giving way to micro-level solutions in which capitalists bear lower costs and are subject to fewer constraints. But at the same time, a devolution of conflict resolution to the level of the firm can have profound consequences for the organizational cohesion and strength of labour. Thus, although the complexity of crisis management will usually involve a combination of forms and levels, a divergence of interests can be detected between the preference of trade unions for solutions defined at the sectoral level and the concern of capitalists — dictated in part by the pressures of competition — to decentralize and differentiate in their response to the crisis. The extent to which the sector or the firm becomes the locus of crisis management will depend on a number of factors, including the respective organizational strength of capital and labour and the role played by the state in regulating social relations. The aim of this paper is to consider the determinants of the forms and levels of crisis management, their consequences for interest organization and articulation on the part of capitalists and trade unions, and the degree to which a convergence or divergence may be occurring in strategies of industrial adjustment.

West Germany
The West German approach to crisis management in steel has been distinctive for the high degree of collaboration and consensus achieved among the major actors of the sector. Regional 'crisis cartels' in the Saarland and the Ruhr (the two principal areas of German steel production) have been based on a functional association of management, organized labour (the engineering union, IG-Metall, and company works councils), regional authorities and the federal government in a joint effort to regulate rationalization and ease the employment impact of contraction. This meso-corporatist strategy, involving the IGM and works

councils in both shaping and implementing policy, has been facilitated by favourable objective circumstances — German market dominance in European steel has allowed a more gradual adjustment cycle then elsewhere — and by institutional structures and a prevailing ideology conducive to a collaborative mode of crisis management: the principles of the social market economy, a firmly based tradition of industrial co-management and an elite network linking industry closely with the financial system.

During the first phase of the steel crisis, from 1975 to 1981, these classical features of 'modell Deutschland' enabled a relatively painless adjustment to new market conditions — assisted, it should be added, by increasing, albeit largely indirect, amounts of federal and regional government aid. Since 1982, however, a number of developments have weakened the potential of the German system for crisis regulation: a growing reluctance on the part of the banks to underwrite the costs of adjustment; an absence of cooperation among the steel companies in confronting the crisis; tensions between the trade unions and the Conservative government elected in autumn 1982; and strains within the labour movement between the national IGM and the local-level works councils. The collapse of the government-sponsored rationalization plan for the industry in 1983 has confirmed the tendency, under market pressures, towards fragmentation among capitalist interests and suggests that a parallel development may well be occurring within the labour movement, posing serious problems for union organization and militating against crisis management at the supra-company level.

The bank–industry nexus
The West German steel industry has been dominated during the last decade by an oligopoly of seven large firms, all but one of which is in the private sector: Thyssen Gruppe, Hoesch Werke AG, Arbed Soarstahl, Krupp Stahl AG, Klöckner Werke AG, Mannesmann AG Hüttenwerke and the state-controlled Stahlwerke Peine Salzgitter. The strength, diversification and capacity for adjustment of the German firms in the pre-crisis period can be attributed to their close links with universal banks and to inter-company cooperation during the 1960s and 1970s through regional marketing cartels ('Walzstahlkontore') and rationalization agreements ('Rationalisierungsgrupen'). While marketing cartels allowed the maintenance of price discipline, the rationalization agreements provided a framework for market organization, product substitution among plants and surplus capacity management. Both increased efficiency while enabling the companies involved to remain formally independent (Messerlin, 1981; Stegemann, 1977). Coordination within this system was

assisted by close links between the steel firms, banks and large
insurance companies, the most important of which have been the
Deutsche Bank (which in the 1960s worked in conjunction with the
German Iron and Steel Association in facilitating agreements
among individual firms) and the Münchener Rückversicherung
Allianz AG (Hayward, 1974). 'Hausbanken' have not only provided
investment capital and financial security during downturns but have
been involved in investment-steering through representation on the
supervisory boards of the steel firms, interlocking directorships
forming the binding links in the bank–industry nexus (Dyson, 1983).

Given the almost 'para-statal' role played by the banks and the
associational strength of the industry itself, state intervention has
traditionally been limited to the maintenance of a favourable
economic climate. It should be noted, however, that the state has
directly and indirectly subsidized the industry to a level, before the
1970s (and again since 1977–78) equal to that of the French and
Belgium industries (Messerlin, 1981). Its direct involvement in the
rescue of Krupp Stahl in 1967 — often considered a prime example
of private corporate crisis management — should also be mentioned: the provision of fresh capital by the Deutsche and Dresdner
Banks following Krupp's financial collapse was tied to an equivalent
sum in government credit and guarantees (Stora, 1979: 227). It is
none the less true that, until 1983–84, the German government has
not had an explicit industrial policy for the sector. Under the
pressure of the crisis, however, this highly developed form of
'organized capitalism' has gradually been undermined, involving a
shift from a market to a corporatist mode of state intervention: both
federal and regional levels of government have assumed a new role
in mediating between capital and labour, in providing financial aid
to firms for negotiated programmes of adjustment and in absorbing
the social costs of restructuring.

Co-determination and union strength
The form taken by steel crisis management in Germany since the
late 1970s has been heavily conditioned by the nature of German
industrial relations, which, like the industry itself, have been well
regulated and organized along legal–rational lines. While direct
state intervention has been weak, a pervasive but diffused state
presence through formal law, and the organizational strength of
German unions, have ensured that bargaining and conciliation
occur and have contributed to a 'virtuous circle' of industrial
relations peace, high productivity and bargained rewards for
workforce moderation (Streeck, 1982a; 1982b). German industrial

unions are centralized, highly professional organizations with a strong financial base (funded by a computerized, automatic dues check-off system), a monopoly of representation and, in coal and steel, high membership density ratios. Organizational strength and stability have been sustained by the formal division of labour between the national industrial unions (in steel, the IGM) and the officially autonomous works councils ('Betriebsräte'): while the former have a legal monopoly on strike action and wage bargaining, the latter, through the co-determination laws (applied since 1952 in iron and steel), are formally restricted to shop-floor, job security issues, in many of which they share decision-making. In steel, workforce representatives share membership of company supervisory boards ('Aufsichtsräte'), and a labour director (usually connected to the union) sits on the company managment board ('Vorstand') (Bain, 1983). The 1972 revision of the 1952 Works Constitution Act made legal provision for company workers councils ('Gesamtbetriebsräte') comprised of delegates from the separate works councils of multi-plant firms. Within this dual structure of representation, co-determination has complemented collective bargaining and horizontal and vertical coordination have been ensured by the de facto control by unions of the works councils (the latter are usually composed of a majority of union officials and are dependent on services provided by central unions) and by the distribution of the fruits of economic growth in the form of high wages and job security (Streeck, 1982a; 1982b).

During the first phase of the steel crisis, this system of industrial relations provided a solid institutional framework for neo-corporatist crisis management. Co-determination has had a decisive influence on restructuring (which the labour courts have decreed as bargainable) and in mediating the impact of technological change: works councils have encouraged new forms of work organization if employment and wage levels are maintained (Bain, 1983). Collaboration has been favoured by a consensus between management and unions on the need for modernization as long as the core workforce (young, German, male) is protected. More recently, however, the uneven impact of continuing crisis across the industry has accentuated workforce divisions among and within companies, and new particularist plant-level demands pose a threat to union mobilization along class lines. As the employment impact of the crisis extends to the core of union membership — the skilled workers — a union–management compromise on layoffs will be more difficult to achieve. Furthermore, rationalization shifts the focus of union action away from quantitative issues to qualitative, shop-floor issues and signals a transfer of authority from the

198 Organized interests and the state

national unions to the works councils, increasing competition within the union hierarchy (Alexis, 1983; Streeck, 1982a). Recent events (see below) suggest that these developments may contribute, along with the fragmentation of capitalist interests, to the emergence of 'coalescing power' (Adams and Brock, 1983–84) at the company level as works councils lobby alongside managers for preferential state subsidies and enter into micro-level pacts with their companies or plants on issues of job security and work organization (cf. Goldthorpe, 1984).

The steel 'crisis cartels'

In the most important and complete example of 'crisis regulation by political cartel formation' (Esser and Väth, 1985), the threat of Neunkircher Eisenwerke and Röchling-Burbach Gmbh. to close their steel plants in the Saarland in the face of mounting losses, was countered by a rescue plan involving the Luxemburg steel group, Arbed, but sponsored and financed by the state. Industrial conflict, sparked by the announcement in March 1977 of 1300 redundancies without prior works council consultation, was resolved through negotiations between the federal and regional governments, the shareholders of the respective firms, the central executive of the IGM and Arbed, leading to the creation of a new company, Arbed Saarstahl, and an industrial and regional development programme based on federal and Land aid for investment and employment creation. The IGM played a central role, first in placating the workforce (which had initially called for nationalization) and then in negotiating a plan for employment adjustment providing for early retirement at 55 with 90 percent of take-home pay; the extension of future wage increases to early retirees; wage-level maintenance for five years for workers transferred to less well paid jobs; and co-management involving the works councils closely in implementing the agreement. The main concerns of the unions were to influence the methods of removing workers from the labour market; to secure early retirement for as many workers as possible while avoiding significant material loss; and to determine the categories of labour made redundant, marginalizing the older and least productive workers and providing immigrant labour with little or no protection (Erbes-Seguin and Volz, 1979; Esser and Fach, 1981; Esser and Väth, 1985).

This process of cartel formation was replicated in the Ruhr in 1980. Owing to a refusal of the Deutsche and Dresdner banks to extend further credit, Hoesch and Krupp were under increasing pressure to close obsolete capacity and cut back employment. Successfully exercising 'coalescing power' — contrary to the social constitution, which requires competition among associations of capital and labour (Schwerdtner, 1979: 470) — Hoesch, in alliance with its works councils and the IGM, had lobbied for and obtained hidden subsidies from the federal and Land governments. But this tactical coalition was now broken by a modernization plan requiring the loss of 5000 jobs. Strike action initiated by the workforce was directed into cooperative channels by the IGM; and, following a conference between Hoesch, the trade unions and the city of Dortmund, an agreement was reached on a corporate plan in May 1981. In October, a joint plan formulated by Hoesch and Krupp along the lines of the Saarland agreement was presented to the North Rhine–Westphalia Land government and the Economics Ministry in Bonn. It had not been submitted to co-determination procedures, however, and following a union veto the draft plan had to be withdrawn. After consultation with the unions, a new plan was agreed to in early 1982. This proposed a merger of Krupp and Hoesch creating Ruhrstahl AG, rationalization, and phased employment reductions mediated by co-determination and regulated by a 'Sozialplan' based on the Saar model (Esser and Väth, 1985).

The Saarland and Ruhr agreements reveal the utility of crisis cartel regulation for the unions, the state and the steel companies. While the state had become increasingly implicated in restructuring through its role as provider of investment capital and social aid and as mediator between capital and labour, 'selective corporatism' (Esser and Fach, 1981) allowed it to avoid direct responsibility and to insulate sectoral crisis management from the wider political system (Dyson, 1983). Although the steel companies are compelled to respect the conditions of the social plan, in return they gain access to state resources which are crucial for regaining competitiveness and their private sector status remains intact. The agreements also reveal the leverage gained by the trade unions from the dual structure of industrial relations and their capacity for maintaining internal cohesion. While the IGM can act effectively at the political and sectoral levels through lobbying and negotiation, the legal rights given to the works councils allows the translation of agreements into effect under union scrutiny. Requirements on management to respect these rights reinforce, in turn, the bargaining strength of the IGM. Horizontal cohesion among plant unions is vital for the maintenance of this strength, and this was enhanced by the creation of a number of coordinating mechanisms, notably a regular exchange of information between labour directors and works councillors in the steel firms concerned (Esser and Väth, 1985).

The limits to meso-corporatism
Developments since 1982–83 have revealed the limits to this model
of crisis management. In both the Saar and the Ruhr, the steel firms
have been progressively weakened by the continuing recession in
the industry and, in the absence of bank support, have asked for
increased state aid. By late 1982, and despite subsidies amounting to
DM2.2 billion since 1978, Arbed Saarstahl required a further
DM310 million. But this aid was agreed to by the new Conservative
government only following a sacrifice by the workforce of their one
month's salary Christmas bonus. It should be noted that the IGM
initially refused to make this concession, but was forced under
pressure from the Arbed workers to negotiate the bonus as an
interest-free loan. In October 1983, Arbed asked for a further
DM658 million in subsidies for 1983–85 and proposed a restructuring plan involving a reduction in employment by 5000. In return, the
federal government asked for a 25 percent reduction in board
members' salaries, cuts in payments to workers made redundant
under the Saarland 'Sozialplan' to 82 percent of previous salary, and
a wage freeze in 1984. Under the threat of the company's collapse,
the IGM and the works council agreed to the modification in the
redundancy agreement, but in order to gain a wage freeze, the
federal government asked Arbed to resign from the Employer's
Association of the Iron and Steel Industry in order to bypass the
established process of wage bargaining between the latter and the
IGM. This has been seen as a direct attack on the traditional
procedures (and rigidities) of neo-corporatist industrial relations,
but also as evidence of the continuing power of the unions, given
that this attack selected the employers' organization as the weakest
link in the neo-corporatist chain (Streeck, 1984).

The failure of the 1982 proposal to merge Krupp with Hoesch in
Ruhrstahl led the federal government in 1983 to sponsor a
rationalization plan, designed by three independent moderators,
which envisaged a consolidation of the industry within two large
groups — a 'Rhine group' (Thyssen and Krupp) and 'Ruhr group'
(Hoesch, Klöckner and the state-owned Salzgitter). State aid of
DM3 million was provided as an incentive for the mergers.
However, after two months of negotiations, all that remained of the
plan was a proposal by Salzgitter and Hoesch to cooperate in some
areas of steel-making (Dyson, 1984). A number of factors account
for this failure, including the belief (since confirmed) of the various
firms that the government would provide the aid even if mergers
failed to proceed, and the hope (unrealized) that Klöckner would go
bankrupt, cutting overall capacity and easing the pressure on the
other companies. Most importantly for the present discussion, an

attempt by the federal government to create a new crisis cartel between the steel companies, the national unions and the Länder concerned (a meso-corporatist design) broke down owing to a defensive coalition of political, union and managerial interests at company level. Beyond the general concern of the IGM that large industrial groups would be able to bypass effective union mediation in resolving employment problems (undermining the role of the works councils and provoking hierarchical disintegration in union structures), company councils ('Gesamtbetriebsräte') in alliance with managers and Länder politicians, did their utmost to prevent arrangements requiring a sacrifice in production or employment at their own sites (Buchan, 1983).

Continuing crisis in steel has provoked a parallel fragmentation of interests along company lines within both capital and labour which militates against sectoral crisis management and poses potentially serious problems for trade union organization at the industry level. Under market pressure, the more dynamic individual steel firms have fallen back on their own organizational resources and are unwilling to participate in state-sponsored plans which aim to save the weak by combining them with the strong. The healthier firms therefore have a greater interest in lobbying individually for state aid than in collective action and hope that those firms in greater difficulty will be allowed to collapse, thereby surrendering their market shares and easing overall problems of excess capacity. This individualist response on the part of the steel firms threatens to intensify the organizational difficulties of the trade unions as their countervailing powers, exercised at the industry level, are sapped by the emergence of 'coalescing power' between management and works councils at the company level. The development of micro-level collaboration seems already to be favoured by the workplace impact of technological change and a decline in collectivist ideology among the workforce (Streeck, 1982b); while the growing import-ance of shopfloor issues transfers authority from the industrial unions to the works councils, an absence of solidarity among works councils will mean that they will be less amenable to coordination by the centre. As Wolfgang Streeck (1984: 34) suggests, the 35-hour week campaign can be seen as an attempt on the part of IG-Metall to reclaim the initiative on restructuring issues which are currently the preserve of the works councils. This may have been achieved to some extent by the IGM's success in obtaining a 38-hour week for the steel industry's 170,000 workers in July 1984 in return for a 1984 wage freeze. The IGM hopes this will prevent the loss of 21,000 jobs which had been forecast before the end of 1985 (Cornwall, 1984). But this on its own is unlikely to prevent what Streeck has referred

to as 'wildcat cooperation' between works councils and management, either on shop-floor issues (the reorganization of the work
process in line with international 'best practice', for example) or in
joint lobbying against the works council–management coalitions of
other companies for privileged access to state resources.

France

The pattern of organized interests in French steel, and in consequence, the mode of crisis management employed, contrast in
almost every aspect with the German experience. The French state
has been involved in the industry's affairs, mediated by a powerful
trade association, the Chambre Syndicale de la Sidérurgie (CSSF),
for most of the postwar period. It has been an important source of
investment funds and has increasingly socialized the costs of
restructuring since the mid-1960s. This relationship between the
industry and the state has taken the form of a 'bipartite meso-
corporatism', consolidated in 1966 by a joint government–industry
modernization plan, the Convention Etat-sidérurgie. This relationship persisted, largely unmodified, until the quasi-
nationalization of steel by the liberal government of Raymond
Barre in 1978, which, in suppressing the mediation of the trade
association, illustrated the limits of sectoral or meso-corporatism
when corporate crisis management requires a more selective mode
of intervention. The trade unions, although more influential in steel
than in many sectors, suffer from low membership and meagre
resources, are divided ideologically, have been excluded from
decision-making at the industry level by an institutionalized system
of closure designed by employers and the state, and have been
denied an effective presence within the firms. The legal framework
for industrial relations has been ambiguous and ineffectual, and
securing negotiations with employers and governments on restructuring issues has required often violent social conflict.

As with French relations in general, crisis management in steel
has been highly politicized. It is largely for this reason that the
'charismatic' French unions have been able to achieve concessions
for their members similar to those gained by their 'professional–
bureaucratic' German counterparts (Maurice and Sellier, 1979).
Strike action more often than not escapes union control, and, in the
case of steel, has often taken insurrectionary forms. Under these
circumstances, generous social plans for steel workers can be
attributed more to the threat of physical disruption and electoral
damage to the ruling majority at both regional and national levels
than to union bargaining strength per se. In order to reduce the
political profile of industrial conflict, governments have constrained

employers and unions to negotiate and agree on methods of employment reduction with the threat of withholding financial aid. Once negotiated, the industry's managers have been able to implement these agreements without union involvement or state scrutiny. Under the Socialist government, elected in May 1981, this traditional pattern of labour–management relations remains fundamentally unchanged, nationalization and reformist labour legislation notwithstanding. If anything, management control in the steel industry has been enhanced by a number of factors: a decline in union base support owing to falling employment levels and workforce disillusion with intra- and inter-union conflict; the new element of uncertainty introduced into government–union relations by the Socialist victory and subsequent austerity policies; and, most importantly, a new social strategy at the company and plant levels which, consciously emulating Japanese management practices, endeavours to integrate workers more closely with the firm — and bypass union shopfloor influence — through the use of quality circles, management information systems and productivity incentives. Together, these factors threaten to decrease internal union cohesion, undermine the already limited bargaining strength of the metal federations at the industry level, and limit the effect of collective agreements already in force (Lévy, 1984).

The demise of 'bipartite corporatism'
The postwar strength of the steel industry's trade association, the CSSF, was inherited in large part from the early decades of the twentieth century when the steel barons dominated French employers' organization through the renowned Comité des forges. The experience of Vichy streamlined the steel association and accustomed its professional staff to dealing with a dirigiste state. In the 1950s and 1960s, the CSSF played a central role of mediation between the state and the steel firms through the planning process, as a lobby for special access to state resources and in raising investment capital for the industry through the issue of debenture loans.

The advantage for the firms of this mediation lay in several areas. First, it meant that the industry enjoyed both a formal relationship with the state through the planning system (which it was able to dominate owing to the CSSF's monopoly of statistics and information) and an informal relationship through day-to-day contacts between CSSF staff and the key ministries of state. This gave the industry an access to the state and decision-making denied to other interests restricted to the formal channels and provided it with an alternative and discreet means of exerting influence (St Marc, 1961;

McArthur and Scott, 1970). Second, it meant that the individual steel firms could avoid direct government intervention in their affairs, although it seems that the Ministries of Industry and Finance were able to influence to some extent the distribution of investment funds raised through the industry's collective debenture issues. Third, the ability of the industry to issue these debentures through a subsidiary organization of the CSSF, the Groupement de l'industrie sidérurgique (GIS), gave the firms an access to finance which bypassed banks and other financial institutions, and allowed them a certain insulation from market forces. An effective state guarantee for these loans meant that subscribers need never doubt that in the long term their money would be safe, in spite of the often poor performance of the steel firms on the Paris Bourse. Easy credit on these terms also meant that development could proceed without traditional patterns of control being compromised by the need to merge or forge alliances with sources of finance capital. One consequence of this was a slow merger movement, insufficient rationalization and declining productivity (Freyssenet, 1979; Stora 1979). By the mid-1960s, increasing debt and the scale of the social problems associated with retarded modernization were demanding a new form of relationship between the steel industry and the state.

In the 1960s, formal indicative planning procedures gave way to new forms of contractual relationship, initially between the government and individual firms but after 1966 with the sector as a whole: the industry required financial aid (in compensation, it was claimed, for indiscriminate government price fixing); the government wanted modernization (steel having been assigned 'national champion' status); and the natural go-between was the CSSF, led by the professional 'diplomat' between steel and the state, M. Jacques Ferry. In return for a large capital infusion through low interest loans, the industry agreed to a programme of mergers and modernization. Although as co-manager of the 1966 plan the CSSF was attributed quasi-public status, the contractual nature of the agreement should not be overestimated: reciprocal obligations were ill-defined and easily evaded, and the CSSF, through its monopoly of information and skilful exploitation of divisions within the state, was able to reduce the role of government to that of a sleeping partner. The general agreement with the CSSF was followed by a series of specific contracts with the steel companies themselves, but no effective mechanisms for monitoring the deployment of public funds were created. Although legal provisions were made for ensuring the industry's respect of certain obligations, including the repayment of loans as profit levels rose, in practice these were not enforced (Boy and Pirovano, 1983). The legitimacy traditionally granted to employers' organizations by the French state (Suleiman, 1974) and the dependence of civil servants on the expertise of the industry's professional staff combined to create a consensus on the desirability of publically financed, privately managed growth (Stoffaes, 1978: 492–505; Padioleau, 1981). The precise nature of this growth received little critical attention, and by the early 1970s, despite the state-sponsored merger of the sector's firms into two large groups, Usinor and Sacilor, the financial condition of the steel companies had further deteriorated, largely owing to inadequate rationalization and their concentration of production in low value-added bulk steel (Freyssenet, 1979).

The steel–state consensus was broken by the onset of the crisis in 1974, although effective action and a shift in the balance of power were delayed by the electoral constraints of the 1970s: the presidential election of May 1974, in which Giscard d'Estaing only narrowly defeated François Mitterrand, opened a campaign which, spanning the March 1976 cantonal elections and the March 1977 municipal elections, came to a close with the defeat of the left in the legislative elections of March 1978. In 1975 and 1976 the Chirac government prevented the steel firms from reducing employment; in 1977 an interim plan (the 'Plan Acier') created an interministerial committee to supervise a rationalization programme agreed to in return for state aid, but left the existing balance of power between the government and the industry unchanged. Following the victory of the right in 1978, the 'liberal' government of Raymond Barre formulated a new plan with the creditors of the bankrupt industry, transforming debts into shareholdings, making available state 'participatory loans' which, in effect, could be used as equity and implied no socialization of management (Gourdet, 1983), and encouraging a closer integration of bulk steel with special steel production (Dahmani, 1983).

Most importantly for the present discussion, one aim of the Barre plan was to ensure a more direct line of command between the state administration and the two major companies, Usinor and Sacilor, and to prevent the financial holdings of these companies from shifting their resources to their profitable divisions while leaving the loss-making divisions in the hands of the state. This required that the industry's trade association, the CSSF, be deposed from its mediating position along with its chairman, Jacques Ferry, and direct links be established with the two steel companies through the appointment of government-nominated general managers. Although formally the independence of the new managers was to be respected, the government now had the means to intervene directly at the company level. Full nationalization under the Socialists has done little to alter this design (Sueur, 1983), although, whereas the previous government limited its intervention largely to financial affairs and left industrial matters to its managers, the Socialists have intervened more directly in defining the sector's industrial strategy and on occasion have imposed decisions on the firms. To this extent there has been a shift in state intervention from a corporatist mode (in which the allocation of resources is bargained — but not in this case implemented by — producers and the state) towards a bureaucratic mode (state capitalism), in which investments and strategy are determined by political command (Cawson, 1982).

Industrial relations and social closure
In France, a close relationship between capital and the state has generally entailed the exclusion of labour from policy influence. Company paternalism, weak institutions of statutory representation and the state's view of organized labour as a lobby of low status have created a broad structure of social closure which marginalizes the unions, contributes to their weakness and helps perpetuate politicized unionism and ideological positions hostile to management (Gallie, 1980). The power of organized labour is further weakened by plural unionism, with the three major unions — the Communist CGT, the Socialist CFDT and the reformist CGT-Force Ouvrière — competing for members, workplace influence and ideological supremacy (Rand Smith, 1984). Potential solidarity in bargaining is sapped by the applicability of collective agreements to the entire workforce of an industry even if they are signed by the smallest and least representative unions. Also, conflict within the labour movement is often precipitated by the parties of the left which, especially in the case of the Communist Party (PCF), contest the claim of the unions to be the sole, legitimate representatives of the working class.

In steel, this structure of closure and organizational assymetry between capital and labour have been reinforced by specific institutional mechanisms restricting bargaining to limited levels and areas of influence, a strategy supported by a legal framework which distinguishes clearly between the domains of economic decision-making (reserved for employers) and social matters where a degree of legitimate union influence is recognized (Lyon Caen, 1979). At the level of the firm, this restricts works councils ('comités d'entreprise') to a purely consultative function (Oheix, 1979) and at the level of industrial bargaining it restricts union federations to negotiating the terms of employment reductions (Bonnechère, 1979). The government has been as keen as employers to resist union demands for tripartite bargaining on industrial and financial matters, in order partly to prevent a conspiracy between the steel firms and the unions in lobbying for subsidies and concealing the real extent of employment reduction required (Sellier, 1970; Mohamed Salah, 1983). Employers have been concerned to minimize any constraint on their managerial autonomy by refusing to bargain restructuring plans. For these reasons, each of the steel plans negotiated between the steel producers and the state has been followed by separate social negotiations between employers' representatives and the unions.

This system of bargaining has been replicated several times (1977, 1979, 1984) since the first 'convention social' of 1967. In each case, concessions have been gained only after serious social conflict in the steel regions, and the unions have contested the form as much as the content of the negotiations. But, given their own divisions and the strength of the opposition, the capacity of the unions to alter the rules of the game has been limited. At each stage they have demanded global negotiations covering both social and economic questions, but to no avail: in 1979 the industrial plan was discussed with them for the first time, but they were unable to modify its content. Also for the first time in 1979, the unions attempted to develop effective counter-proposals for the industry's development and thereby to enhance their credibility as bargaining partners. This strategy failed for a number of reasons. The proposals themselves, and particularly those of the CGT, were still linked to global alternatives to capitalist development and provided little ground for negotiation on specific issues. At the same time, the central union intellectuals were unable to secure workforce mobilization behind the proposals because of their abstract nature and an absence of genuine consultation with the base. More generally, the new strategy was undermined by the politicization of the dispute by the Communist Party and the Socialist Party (each attempting to exploit it for their own electoral purposes following the rupture of the union of the left) and by the inability of the central union federations to discipline the forms of protest in the steel regions and to channel it in support of particular demands. This problem points to one of the major obstacles to trade union participation in decision-making and to the development of neo-corporatist type relationships in France: if the unions are unable to marshal their troops behind particular policies and to ensure their compliance with bargains struck with capital and/or the state, then the latter have little incentive for modifying their exclusionary strategies (Schain, 1980; Cox and Hayward, 1983). In the case of the 1979 strike, the impact of union protest was quickly undermined by the government's offer of lump-sum severance payments ('primes de départ') of Fr50,000 which circumvented the unions and demobilized the workforce, reducing the strike to a few remaining pockets of resistance.

Union weakness, dualism and management control
Developments since 1979, both in industrial bargaining and on the shop-floor, confirm increasing organizational weakness in the labour movement. The widening division of the left after 1978 and conflict within and between the unions before the election of the Socialist government in May 1981 led to a loss of membership and an attrition of base-level leadership. Since 1981, effective union action has been prevented by the dilemmas of dealing with a left-wing government whose policies have increasingly come to resemble those of the right. Competition between parties and the unions for primacy as representatives of the working class has also increased, and many workers have taken party cards while allowing their union membership to lapse.

These general trends have been accentuated in the case of steel by the severe impact of the crisis in the sector, the repercussions of inter-union conflict and the defeat of the labour movement in the 1979 strike: CGT and CFDT membership has fallen sharply in favour of the moderate Force Ouvrière; the limited degree of coordination existing between the federal, regional and plant levels of the metal unions has disappeared, although unity at the base has persisted in a number of isolated cases; and the workforce has become increasingly disoriented — and demobilized — by the equivocal response of the central unions to Socialist-directed restructuring. Under these circumstances, the unions have been unable to alter the established system of bargaining in their favour and on several occasions have been refused access to industrial negotiations and information on redundancy plans by a government concerned to keep management free from constraints (Pakradouni, 1984).

Trade union divisions and workforce disillusion have also given the industry's management an opportunity to pre-empt Socialist legislation on worker participation by extending its shop-floor control and marginalizing the role of the unions within the firm. This has occurred across French industry in anticipation of new statutory rights at decision-making levels for workers' representatives (Mothé, 1983). In steel, there has been a 'Japanization' of work relations in the most modern plants (Fos and Dunkirk) which bypasses union mediation between management and workers and seeks to imbue employees with a 'company spirit' through the use of quality circles, the creation of information systems under management control and the introduction of various forms of bonuses for productivity increases and participation in work life improvement schemes (Gourc and Gourc, 1981; Lévy, 1984; Barisi, 1984). The specific target of these innovations are the shop-stewards ('délégués du personnel') who have traditionally been trade union militants. At the same time, internal labour market flexibility has been increased by the use of subcontracting and part-time work, a practice well established in the French steel firms since the end of the 1960s and introduced, in part, to evade the constraints placed on hiring and firing by labour legislation after May 1968 and by collective agreements (Berger and Piore, 1980: 33–41; Broda et al., 1978).

Unlike their Italian counterparts, the French steel unions have been unable to resist developments which, together, signal the emergence of an accentuated dualism between a protected core of workers and a periphery of largely non-unionized, part-time and subcontract workers. It is too early to predict the impact of Socialist legislation in favour of greater worker participation (the 'lois Auroux') on French workplace politics, but, given the weakness of French industrial unions and the strength of management control, a scenario similar to that emerging in West Germany can be predicted: company unionism involving the cooptation of workforce representatives, fragmenting the union hierarchy and breaking solidarity among plants.

Italy

Both the French and the German cases have revealed the limits under crisis conditions to corporatist arrangements (whether bipartite or tripartite) at the sectoral level and appear to confirm the supposition that neo-corporatism is, in general, a fair, or at best a mild, weather creature. However, while crisis management is a recent phenomenon in the Italian experience, its emergent forms indicate that, under certain political and economic circumstances, corporatist type solutions may provide a useful means of interest accommodation and policy outcomes beneficial to all parties. But equally, the Italian case reveals the limits to such arrangements and the tensions and imbalances of power that inevitably persist within them.

The nature of state intervention and the pattern of interest organization in the Italian steel sector differ markedly from the previous two cases. Its most distinctive features have been: (1) the co-existence of a large public sector — producing flat products (plates and sheets) from coastal, integrated steel plants — with a dynamic private sector, concentrating on special steels and long products (beams and concrete reinforcing bars) and using more flexible, cost-efficient, electric furnaces; (2) the highly politicized character of policy-making owing to the fragmentation of the Italian state and the internal strains of Italy's makeshift coalition governments; and (3) a strong federal union, the Federazione Lavoratori Metalmeccanici (FLM), which has exerted considerable influence over industrial policy at sectoral level, (successfully resisting privatization and reductions in employment) and at plant level, mediating modifications to the work process (automation and computerization) and extending employment protection to the workers of subcontracting firms connected to steel companies. This countervailing power has been exercised primarily within the public sector; the unions have had less success in the highly individualistic private sector firms.

During the 1960s and 1970s, industrial relations were highly conflictual, and consistent policy-making was impossible owing to political divisions and the absence of a stable policy network insulated from the day-to-day pressures of political bargaining, factionalism and patronage (Eisenhammer and Rhodes, 1985). The private sector, traditionally more profitable and adaptable to changing market conditions than the public companies, was concerned above all to retain its entrepreneurial autonomy while gaining advantages from the state in the form of tax concessions and indirect subsidies (primarily preferential energy prices). More recently, the impact of the recession and directives from Brussels on capacity reduction under the European crisis regime have forced each of the major actors in the sector to adopt more conciliatory positions and to cooperate in formulating and implementing a sectoral plan spanning both public and private companies. While the eventual form and outcomes of this plan are as yet uncertain, an analysis of the forces militating both for and against the creation of a sectoral 'crisis cartel' in Italian steel will provide useful insights into the conditions required for 'meso-corporatist' solutions to crisis management problems.

The state and organized labour in the development of Italian steel
In order to understand the form of interest accommodation required for effective crisis management in Italian steel, it is necessary first to take a brief detour to examine the nature of policy-making in the sector, and the role played by the unions, during the period of expansion.

The Italian steel industry differs from its French and German competitors in that it is largely a creation of the postwar period. For this reason it has avoided the problems caused by the location of outdated plant in single-industry, coal or iron-ore-bearing regions. Most of the Italian industry's raw materials are imported and its production is concentrated in comparatively modern plant. During the 1950s and 1960s, it enjoyed the fastest rate of growth in the European Coal and Steel Community (De Rosa, 1978). Paradoxically, rapid expansion, unaccompanied by a parallel evolution of strategic planning or industrial relations, explains many of the steel industry's contemporary problems. Concentration on quantitative growth neglected the other conditions of profitable long-term development: a sound financial base, a controllable commercial network, and integration downstream with firms transforming bulk steel into high value added products. This meant that, even before the crisis of the mid-1970s, Italian steel was financially unsound (14.2 percent of investment only from equity in 1974) and vulnerable to import penetration. As the crisis has deepened, these problems have compounded one another. Further difficulties derive from poor industrial relations, giving Italian steel the worst strike record and the highest labour costs in Europe (ASSIDER, 1980).

Policy choices made in the 1970s reflected the optimism of the industry in the future of steel production, but they were also shaped increasingly by political and trade union influence. At this stage, public sector managers were planning expansion along Japanese lines, involving a rationalization of existing plants and the construction of giant coastal steel complexes. Managerial autonomy was reduced, however, by pressure from the left, powerful sections of the centre right and the three metal unions (CGIL–FIOM, CISL–FIM and UIL–UILM) which, after 1971–72, united within the FLM and became the driving force behind the growth and unification of the labour movement. In steel, the unions have been at their most powerful when they have managed to forge alliances with political parties at the national and local levels. By mobilizing such support, the FLM has successfully managed to lobby in favour of investment and employment creation in the South and against closures, redundancies and the privatization of public sector firms: employment levels in steel were maintained until 1980, a plan to shift certain public special steel plants to private management under FIAT was successfully vetoed in 1977, and several attempts to run down production at Bagnoli in Naples have been prevented by FLM and local opposition (Barisi, 1982). As has been the case for the public sector in general, steel policy has been subject to wider political and social constraints (Grassini, 1980): Italy's fourth integrated steel complex was constructed at Taranto in the South contrary to the wishes of Finsider (the steel subsidiary of the state shareholding, IRI); similarly, political and social criteria dictated a location for a fifth steel complex (since abandoned) at Gioia Tauro in Calabria. Influence of this type could be exerted because of the fragmentation of the policy process (which institutional reform in the mid-1970s singularly failed to rectify) and the important role of party influence within it (Eisenhammer and Rhodes, 1985).

The trade unions have also been highly influential within the various steel plants. Unionization rates have been high, the workforce militant, the the 'consigli di fabbrica' (workers' councils comprised of shop-floor delegates) have played a central role in mediating the introduction of new technology and changes to the work process: at the Cornigliano (Genoa) works in the mid-1970s, 69 percent of the workforce paid union fees, each worker spent an average of 39 hours per year on strike, and there was one shop-floor delegate for every 40 workers. Until 1977, the union's preferences usually prevailed on workplace issues and particularly on minimizing the detrimental impact of computerization on social relations in the plant. In public sector steel, the dualism for which the Italian labour market is notorious has largely been avoided: after an important conflict in 1975, subcontractors on the site were absorbed into the company and given protection and status equivalent to that of other workers (Barisi, 1984). Unlike in Germany, there have been direct links between plant and federal levels of union representation and this has prevented hierarchical fragmentation.

Further constraints have been placed on steel management by the divisions of consecutive coalition governments and by the general crisis of Italian public sector finance. This has meant that managers have had to operate under conditions of considerable uncertainty and have been unable to depend on a steady and reliable flow of credit. Conflict within the Cabinet (typically between the Minister for State Shareholdings and the Ministers of the Treasury and Budget) has often prevented funds promised from being disbursed. More generally, the refusal of special credit institutions to supply finance in the absence of reliable government guarantees for repayment has left the steel firms heavily under-capitalized. In these circumstances, they have had little option but to turn to the private credit market and contract loans at often exorbitant interest rates. The consequence has been massive debts: in 1980, 40 percent of Finsider's total capital investment was covered by expensive short-term loans, while equity accounted for only 5 percent (CIPI, 1981). In 1981 its accumulated debt equalled its turnover.

Crisis management and interest realignment

Despite serious financial problems, the severity and structural nature of the steel crisis was fully recognized by the Italians only in 1981–82. They attributed their problems in the main to under-capitalization, however, and requests for capacity cuts from the

European Commission were refused on the grounds that Italian plant was more modern than that of other European countries and that sustained demand in certain product lines justified capacity maintenance. This ignored the structural problems of the industry — bad downstream connections, obsolete plant, insufficient economies of scale, and an inadequate articulation of production with distribution (Liberati, 1981; Moro, 1984). In June 1983 the European Commission delivered an ultimatum to the Italian government, requesting capacity cuts across the industry totalling 5.8 million tonnes. Within Italy, certain influential political figures — chief among them Romano Prodi, the chairman of IRI — agreed that such cuts were necessary: steel was now largely responsible for IRI's enormous losses (L2672 billion in 1982). Prodi also advocated a reduction in employment in the industry by at least 25,000. For this programme of adjustment to proceed, fundamental policy innovation and a reconciliation of contradictory interests would be required.

In Italy, the weakness of the state and the political and shop-floor strength of the trade unions demand a multilateral approach to industrial adjustment. However, a bargained response to the steel crisis depends on a degree of consensus on the distribution of the costs and an institutional and legislative framework for policy implementation. Until recently, neither of these preconditions have existed. Industrial location planning and an active public manpower policy have both traditionally been absent. As for employment adjustment, trade unions have tied labour market concessions to greater influence over investments and industrial strategy, areas in which employers have been reluctant to concede autonomy. Within the labour movement itself, the unions, in particular the CGIL, have been opposed to German style co-management at the enterprise level: it has been feared that institutionalized participation would reduce union autonomy, direct conflict into less rewarding conciliatory channels and undermine the influence exerted by the central unions on macroeconomic policy (Caloia, 1979). In industry, private sector firms have been hostile to collaboration with the public sector for fear of a loss of independence. Corporatist relationships also depend on the capacity of the state for providing material rewards or conferring public status in return for interest group cooperation: in Italy, a fragmented bureaucracy and fragile coalition governments have prevented the fulfilment of this condition (Ferraresi, 1983; Regini, 1982; 1983). Given these constraints, crisis management in Italy has largely been limited to the extended use of the state-assisted 'Cassa Integrazione Guadagni' (Wage Supplementation Fund) which provides income stability and continued employment status for the surplus work-force. In steel, however, a number of novel developments have occurred under the pressure of market deterioration and directives from Brussels. Together, these have provided the conditions for a crisis management strategy for the sector spanning both public and private sector firms and involving the unions closely in implementation.

The two major problems facing the steel industry are excess production and surplus employment, but any attempt to reduce either inevitably faces the combined opposition of unions and political interests in the steel areas. A restructuring plan for the sector must therefore seek to reconcile economic necessity with the preservation of social order and political legitimacy. New legislation provides two means of doing so. Early retirement at 50 is now available to steel workers and will cater for some 19,000 of the 26,000 due to leave the industry. This measure is acceptable to the unions and represents a saving to the state over further recourse to the Cassa Integrazione. Second, government approval of subsidies to private producers wishing to scrap their plant simultaneously provides a solution to a number of problems. It allows the cuts demanded by Brussels to be spread over the sector as a whole and eases the burden on the more heavily unionized public companies. It also eases the financial difficulties facing the private electric furnace producers caused by the soaring price of scrap steel (their main material input).

Moreover, subsidies to the private sector may permit the preservation of public sector employment. A recently negotiated public–private deal for rescuing part of the Cornigliano (Genoa) works aims to save 1500–2000 jobs by transferring majority control from Italsider to a consortium of private producers. In return for participation in the plan, the consortium members will be able to produce oxygen steel more cheaply than electric steel and will receive further aid for scrapping their own mills. Private–public cooperation is also occurring within joint rationalization plans: Falck, the largest private producer, is working with the state-controlled Dalmine to avoid product duplication and redistribute steel tube production among their most efficient plants. At the sectoral level, it has been suggested by a number of influential politicians and businessmen that the trade association of the small private sector producers, ISA, merge with ASSIDER, the association of the large private and public sector firms. This, it is thought, would enhance sectoral coordination and provide the Italian industry as a whole with greater bargaining power with Brussels on restructuring issues (Eisenhammer and Rhodes, 1985).

The trade unions have a central role in shaping and implementing the new Italian steel plan. It should be noted that the FLM has been considerably weakened in recent years. Its greatest defeat was during the six-week FIAT dispute in 1980, when 40,000 workers marched through the streets calling for an end to the strike. Since then it has been deserted by its base, and financial problems have reduced its professional staff and diminished its shop-floor presence. More recently it has fallen victim to the general collapse of solidarity among the union confederations (CGIL, CISL and UIL) and is divided internally among its three component metal unions. In steel, it has been unable to prevent conflict among plants over employment and capacity maintenance. None the less, the government and the industry have had to take union policy closely into account in formulating the new plan, and the FLM remains an indispensable partner in ensuring its effective implementation.

Several reasons can be suggested for this. First, the union retains considerable shop-floor strength, and its capacity for striking common cause with local and national political interests remains an important weapon. Shop-floor strength also provides it with an important resource that its French counterparts lack: since the late 1970s, the FLM has become involved in a process of exchange whereby steel management has conceded ground on investment and employment issues in return for greater control of the work process and technological change. This has been accompanied by a degree of centralization within the union, but the influence and legitimacy of the *consigli di fabbrica* remain intact. The government and management clearly prefer to deal with the federal FLM, however, and it has recently become an important agent of control in the restructuring process. Having obtained sacrifices from the workers of other plants in the industry, the FLM was faced with opposition from the *consiglio* of Bagnoli (Naples) to an agreement it had signed with Finsider on employment at the plant. The FLM responded by holding a referendum of the plant's workforce which undermined the legitimacy of the strike called by the delegates: a majority voted in favour of the FLM–Finsider agreement, and the *consiglio* was disciplined by dissolution.

The Bagnoli episode clearly revealed the utility for the government and management of a strong national union, but also indicated a source of potentially serious conflict between the union and its base: in the event of a more radical restructuring programme, the FLM's representative functions will inevitably clash with its crisis management role. Further problems for internal union organization may arise for the same reasons as in Germany and France: as workplace politics are transformed by the adoption of Japanese management techniques (which, as elsewhere, aims to bypass union mediation between management and labour and integrate workers more closely with the firm), the potential for labour–management coalitions at company level will increase, provoking fragmentation at the union base and a loss of hierarchical control. In certain plants such as Taranto, close collaboration with Japanese consultants has sought specifically to increase direct worker participation and has circumvented traditional union representatives (Masi, 1985).

The tentative 'crisis cartel' of Italian steel rests on a precarious compromise which, in the final analysis, depends on continuing state financial support for its survival. Factors working in its favour are the Italian state's incapacity for implementing a policy of such radical dimensions independent of support from powerful interest groups, and the presence of a common external enemy, the European Commission. 'Sectoral consciousness' has been raised by the impact of the recession and, once again, by the inequitable treatment that both private and public sector producers feel they have received from Brussels. Factors working against the consolidation of this tactical coalition into a more formal crisis cartel are: conflict within the private sector between those producers who are given special access to state resources and those who are not; disagreement between private sector and public sector firms over the distribution of capacity cuts; clashes between unions and management over the extent and methods of employment reduction and, in the case of joint public–private salvage operations, over the preservation of public sector work practice, salary and status agreements; divisions within the state over the provision of continued aid to the sector; and, finally, conflict within the unions themselves, both horizontally among plants and vertically between plant, regional and federal levels. In these circumstances, the most likely medium-term scenario for sectoral crisis management in Italian steel is for continuing tension among the partners to the bargain and the need for a constant renegotiation of its terms.

Conclusions

In each of these three case studies, attention has been given to the form and levels of conflict resolution in crisis management. As has been shown, the impact of industrial crisis primarily concerns the company and its plants: the crucial questions, however, are, first, the extent to which the response to the crisis is determined at this level or is mediated by the national institutions of capital and labour; and, second, the degree to which the strategy adopted excludes or includes trade union representation. As the case studies also reveal, the consequences of the crisis for company- and plant-level politics will also affect the nature of interest organization and articulation beyond the firm: both the exclusion and the co-optation of labour at the micro-level will create organizational difficulties for the union hierarchy and provoke a shift in the balance of power at the meso-level of the sector. Similarly, collaboration or marginalization at the meso-level will modify the relationship between national unions and their members and cause problems of cohesion and control. The management of industry, in contrast, is more flexible in adjusting from one form of conflict resolution to another. As industrial unions are weakened by declining membership and internal fragmentation, management can exploit these problems by decentralizing industrial decision-making and encouraging a diversification between and within centres of production. A major goal of this strategy is to undermine collective bargaining with its costly and time-consuming procedures and, rather than establish norms for regulating crisis management on an industry-wide basis, to allow a differentiation of response according to managerial preferences and to the balance of power in micro-level situations.

The differential capacity for organizational adjustment on the part of capital and labour is closely related to the underlying structural assymetry of their relationship one to the other (Offe and Wiesenthal, 1979) While capitalist associations (both peak and sectoral) may well see their role and influence decline with a devolution of crisis management, the margin for manoeuvre of their members will be increased. In the process, a new division of tasks is likely to be established in which the employers' associations are restricted to their traditional role as lobbyists and industrial relations becomes the preserve of the individual company. But within this process of devolution, capitalists remain the primary organizers, and, in the absence of powerful and highly cohesive industrial unions, their organizational response will dictate in many ways the response of labour. Their power at the micro-level does not ultimately depend on association at the meso-level — even though they have a variety of associational forms from which to choose (cartels, flexible rationalization agreements, employers and trade associations) — whereas the micro-level power of labour seems closely linked with its ability to organize collectively. Although certain élite categories of the workforce may retain their capacity for striking preferential bargains with management in the absence of collective organization or solidarity — and, indeed, they may well prefer to do so — as the three national case studies of steel have shown, the ability of labour to exercise countervailing power at the micro-level depends on hierarchical control within unions and on their capacity for mobilization. In certain conditions, capitalists will combine in order to strengthen their sectoral defences against other capitalists and disruptive market forces, or to reinforce their powers of lobbying national or as in the Italian case, supra-national, government. In other conditions — in the German case, prolonged crisis — capitalists will prefer to fall back on their own organization-al resources, lobby independently for state resources and avoid the political and economic costs of sectoral crisis management.

Thus, while Wassenberg (1982) has suggested that sectoral or meso-corporatism may provide a useful means of conflict resolution and policy formation — avoiding conflicts of loyalty within trade unions and in the body politic in general — in those industries undergoing rapid transformation, such solutions are likely to be unstable and temporary even where, as in Germany, conditions conducive to the emergence of neo-corporatist forms exist. For capitalists, or at least for those with a future, sectoral strategies are inconvenient for a number of reasons and will be adopted only as second-best solutions. They may, as in the case of West German steel, involve compromise with other, perhaps weaker, companies on the part of the strong and place constraints on labour force management which derive from collective agreements with national unions. They may also involve, as in the cases both of Germany and France, a degree of state regulation either directly (following from government participation in bargaining) or indirectly through the legal system.

Furthermore, the actor with the greatest stake in the maintenance of collective bargaining and in sectoral conflict resolution — the industrial union — would appear to face the most difficulty in preserving its own organizational capacities for achieving and actively participating in such arrangements. First, industrial crisis and employment reduction will inevitably undermine union mem-bership even if at first its impact is restricted to poorly qualified and immigrant labour, neither categories of which have provided important sections of the union constituency. Second, crisis conditions will not only affect the union's capacity to provide the collective goods (purchasing power, job security and so on) required for maintaining membership allegiance (Olson, 1965), but will also increase the demand for non-collective goods such as special protection for older and immigrant workers and assistance in finding new jobs for those made redundant. Crisis management may require a union to trade one collective good for another — a loss in purchasing power in return for greater job security, for example — but in so doing it will risk losing support from those highly skilled core workers whose jobs, at least in the short-term, are not under threat, and who feel that their interests are better served by particularist pacts with management rather than by collective bargaining. A third and related point is that restructuring will increasingly differentiate between membership units (companies and plants) and will encourage competition among workers for a diminishing number of available jobs. This will provoke fragmentation at the union base — exacerbated in some cases by labour–management coalitions — and undermine, in turn, coordination in the union hierarchy. Finally, organizational cohesion between levels of union representation may be undermined by the adoption of new managerial strategies at the micro-level ('Japanization') which aim to bypass union shop-floor delegates and integrate the core workforce more closely with the firm. Both of the latter two developments will contribute to the emergence of 'company consciousness' among workers at the expense of union sectoral or class identity.

Together, these tendencies threaten to weaken industrial unions and to diminish the need or incentive for capitalists to partake in sectoral-level bargaining and conflict resolution. Their ability under propitious economic and political conditions (the prolonged crisis of Western capitalist economies) to decentralize industrial adjustment strategies and segment social relations by company and plant attests to the organizational power of capital. But it also reveals the constraints on capitalists to conform with the norms of international 'best practice' set by their fiercest competitors. Hence the tendency (more pronounced in some sectors and countries than in others) for a devolution of industrial crisis management to the level of the firm, and the attempt to increase participation in management-inspired workplace democracy. Depending on union concern and bargaining strength, and on the legal regulation of employment contracts, this strategy may also involve an increasing differentiation between a stable core of skilled workers and a periphery of part-time and subcontract workers who can be hired and fired at ease and who enhance the capacity for adjustment of the firm. Inclusion — in the form of class collaboration — at the micro-level may thus proceed simultaneously with a greater or lesser degree of exclusion for certain sections of the labour force. If the state is also involved in sponsoring or bargaining the terms of such strategies (as part of a policy of selective support for 'national champions', for example), it is conceivable that corporatism and dualism may be complementary rather than mutually exclusive strategies (cf. Goldthorpe, 1984). They may also, together, constitute the most effective institutional forms for industry to adopt in its attempts to counter the commercial threat posed by the Japanese.

Under certain circumstances, as in the Italian case, a sectoral strategy of crisis resolution and policy formation may continue to be more appropriate. In Italy, the recent response to the steel crisis along these lines has been attributed to the sustained strength of the sector's industrial union, the FLM, to the weaknesses and divisions of the state, and to the common cause created between private and public sector producers by the EEC Commission's demand for cuts. But, as was also indicated, this strategy is subject to a number of strains, some of which derive from the organizational problems of the FLM. In other cases, the state may be an important factor in preventing the firm from becoming the privileged site of crisis management and in sponsoring collaborative strategies. In France, new labour law reforms have aimed to strengthen union representation within firms, to create company-level workers' councils similar to the German 'Gesamtbetriebsträte' and to legislate against labour market dualism in the form of part-time work and subcontracting. They have also attempted to strengthen bargaining within firms, and it is at the micro-level that negotiation between capital and labour would appear to have its greatest future. Otherwise, these measures have been under fierce attack from both employers' organizations and opposition parties; and, given the poor electoral standing of the Socialist government, their likelihood of long-term success is open to doubt. Above all, as in Italy, Germany and elsewhere, companies are concerned to retain their autonomy of labour use and to avoid the restrictions of compromise solutions with national unions which span entire industries. The July 1984, 'Convention sociale' between the nationalized steel companies and the sector's unions (the CGT excepted) represents an exception in a country where the future of collective bargaining is highly uncertain. As elsewhere in Western Europe, the crisis of industrial unions and the decline of collective bargaining are the consequences of more general changes, both in the structure of production and in the nature of employment. Under these circumstances, the time of meso-corporatism as mode of crisis management would seem to have passed.

Note

I would like to thank Alan Cawson and Philippe Schmitter for their critiques of an earlier version of this paper.

11
Conclusion: some implications for state theory

Alan Cawson

The scope and applicability of meso-corporatism
If we consider corporatism at the macro-level, we can specify some preconditions for its emergence — principally, monopoly peak organizations of capital and labour — and describe the kinds of factors which encourage its development in terms of the calculative strategies and organizational cohesion of the principal collective actors with respect to encompassing class issues. It appears from such studies that macro-corporatism has been an accurate description of the political economy of several West European countries at least for some periods of their history, but in some other countries, such as Britain, attempts to sustain macro-corporatist bargaining over a long period have met with failure. One of the reasons for this, as discussed by Vickerstaff and Boston in their chapters, is the inability of interest organizations to reconcile what we may, following Schmitter and Streeck (1981), call the politics fo membership and the politics of influence. These two sets of opportunities and constraints tug in different directions, and their contradictory impulses can best be tamed in a buoyant economic context which maximizes the potential for influence and the payoffs that can sustain member allegiances.

When we fix our sights below the peaks of class organization, and study organization and interest intermediation within specific sectors and policy fields, a much more complex picture appears. Can we now be as confident as the 'first generation' of studies that corporatism has little relevance in countries which exhibit a fragmented and fissured associational system at the peak?

The essays in this book have examined aspects of meso-corporatist interest intermediation in several industrial sectors of seven countries. Only one of those countries, West Germany, shows up as even moderately corporatist when attention is focused on the macro-level (Schmitter, 1981; Lehmbruch, 1982; Schmidt, 1982). Canada and the USA vie for the title of the weakest example of macro-corporatism, yet at the provincial level in Canada, as chapters 2 and 6 demonstrate, there is evidence of strongly meso-corporatist patterns in particular sectors. In chapter 8 it was argued that the chemicals sector in the USA is strongly pluralist, in terms of its interest organizations, when compared with the same sector in West Germany. Two authors (Salisbury, 1979; G.K. Wilson, 1982) have argued the case that there is no corporatism in the USA, and Schneider's analysis of the chemicals sector (chapter 9) seems to confirm this by finding little evidence of meso-corporatism. Yet we should be careful not to leave the matter there, and we should allow for the possibility of meso- or micro-corporatist practices in other sectors or below federal level. This point has now begun to be recognized, and a discussion of corporatism as interest intermediation in the USA (rather than apocalyptic discussions of the arrival of the 'corporate state', or the equation of corporatism with corporate capitalism) is beginning to emerge with the identification or corporatist practices at state government and city level (Milward and Francisco, 1983).

Consider the following extract from the conclusion to a study of urban policy in the USA:

> the organization of the state mediates the relationship among social groups. The structure of the state is a source of power because the organization of political authority differentially affects the level and effectiveness of different social groups' participation. In this viewpoint, the state is not a competitive marketplace where interests are brokered by the government, but a structured battleground where some groups are strategically placed while others are located far from the real centers of power. The structure of the state selects which demands can be handled by the government, and thus which kinds of participants will most easily gain access. It also channels participants into government locations with differential capacities to respond to their demands. Finally, by implication, the state organizes the political relationship among social groups, such that some groups must regularly confront each other while others rarely do. (Friedland, 1982: 211–12)

The term 'corporatism' nowhere appears in Friedland's book, yet his analysis and conclusions are strikingly similar to those uncovered in explicitly corporatist research, and the above passage is a good summary of the relationship between the state and interest organizations within corporatism. Any satisfactory answer to the question, 'Why no corporatism in America?', must contest the basic premise of the question. A less superficial response than so far available would be that there may well be no macro-corporatism in America, but if we adopt a sectoral approach — if we look below the level of federal government and focus on a meso-level of government — we are likely to find some networks of relationships between interest groups and state agencies which do not at all fit the pluralist or neo-Marxist models. Moreover, if this is true of the

USA, the empirical and intellectual heartland of pluralism, then it should not need much further argument to secure the place of corporatism on the research agenda for other countries.

The study of interest intermediation at the meso-level is not, however, simply a matter of uncovering corporatist practices, one after another. It is not corporatism *per se* which is of interest to the authors of the chapters in this book; it is, rather, the contribution that corporatism can make to the explanation of public policy-making. What is evident from these studies is the variety and considerable complexity of these political relationships, and the relative crudeness of the conceptual tools we are working with. We are far from being able to explain why it is that interests are organized pluralistically in one sector but monopolistically in another, or in the same sector in a different country, but a number of interesting hypotheses are beginning to emerge. We can, for example sharpen our descriptions of these differences, and say something about their effects in terms of whether particular kinds of interventionist public policies require a specific pattern of interacting interest organizations. Some of the chapters are drawn from material collected in a large comparative project on the organization of business interests in four sectors across ten countries, and, at least for that interest category, the results are likely to deepen our understanding of what factors account for observed differences in associational patterns (Schmitter and Streeck (forthcoming)).

The question of the state
There is still, as evidenced by these essays and in the companion volumes to follow (see the Preface to this book), a lively discussion about the concept of corporatism itself, and about what is not corporatism; but it is equally clear that the different approaches have not hindered empirical study. Indeed, there is good reason to believe that corporatism, like other concepts in political inquiry, such as power, is 'essentially contestable' (Lukes, 1979; Gray, 1983). Disputes over meanings will never be settled once and for all, because they cannot be separated from the political struggles which they interpret. A conflict-free social science presupposes the transcendence of politics itself (Connolly, 1983: 227), which is neither possible nor desirable. What can be claimed with some confidence is that theoretical progress is a dialectical process of interrogating the real world through abstract conceptions of it, and a deeper understanding of political processes and a greater conceptual clarity, may be obtained without any presumption of a theoretical 'final solution' or 'last instance'.

There is, however, some *convergence* of meaning within the writings of those who study neo-corporatism, and a common recognition of the significance of the organizational dimension in the study of politics, especially in respect of the relationships of interest categories to the state system. The latter remains relatively little elaborated in the corporatist literature, and future research will have to pay a great deal more attention than hitherto to the issue of intra-organizational relationships *within* the state system. Even at this stage, however, it is possible to draw two inferences from the corporatist literature which are crucial for the development of state theory. The first is that different parts of the state system — bureaus, ministries, commissions — at different levels — central or federal, regional, local — interact with social organizations in a variety of different ways, and as yet we know little about how these interactions are affected by the structures and activities of different parts of the state system. We do however know enough to reject the assumption that there is some mystical 'essential unity' within the state which gives it a power beyond its organizational capacity to marshall overt or latent coercion. The second vital dimension which a corporatist perspective on state–society interactions adds to a theory of the state is the recognition that state systems cannot be understood solely in terms of their internal characteristics, their public policy goals or the external pressures upon them. Corporatism forces a study of *relationships* and interactive exchanges, and suggests that state theory may be enriched by the systematic empirical study of these processes.

Corporatist interest intermediation is *one* possible form that the relationship between state structures and political interests may take. Other forms expressed in ideal-typical terms (Cawson, 1982, chapter 5) include bureaucracy and the market, and we should expect actual examples of policy processes to combine these elements in different degrees. Moreover, meso-level corporatism seems to be not only qualitatively significant (in terms of the power of the organizations involved and the impact of the policies negotiated), but also increasingly resorted to (especially in the field of industrial policy) as public authorities attempt to grapple with the deficiencies of the market and the rigidities of bureaucratic structures.

Earlier chapters in this book provide some important clues to the 'state factor' in corporatist arrangements, and hint at the potential contribution that corporatist theory has to make to more general theories of the state in capitalist democracies. In chapter 6 Coleman discusses the important finding that relatively authoritarian modes of state intervention — comparable to those discussed under the heading of 'state corporatism' in the earlier literature (Schmitter, 1974) — can be found even in apparently pluralistic market-oriented polities. Coleman suggests some of the external conditions which might precipitate such interventions at a sectoral level, but there remains scope for further investigation of the conditions under which such coercive capacity can be organized, and the issue of what interests can be attributed to state systems at different levels. It seems a persuasive argument that an important prerequisite within the state system is its centralization and differentiation, but these processes themselves require explanation.

One possibility suggested by Badie and Birnbaum (1983), the implications of which in the British case are discussed in Burgi's chapter (chapter 7), is that different degrees of state autonomy are related to the particular historical pattern of the resistance to economic modernization, by which they mean the penetration of capitalism. They suggest implicitly a continuum between societies which developed strong state forms (their ideal type is France) and those in which there were relatively few resistances, where a strong state was unnecessary (Britain and the USA). Applying these arguments to the specific issue of corporatism, Birnbaum (1982b) suggests that corporatism is impossible in societies where the state is either too weak or too strong.

Corporatism seems to require a state system which is strong enough to preserve its autonomy from societal interests, yet not strong enough for an independent conception of a transcendent interest to be enforced upon society in a directive mode without the participation of interest organizations. It may be useful to envisage this in the form of a continuum:

Strong	State	Societal	Weak
state $\longrightarrow$	corporatism $\longrightarrow$	corporatism $\longrightarrow$	state

where the underlying variable is the degrees of autonomy of the state. If we apply this idea to the macro-level within capitalist democracies (although the idea may be useful for non-capitalist systems as well), we find that countries such as France are to the left of the corporatist part of the continuum; countries such as Britain, France and the USA, with weakly differentiated state systems, are to be found at the right-hand end. If we apply it at the meso-level, however, we find a more complex pattern, with considerable variations in autonomy (from sectoral interests) on the part of different state agencies (Pitt and Smith, 1981), and thus no necessary correspondence between the incidence of meso-corporatism and that of macro-corporatism.

Moreover, evidence from policy-making in specific sectors seems at least partially to contradict the Badie–Birnbaum thesis of a state sufficiently strong to remove the need for corporatist intervention. The French state has shown some weakness in its industrial policy, as Rhodes (chapter 10 above) points out with respect to the steel industry, and as Estrin and Holmes (1983a; 1983b) emphasize with respect to planning agreements. Only if we concentrate on the *macro-level* is corporatism invisible in France; sectoral corporatist policies at meso- and micro-levels have been pursued, and as elsewhere the agricultural sector is strongly meso-corporatist (Keeler, 1981).

Leo Panitch (1979a: 124–5) alleged that corporatist theory is deficient in its lack of a rigorous theory of the state. Some alternative approaches make up in rigour what they lack in plausibility or empirical application and progress will always be something of a compromise. It may be doubted that there is a theory of *the* state, when the patterns of state intervention are so diverse, even within a single country. The need is for state theory to comprehend the coexistence of corporatist practices and competitive pressures, and the complex interplay of levels, sectors and classes, and this cannot be met without a theory of corporatism. Conversely, a concept which is defined in terms of a relationship between the state and organized interests cannot but give equal emphasis to both sides of the relationship. We need both state theory *and* corporatist theory, and this book represents a modest contribution to that goal.

References

Adams, Roy J. (1982) 'The Federal Government and Tripartism', *Industrial Relations*, 37 (4): 606–16.

Adams, W. and Brock, J.W. (1983–84) 'Countervailing or Coalescing Power? The Problem of Labor/Management Coalitions', *Journal of Post-Keynesian Economics*, 6 (2): 180–97.

Addison, John (1979) *Wage Policies and Collective Bargaining Developments in Finland, Ireland and Norway*. Paris: Organization for Economic Cooperation and Development.

Alchian, Armen A. (1973) *The Economics of Charity*. London: Institute of Economic Affairs.

Alexis, M. (1983) 'Neo-Corporatism and Industrial Relations: The Case of German Trade Unions', *West European Politics*, 6 (1): 75–92.

Allen, V.L. (1981) *The Militancy of British Miners*. Shipley: The Moor Press.

Almond, G.A. (1983) 'Corporatism, Pluralism and Professional Memory', *World Politics*, 35: 245–60.

Anderson, Charles W. (1977) 'Political Design and the Representation of Interests', *Comparative Political Studies*, 10: 127–52.

Anderson, Charles W. (1978) 'The Logic of Public Problems: Evaluation in Comparative Policy Research', pp. 287–327 in D.E. Ashford (ed.), *Comparing Public Policies*. Beverly Hills and London: Sage Publications.

Ashford, Nigel (1984) 'Intellectual Sources of Economic Policy: Thatcher and Reagan'. Paper presented to European Consortium for Political Research Workshops, Salzburg.

ASSIDER (1980) 'Prospettive e problemi della siderurgia italiana'. Unpublished paper. Rome: ASSIDER.

AUEW/TASS (1982) *TASS on Training*. Richmond: AUEW/TASS.

Badie, B. and Birnbaum, P. (1983) *The Sociology of the State*. Chicago and London: University of Chicago Press.

Bain, T. (1983) 'German Co-determination and Employment Adjustment in the Steel and Auto Industries', *Columbia Journal of World Business*. 18 (2): 40–7.

Balogh, Thomas (1970) *Labour and Inflation*, Fabian Tract 403. London: Fabian Society.

Barichello, Richard B. (1981) *The Economics of Canadian Dairy Industry Regulation*. Ottawa: Economic Council of Canada.

Barisi, G. (1982) *Relations collectives de travail et stratégies des acteurs sociaux dans la sidérurgie à participation d'Etat en Italie (1868–1982)*. Thèse de troisième cycle. Université de Paris VII.

Barisi, G. (1984) 'Informatique, relations sociales, contrôle ouvrier', *Travail*, 4: 36–40.

Barnett, Joel (1982) *Inside the Treasury*, London: André Deutsch.

Barry, Brian and Hardin, Russell (eds) (1982) *Rational Man and Irrational Society?* Beverly Hills and London: Sage Publications.

Batstone, Eric (1985) 'Bureaucracy and Shop Steward Organization in the Depression' in O. Jacobi et al., *Technological Change, Rationalization and Industrial Relations*. London: Croom Helm.

227

BEC (1957, 1958) *Annual Report*. London: British Employers' Confederation.

Bedarida, F. (1977) 'Le socialisme en Grande Bretagne', in J. Droz (ed.), *Histoire générale du socialisme, Vol. III*. Paris: Presses Universitaires Francaises.

Beer, S.H. (1969) *Modern British Politics*, 2nd ed. London: Faber and Faber.

Berger, S. (1981) 'Introduction', in S. Berger (ed.), *Organizing Interests in Western Europe: Pluralism, Corporatism and the Transformation of Politics*. Cambridge: Cambridge University Press.

Berger, S. and Piore, M. (1980) *Dualism and Discontinuity in Industrial Societies*. Cambridge: Cambridge University Press.

Birnbaum, P. (1982a) *La Logique de l'Etat*. Paris: Fayard.

Birnbaum, P. (1982b) 'The State Versus Corporatism', *Politics and Society*, 11 (4): 477–501.

Blair, E.H. (1976) 'Wherein It is Argued that Regulators are Threatening and Inhibiting Science', *New York Times*, 17 January: 252.

Blair, E.H. and Hoerger, F.D. (1976) 'Toxic Substances Legislation — Regulators vs. Science', *Environmental Policy and Law*, 2 (2/3): 133–40.

Bolton Committee (1971) *Report of the Committee of Inquiry on Small Firms*, Cmnd 4811. London: HMSO.

Bonnechère, M. (1979) 'Le contrôle par les travailleurs des restructurations et leurs conséquences sur l'emploi', *Revue de Droit Ouvrier*, August: 273–92.

Booth, Alan (1985) 'Liberal Strategies and Corporatist Structures in Britain 1945–83'. Paper presented to a conference on 'Economic Crisis and the Politics of Industrial Relations', King's College, Cambridge.

Bosanquet, Nick (1983) *After the New Right*. London: Heinemann Educational Books.

Boston, Jonathan (1983) 'The Theory and Practice of Voluntary Incomes Policies With Particular Reference to the British Labour Government's Social Contract, 1974–1979'. DPhil. thesis, University of Oxford.

Boy, L. and Pirovano, A. (1983) 'Dirigisme privé et dirigisme public dans l'industrie sidérurgique', pp. 16–73 in TAPSES, *Siderurgie et Droit de Crise*. Paris: Presses Universitaires de France.

Brickman, R., Jasonoff, S. and Ilgen, T. (1982) *Chemical Regulation and Cancer: A Cross-national Study of Policy and Politics*. Ithaca, NY: Cornell University Press.

British Institute of Management (1980) *Skilled Manpower and Training Policies: A Management View*. London: BIM.

Brittan, Samuel and Lilley, Peter (1977) *The Delusion of Incomes Policy*. London: Temple Smith.

Broda, J. et al. (1978) 'Crise de la siderurgie et recomposition du procès de travail: la sous-traitance à la Solmer', *Sociologie du Travail*, 4: 423–47.

Brown, William (1979) 'Engineering Wages and the Social Contract, 1975–77', *Oxford Bulletin of Economics and Statistics*, 41: 51–61.

Buchan, J. (1983) 'Limits to Benefits of Steel Rationalization', *Financial Times*, 4 May.

Buckley, Peter and Casson, Mark (1976) *The Future of the Multinational Enterprise*. New York: Holmes and Meier.

Buksti, J.A. and Johansen, L.N. (1979) 'Variations in Organizational Participation in Government', *Scandinavian Political Studies*, 3: 197–220.

Bundesminister des Inneren unt Umweltbundesamt (1980) *Act on Protection Against Dangerous Substances (Chemicals Act) of 16 September 1980*. Federal Law Gazette I: 1718.

Bundesminister für Inneren (1982) *Bericht der Bundesrepublik Deutschland zur Umweltpolitik* (Report on the Environmental Policy of the Federal Republic of Germany). Bonn: Bundesminister fir Inneren.

Caloia, A. (1979) 'Industrial Relations in Italy: Problems and Perspectives', *British Journal of Industrial Relations*, 17 (2): 259–67.

Canada, Industry, Trade and Commerce (1979) *Health Care Products Industry*. Ottawa: Supply and Services Canada.

Castle, Barbara (1980) *The Castle Diaries 1974–76*. London: Weidenfeld and Nicolson.

Cawson, A. (1982) *Corporatism and Welfare: Social Policy and State Intervention in Britain*. London: Heinemann Educational Books.

Cawson, A. (1983) 'Functional Representation and Democratic Politics: Towards a Corporatist Democracy?' in G. Duncan (ed.), *Democratic Theory and Practice*. Cambridge: Cambridge University Press.

Cawson, A. (1985) 'Is There a Corporatist Theory of the State?' in G. Duncan and R. Alford (eds), *Democratic Theory and the Capitalist State*. Cambridge: Cambridge University Press.

Cawson, A. and Ballard, J. (1984) 'A Bibliography of Corporatism'. Florence: European University Institute Working Paper no. 115, October.

Cawson, A. and Saunders, P. (1983) 'Corporatism, Competitive Politics and Class Struggle', in R. King (ed.), *Capital and Politics*. London: Routledge and Kegan Paul.

CBI (1968) Supplement to CBI Education and Training Bulletin. London: Confederation of British Industry (September).

CBI (1971) *Supplement to Education and Training Bulletin*. London: Confederation of British Industry (February).

Central Policy Review Staff (1980) *Education, Training and Industrial Performance*. London: HMSO.

Chester, Sir N. (1975) *The Nationalization of British Industry 1945–1951*. London: HMSO.

CIPI (1981) *Piano della siderurgia a partecipazione statale*. Rome: CIPI.

Cliche Commission (1974) *Commission de l'enquête sur l'exercice de la liberté syndicale, Rapport*. Québec: Editeur officiel.

Cohen, C.D. (1975) 'The Social Contract and the Standard of Living', *National Westminster Bank Quarterly Review*, August: 44–56.

Coleman, William D. (1984a) *The Independence Movement in Quebec, 1945–1980*. Toronto: University of Toronto Press.

Coleman, William D. (1984b) 'The Political Organization of Business Interests in the Canadian Construction Industry'. Berlin: International Institute of Management Discussion Paper, IIM/LMP 84–11.

Collard, David (1978) *Altruism and Economy: A Study of Non-selfish Economics*, Oxford: Martin Robertson.

Congdon, Tim (1982) *Monetary Control in Britain*. London: Macmillan.

Connolly, W.E. (1972) 'On "Interests" in Politics', *Politics and Society*, 2: 459–77.

Connolly, W.E. (1974) 'Theoretical Self-consciousness', in W.E. Connolly and G. Gordon (eds), *Social Structure and Political Theory*. Lexington, Mass.: D.C. Heath.

Connolly, W.E. (1983) *The Terms of Political Discourse* (2nd ed.). Oxford: Martin Robertson.

Cornwall, R. (1984) 'West German Steelmen Win 38-hour Week', *Financial Times*, 18 July.

Cox, A.W. (1981) 'Corporatism as Reductionism: The Analytic Limits of the Corporatist Thesis', *Government and Opposition*, 16 (1): 78–95.

Cox, A.W. and Hayward, J. (1983) 'The Inapplicability of the Corporatist Model in Britain and France: The Case of Labour', *International Political Science Review*, 4: 217–40.

Crouch, C. (1977) *Class Conflict and the Industrial Relations Crisis: Compromise and Corporatism in the Policies of the British State*. London: Heinemann Educational Books.

Crouch, C. (1982) *Trade Unions: The Logic of Collective Action*. London: Fontana.

Crouch, C. (1983a) 'Pluralism and the New Corporatism: A Rejoinder', *Political Studies*, 31 (3): 452–60.

Crouch, C. (1983b) 'New Thinking on Pluralism', *Political Quarterly*, 54: 363–74.

Dahmani, A. (1983) 'La sidérurgie: le poids de l'assistance permanente', pp. 121–56 in B. Bellon and J.–M. Chevalier (eds), *L'Industrie en France*. Paris: Flammarion.

Daniel, W.W. (1976) 'Wage Determination in Industry', *PEP Broadsheet*, 42 (563).

Daniel, W.W. and Millward, Neil (1983) *Workplace Industrial Relations in Britain*. London: Heinemann Educational Books.

De Rosa, L. (1978) 'La siderurgia italiana dalla ricostruzione al quinto centro siderurgico', *Richerche Storiche*, 8 (1): 161–88.

Department of Employment (1972) *Training for the Future*. London: HMSO.

Department of Employment (1973) *Employment and Training: Government Proposals*, Cmnd 5250. London: HMSO.

Department of Employment (1981) *A New Training Initiative*, Cmnd 8455. London: HMSO.

Department of Employment/MSC (1976) *Training for Vital Skills*. London: HMSO.

Diamant, Alfred (1981) 'Bureaucracy and Public Policy in Neo-corporatist Settings', *Comparative Politics*, 14 (1): 104–24.

Dolzer, Rudolf (1982) 'Verwaltungsermessen und Verwaltungskontrolle in den Vereinigten Staaten', *Die öffentliche Verwaltung*, 14: 578–90.

Donovan Commission (1968) *Report of the Royal Commission on Trade Unions and Employers Associations*, Cmnd 3623. London: HMSO.

Dorfman, Gerald A. (1983) *British Trade Unionism Against the Trade Union Congress*. London: Macmillan.

Dudley, G. (1983) 'The Road Lobby: A Declining Force?' pp. 104–28 in D. Marsh (ed.), *Pressure Politics: Interest Groups in Britain*. London: Junction Books.

Dunleavy, P. (1979) 'The Urban Bases of Political Alignment: Social Class, Domestic Property Ownership and State Intervention in Consumption Processes', *British Journal of Political Science*, 9 (4): 409–43.

Dunleavy, P. (1980a) 'Some Political Implications of Sectoral Cleavages and the Growth of State Employment', *Political Studies*, 28: 364–83 and 527–49.

Dunleavy, P. (1980b) *Urban Political Analysis: The Politics of Collective Consumption*, London: Macmillan.

Dyson, K. (1983) 'West Germany: The Search for a Rationalist Consensus', in J.J. Richardson (ed.), *Policy Styles in Western Europe*. London: Allen and Unwin.

Dyson, K. (1984) 'The Politics of Corporate Crises in West Germany', *West European Politics*, 7 (1): 24–46.

Eisenhammer, J. and Rhodes, M. (1985) 'The Politics of Public Sector Steel in Italy: From the "Economic Miracle" to the Crisis of the 'Eighties', in Y. Meny and V. Wright (eds), *The Politics of Steel: The European Community and the Steel Industry in the Crisis Years (1974–1984)*. Berlin: De Gruyter/European University Institute.

Erbes-Seguin, S. and Volz, R. (1979) *Les syndicats face à l'évolution économique en Allemagne Fédérale et en France.* CNRS–Université de Paris VII, Groupe de sociologie du travail.

Esser, J. and Fach, W. (1981) 'Korporatistische Krisenregulierung im "Modell Deutschland"', pp. 158–79 in U. Von Alemann (ed.), *NeoKorporatismus.* Frankfurt: Campus Verlag.

Esser, J. and Vath, W. (1985) 'Overcoming the Steel Crisis in the Federal Republic of Germany', in Y. Meny and V. Wright (eds), *The Politics of Steel: The European Community and the Steel Industry in the Crisis Years (1974–1984).* Berlin: De Gruyter/European University Institute.

Estrin, S. and Holmes, P.M. (1983a) *French Planning in Theory and Practice,* London: Allen and Unwin.

Estrin, S. and Holmes, P.M. (1983b) 'The Role of Planning Contracts in the Conduct of French Industrial Policy'. University of Southampton: Discussion Papers in Economics and Econometrics, no. 8402.

Ferraresi, F. (1983) 'The Institutional Transformations of the Post-Laissez-faire State: Reflections on the Italian Case', in S. Clegg, G. Dow and P. Boreham (eds), *The State, Class and the Recession.* London: Croom Helm.

Fine, B., O'Donnell, K. and Prevezer, M. (1983) 'Coal After Nationalization'. University of London, Birkbeck College Discussion Paper no. 138.

Flanagan, Robert, Soskice, David and Ulman, Lloyd (1983) *Unionism, Stabilization and Incomes Policies.* Washington, DC: Brookings Institution.

Freedman, James O. (1978) *Crisis and Legitimacy: The Administrative Process and American Government.* Cambridge, Mass.: Harvard University Press.

Freyssenet, M. (1979) *La sidérurgie française, 1945–1979: L'histoire d'une faillité, les solutions qui s'affrontent.* Paris: Savelli.

Friedland, R. (1982) *Power and Crisis in the City: Corporations, Unions and Urban Policy,* London: Macmillan.

Friedman, Milton (1977) *Inflation and Unemployment: The New Dimensions of Politics.* London: Institute of Economic Affairs.

Galbraith, John Kenneth (1978) 'On Post Keynesian Economics', *Journal of Post Keynesian Economics,* 1 (1): 8–11.

Gallie, D. (1980) 'Trade Union Ideology and Workers' Conceptions of Class Inequality in France', *West European Politics,* 3 (1): 10–32.

Gamble, Andrew (1974) *The Conservative Nation.* London: Routledge and Kegan Paul.

Gaynor, Kevin (1977) 'The Toxic Substances Control Act: A Regulatory Morass', *Vanderbilt Law Review,* 30 (6): 1149–95.

Giles, F.W. (1969) 'Training After the Act', *Personal Management,* 12: 20–6.

Goldthorpe, J. (1984) 'The End of Convergence: Corporatism and Dualist Tendencies in Modern Western Societies', in J. Goldthorpe (ed.), *Order and Conflict in Contemporary Capitalism: Studies in the Political Economy of Western European Nations.* Oxford: Oxford University Press.

Goodhart, C.A.E. (1984) *Monetary Theory and Practice.* London: Macmillan.

Gordon, Myron J. and Fowler, David J. (1981) *The Drug Industry: A Case Study of the Effects of Foreign Control on the Canadian Economy.* Toronto: James Lorimer.

Gourc, G. and Gourc, J. (1981) 'La structuration de la sidérurgie dans les usines performantes: La Solmer à Fos-sur-Mer', *Critiques de l'Economie Politique,* 15/16: 135–84.

Gourdet, C. (1983) 'Une forme spécifique de financement de la sidérurgie: les prêts participatifs', pp. 77–103 in TAPSES, *Sidérurgie et Droit de Crise*. Paris: Presses Universitaires de France.

Grant, W.P. (1982) *The Political Economy of Industrial Policy*. London: Butterworths.

Grant, W.P. (1983a) 'Gotta Lotta Bottle: Corporatism, the Public and the Private and the Milk Marketing System in Britain'. *Sussex Working Papers in Corporatism*, no. 3, April.

Grant, W.P. (1983b) 'The Organization of Business Interests in the UK Chemical Industry'. Berlin: International Institute of Management Discussion Paper IIM/LMP 83–25.

Grant, W.P. (1984) 'Is Corporatism Necessarily Interventionist? A Discussion of the Thatcher Government in Britain'. Paper presented to a conference on 'The Standestaat in Historical and International Perspective'. Salzburg: Ludwig-Boltzmann Institute.

Grassini, F.A. (1980) 'Vincoli politici e direzione delle imprese pubbliche nell'esperienza italiana', *L'Industria*, 1 (3).

Gray, J. (1983) 'Political Power, Social Theory and Essential Contestability', in D. Miller and L. Seidentrop (eds), *The Nature of Political Theory*. Oxford: Oxford University Press.

Green, D. (1983) 'Strategic Management and the State: France', pp. 161–92 in K. Dyson and S. Wilks (eds), *Industrial Crisis: A Comparative Study of the State and Industry*. Oxford: Martin Robertson.

Gusman, S. (1982) 'Implementing the US Toxic Substances Control Act — An Interim Report', *Zeitschrift für Umweltpolitik*, 4 (2): 161–9.

Gusman, S., Moltke, K., Irwin, F. and Whitehead, C. (1980) *Public Policy for Chemicals: National and International Issues*. Washington, DC: The Conservation Foundations.

Haines, Joe (1977) *The Politics of Power*. London: Jonathan Cape.

Hall, S. and Jacques, M. (1983) *The Politics of Thatcherism*. London: Lawrence and Wishart.

Harrison, M.L. (1984) 'Corporatism, Incorporation and the Welfare State' pp. 17–40 in M.L. Harrison (ed.), *Corporatism and the Welfare State*. Aldershot: Gower.

Hartkopf, G. and Bohne, E. (1983) *Grundlagen der Umweltpolitik*. Opladen: Westdeutscher Verlag.

Hayward, J. (1974) 'Steel', pp. 255–71 in R. Vernon (ed.), *Big Business and the State: Changing Relations in Western Europe*. London: Macmillan.

Hébert, Gérald (1977) *Labour Relations in the Quebec Construction Industry*. Part I: *The System of Labour Relations*. Ottawa: Economic Council of Canada.

Held, D. and Krieger, J. (1984) 'Theories of the State: Some Competing Claims', in S. Bornstein, D. Held and J. Krieger (eds), *The State in Capitalist Europe*. London: Allen and Unwin.

Hennert, J.-F. (1982) *A Theory of Multinational Enterprise*. Ann Arbor: University of Michigan Press.

Hiscocks, G.A. (1981) 'Review of the Canadian Dairy Commission: Background, Creation, Policy and Operations', Appendix 15 in *Report of the Commission of Inquiry into Certain Allegations Concerning Commercial Practices of the Canadian Dairy Commission*. Ottawa: Supply and Services Canada.

HMSO (1980) *Monetary Control*, Cmnd 7858. London: HMSO.

Holland, S. (1975) *The Socialist Challenge*. London: Quartet Books.

Jackman, R. and Layard, R. (1982) 'An Inflation Tax', *Fiscal Studies*, 3 (March): 47–59.

Jacobi, O., Jessop, B., Kastendiek, H. and Regini, M. (eds) (1985) *Technological Change, Rationalization and Industrial Relations*. London: Croom Helm.

Jenkins, C. (1978) *Power at the Top: A Critical Study of Nationalized Industries*. London:

Jenkins, C. and Mortimer, J.E. (1965) *British Trade Unions Today*. London: Pergamon.

Jessop, Bob (1979) 'Corporatism, Parliamentarism and Social Democracy', in P.C. Schmitter and G. Lehmbruch (eds), *Trends Toward Corporatist Intermediation*. Beverly Hills and London: Sage Publications.

Jessop, Bob (1980) 'The Transformation of the State in Post-War Britain', pp. 23–93 in R. Scase (ed.), *The State in Western Europe*. London: Croom Helm.

Jessop, Bob (1982a) *The Capitalist State*. Oxford: Martin Robertson.

Jessop, Bob (1982b) 'Stages of Monetarism and the Prospects for a Monetarist Corporatism'. Unpublished paper, University of Essex Department of Government.

Jessop, Bob (1983) 'Accumulation Strategies, State Forms and Hegemonic Projects', *Kapitalistate*, 10/11: 89–111.

Jessop, Bob, Bonnett, Kevin, Bromley, Simon and Ling, Tom (1984) 'Authoritarian Populism, Two Nations and Thatcherism', *New Left Review*, 147, September/October.

Johansen, C.M. and Kristensen, O.P. (1982) 'Corporatist Traits in Denmark 1946–1976', in G. Lehmbruch and P.C. Schmitter (eds), *Patterns of Corporatist Policy-Making*. Beverly Hills and London: Sage Publications.

Johnson, N. (1978) 'The Public Corporation: An Ambiguous Species', in D. Butler and A.H. Halsey (eds), *Policy and Politics: Essays in Honour of Norman Chester*. London: Macmillan.

Jordan, A.G. (1983) 'Corporatism: The Unity and Utility of the Concept', *Strathclyde Papers on Government and Politics*, no. 13.

Jowell, J. (1977) 'Bargaining in Development Control', *Journal of Planning and Environment Law*: 414–33.

Katzenstein, Peter (1978) 'Conclusion', pp. 306–23 in P. Katzenstein (ed.), *Between Power and Plenty: Foreign Economic Policies of Advanced Industrial States*. Madison, Wisconsin: University of Wisconsin Press.

Keegan, William (1984) *Mrs Thatcher's Economic Experiment*. London: Allen Lane.

Keegan, William and Pennant-Rea, Rupert (1979) *Who Runs the British Economy?* London: Temple Smith.

Keeler, J.T.S. (1981) 'Corporatism and Official Union Hegemony: The Case of French Agricultural Syndicalism', in S. Berger (ed.), *Organizing Interests in Western Europe: Pluralism, Corporatism and the Transformation of Politics*. Cambridge: Cambridge University Press.

Kennedy, J., Donnelly, E. and Reid, M. (1979) *Manpower Training and Development* (2nd ed.). London: Institute of Personnel Management.

Keys, B.A. and Caskie, D.F. (1975) *The Structure and Operation of the Construction Industry in Canada*. Ottawa: Economic Council of Canada.

Kriesi, Hanspeter (1983) 'Regional Differentiation of the Associational System in the Construction Sector in Switzerland'. Unpublished paper, Zurich.

Kurth, James (1979) 'The Political Consequences of the Product Cycle: Industrial History and Political Outcomes', *International Organization*, 33 (1): 1–34.

Laidler, David and Parkin, Michael (1975) 'Inflation: A Survey', *Economic Journal*, 85: 741–809.

Lapalombara, J. (1964) *Interest Groups in Italian Politics*. Princeton, NJ: Princeton University Press.

Latham, Earl (1964) 'The Group Basis of Politics: Notes for a Theory', pp. 32–57 in F. Munger and D. Price, *Political Parties and Pressure Groups*. New York: Crowell.

Laver, Michael (1980) 'The Great British Wage Game', *New Society*, 6 March: 495–6.

Laver, Michael (1981) *The Politics of Private Desires*. Harmondsworth: Penguin.

Layard, R. (1982) 'Is Incomes Policy the Answer to Unemployment?', *Economica*, 49: 219–39.

Lees, D. and Chiplin, B. (1970) 'The Economics of Industrial Training', *Lloyds Bank Review*, 96: 29–40.

Lehmbruch, G. (1979) 'Liberal Corporatism and Party Government', pp. 147–83 in P.C. Schmitter and G. Lehmbruch (eds), *Trends Toward Corporatist Intermediation*. Beverly Hills and London: Sage Publications.

Lehmbruch, G. (1982) 'Introduction: Neo-corporatism in Comparative Perspective', pp. 1–28 in G. Lehmbruch and P.C. Schmitter (eds), *Patterns of Corporatist Policy-Making*. Beverly Hills and London: Sage Publications.

Lehmbruch, G. (1984) 'The Logic and Structural Conditions of Neo-corporatist Concertation', in J.H. Goldthorpe (ed.), *Order and Conflict in Contemporary Capitalism: Studies in the Political Economy of Western European Nations*. Oxford University Press.

Leruez, J. (1972) *Planification et politique en Grande Bretagne, 1945–1971*. Paris: A. Collin and FNSP.

Leruez, J. (1975) *Economic Planning and Politics in Britain*. Oxford: Martin Robertson.

Levine, Robert A. (1980) 'Analyzing US Policy-Making', in C.R. Forster (ed.), *Comparative Public Policy and Citizen Participation*. New York: Pergamon.

Lévy, C. (1984) 'Crise des organisations syndicales et politiques patronales', *Travail*, 4: 28–32.

Liberati, T. (1981) 'Le condizioni dello sviluppo', *Quaderni dell'Economia dell'Acciaio*, Universita Bocconi/ASSIDER.

Locksley, Gareth (1983) 'Europe and the Electronics Industry', in David Marsh (ed.) *Capital and Politics in Western Europe*. London: Frank Cass.

Longstreth, F. (1979) 'The City, Industry and the State', in C. Crouch (ed.), *State and Economy in Contemporary Capitalism*. London: Croom Helm.

Lowi, T. (1979) *The End of Liberalism*, 2nd ed. New York: W.W. Norton.

Luce, Duncan R. and Raiffa, Howard (1957) *Games and Decisions: Introduction and Critical Survey*. New York: John Wiley.

Lukes, S. (1979) 'On the Relativity of Power', in S. Brown (ed.), *Philosophical Disputes in the Social Sciences*. Brighton: Harvester.

Lyon Caen, A. (1979) 'Le comité d'enterprise et la restructuration de l'enterprise', *Droit Social*, 4: 23–34.

MacDonald, I.D. (1969) 'CTC: Advisory or Executive Power?' *Personnel Management*, 6 (1): 34–7.

Macpherson, C.B. (1977) 'Do We Need a Theory of the State?' *Archives Européenes de Sociologie*, 18 (2): 223–44.

Magaziner, I. and Reich, R. (1982) *Minding America's Business*. New York: Random House.

Maital, Shlomo and Benjamini, Yael (1980) 'Inflation as Prisoner's Dilemma', *Journal of Post-Keynesian Economics*, 2 (Summer): 459–81.

Malles, Paul (1975) *Employment Insecurity and Industrial Relations in the Canadian Construction Industry*. Ottawa: Economic Council of Canada.

Marin, B. (1983) 'Organizing Interests by Interest Organizations: Associational Prerequisites of Cooperation in Austria', *International Political Science Review*, 4 (2): 197–216.

Martin, Andrew (1979) 'The Dynamics of a Keynesian Political Economy', in Colin Crouch (ed.), *State and Economy in Contemporary Capitalism*. London: Croom Helm.

Martin, R.M. (1980) *TUC: The Growth of a Pressure Group, 1868–1976*. Oxford: Clarendon Press.

Martin, R.M. (1983) 'Pluralism and the New Corporatism' *Political Studies*, 31 (1): 86–102.

Masi, A. (1985) 'Nuova Italsider-Taranto and the Steel Crisis: Problems, Innovations and Prospects', in Y. Meny and V. Wright (eds), *The Politics of Steel: The European Community and the Steel Industry in the Crisis Years (1974–1984)*. Berlin: De Gruyter/European University Institute.

Maurice, M. and Sellier, F. (1979) 'Societal Analysis of Industrial Relations between France and West Germany', *British Journal of Industrial Relations*, 17 (3): 323–6.

Mayhew, Ken (1981) 'Incomes Policy and the Private Sector', pp. 72–99 in J.L. Fallick and R.F. Elliott (eds), *Incomes Policies, Inflation and Relative Pay*. London: George Allen and Unwin.

Mayhew, Ken (1983) 'Traditional Incomes Policies', *Oxford Bulletin of Economics and Statistics*, 45: 15–32.

Mayntz, R. (1983) 'The Conditions of Effective Public Policy: A New Challenge for Policy Analysis', *Policy and Politics*, 11 (2): 123–43.

Mayntz, R. and Scharpf, F.W. (1975) *Policy-Making in the German Federal Bureaucracy*. Amsterdam: Elsevier.

McArthur, J.H. and Scott, B.R. (1970) *L'Industrie française face aux plans*. Paris: Editions de l'Organisation.

McRoberts K. and Postgate, Dale (1980) *Quebec: Social Change and Political Crisis*, 2nd ed. Toronto: McClelland and Stewart.

Messerlin, P. (1981) 'European Industrial Policies: The Steel Industry Case'. University of Sussex: Sussex European Research Centre.

Middlemas, R.K. (1979) *Politics in Industrial Society: The Experience of the British System Since 1911*. London: André Deutsch.

Middlemas, R.K. (1983) 'The Supremacy of Party', *New Statesman*, 10 and 17 June.

Miliband, R. (1969) *The State in Capitalist Society*. London: Weidenfeld and Nicolson.

Miliband, R. (1983) 'State Power and Class Interests', *New Left Review*, 138: 57–68.

Milward, H.B. and Francisco, R.A. (1983) 'Subsystem Politics and Corporatism in the United States', *Policy and Politics*, 11: 273–93.

Ministry of Labour (1962) *Industrial Training: Government Proposals*, Cmnd 1892. London: HMSO.

Ministry of Labour and National Service (1958) *Training for Skill*. London: HMSO.

Mitchell, Don (1975) *The Politics of Food*. Toronto: James Lorimer.

Moe, Terry (1980) *The Organization of Interests: Incentives and the Internal Dynamics of Political Interest Groups*. Chicago: University of Chicago Press.

Mohamed Salah, M.M. (1983) 'Aspects sociaux de la crise sidérurgique', in TAPSES, *Sidérurgie et Droit de Crise*. Paris: Presses Universitaires de France.

Moro, D. (1984) *Crisi e ristrutturazione dell'industria siderurgica italiana*. Varese: Giuffre Editore.

Morrison, H. (1933) *Socialisation and Transport*. London: Constable.

Mothé, D. (1983) 'What Prospects for Democracy at the Work Place?' *Telos*, 55: 95–104.

MSC (1974) *TSA: A Five Year Plan.* London: Manpower Services Commission.

MSC (1976) *Towards a Comprehensive Manpower Policy.* London: Manpower Services Commission.

MSC (1977a) *Review and Plan 1977.* London: Manpower Services Commission.

MSC (1977b) *Young People at Work.* London: Manpower Services Commission.

MSC (1977c) *Training for Skills: A Programme for Action.* London: Manpower Services Commission.

MSC (1980) *Outlook on Training: Review of the 1973 Employment and Training Act.* London: Manpower Services Commission.

MSC (1982) *Manpower Review.* London: Manpower Services Commission.

NATFHE/AACE (1983) *Adult Unemployment: A Discussion Paper.* London: College Hill Press.

NEDC (1981a) *Energy Task Force.* London: National Economic Development Committee, 81 (15), 27 February.

NEDC (1981b) *Energy Task Force.* London: National Economic Development Committee, 81 (59), 6 November.

NEDO (1975) *The Public Client and the Construction Industries* (Chairman D. Morell and K. Wood). London: National Economic Development Office.

NEDO (1976) *A Study of UK Nationalised Industries. Report to the Government from the National Economic Development Office.* London: National Economic Development Office.

OECD (1979) *The Case for Positive Adjustment Policies: A Compendium of OECD Documents.* Paris: Organization for Economic Co-operation and Development.

Offe, C. (1975) 'The Theory of the Capitalist State and the Problem of Policy Formation', in L. Lindberg, R. Alford, C. Crouch and C. Offe (eds), *Stress and Contradiction in Modern Capitalism: Public Policy and the Theory of the State.* Lexington, Mass.: D.C. Heath.

Offe, C. (1981) 'The Attribution of Public Status to Interest Groups: Observations on the West German Case', pp. 123–58 in S. Berger (ed.), *Organizing Interests in Western Europe: Pluralism, Corporatism and the Transformation of Politics.* Cambridge: Cambridge University Press.

Offe, C. (1983) 'The Capitalist State', *Political Studies*, 31: 668–72.

Offe, C. and Wiesenthal, H. (1979) 'Two Logics of Collective Action: Theoretical Notes on Social Class and Organizational Form', *Political Power and Social Theory*, 1: 67–115.

Oheix, G. (1979) 'L'information du comité d'enterprise en cas de licenciement collectif', *Droit Social*, 4: 49–57.

Olsen, Johan P. (1981) 'Integrated Participation in Governmental Policy-making', pp. 492–515 in P.C. Nystrom and W.H. Starbuck (eds), *Handbook of Organizational Design*, Vol. 2. Oxford: Oxford University Press.

Olson, Mancur (1965) *The Logic of Collective Action: Public Goods and the Theory of Groups.* Cambridge, Mass.: Harvard University Press.

Olson, Mancur (1982) *The Rise and Decline of Nations: Economic Growth, Stagflation and Social Rigidities*, New Haven: Yale University Press.

Oswald, Andrew (1980) 'Wages, Trade Unions and the Welfare Economics of Incomes Policy'. Oxford: Institute of Economics and Statistics, University of Oxford.

Padioleau, J.G. (1981) *Quand la France s'enferre: la politique sidérurgique de la France depuis 1945.* Paris: Presses Universitaires de France.

Page, G.T. (1967) *The Industrial Training Act and After.* London: André Deutsch.

Pakradouni, P. (1984) 'Une négociation peu ordinaire', *Travail*, 4: 28–32.

Panitch, L. (1976) *Social Democracy and Industrial Militancy: The Labour Party, The Trade Unions and Incomes Policy*. Cambridge: Cambridge University Press.

Panitch, L. (1979a) 'The Development of Corporatism in Liberal Democracies', in P.C. Schmitter and G. Lehmbruch (eds), *Trends Toward Corporatist Intermediation*. Beverly Hills and London: Sage Publications.

Panitch, L. (1979b) 'Corporatism in Canada?' *Studies in Political Economy*, 1: 43–92.

Panitch, L. (1980) 'Recent Theorizations of Corporatism: Reflections on a Growth Industry', *British Journal of Sociology*, 31 (2): 159–87.

Panitch, L. (1981) 'Trade Unions and the Capitalist State', *New Left Review*, 125: 21–44.

Parker, J. (1947) *Labour Marches On*. West Drayton, Middlesex: Penguin Books.

Parkin, F. (1979) *Marxism and Class Theory: A Bourgeois Critique*. London: Tavistock Publications.

Pearson, L. (1981) *The Organisation of the Energy Industry*. London: Macmillan.

Pempel, T.J. and Tsunekawa, K. (1979) 'Corporatism Without Labour? The Japanese Anomaly', pp. 213–30 in P.C. Schmitter and G. Lehmbruch (eds), *Trends Toward Corporatist Intermediation*. Beverly Hills and London: Sage Publications.

Perry, P.J.C. (1976) *The Evolution of British Manpower Policy*. Portsmouth: BACIE.

Phelps, Edmund S. (ed.) (1975) *Altruism, Morality and Economic Theory*. New York: Russell Sage.

Pitt, D.C. and Smith, B.C. (1981) *Government Departments: An Organizational Perspective*. London: Routledge and Kegan Paul.

PMAC (n.d.) *Code of Marketing Practice*. Ottawa: Pharmaceutical Manufacturers Association of Canada.

Pollard, S. (1982) *The Wasting of the British Economy*. London: Croom Helm.

Polsby, Nelson (1971) *Congress and the Presidency*. Englewood Cliffs, NJ: Prentice-Hall.

Poulantzas, N. (1973) *Political Power and Social Classes*, London: New Left Books.

Prewitt, K. and Verba, S. (1977) *An Introduction to American Government*, rev. 2nd ed. New York: Harper.

Radcliffe Committee (1960) *Principal Memoranda of Evidence Submitted to the Committee on the Workings of the Monetary System*, Vol. 2. London: HMSO.

Rand Smith, W. (1984) 'Dynamics of Plural Unionism in France: The CGT, CFDT and Industrial Conflict', *British Journal of Industrial Relations*, 22 (1): 15–33.

Reade, E. (1982) 'Section 52 and Corporatism in Planning', *Journal of Planning and Environment Law*: 8–16.

Rees, T.L. and Atkinson, P. (eds) (1982) *Youth Unemployment and State Intervention*. London: Routledge and Kegan Paul.

Regini, M. (1982) 'Changing Relationships Between Labour and the State in Italy', pp. 109–32 in G. Lehmbruch and P.C. Schmitter (eds), *Patterns of Corporatist Policy-Making*. Beverly Hills and London: Sage Publications.

Regini, M. (1983) 'The Crisis of Representation in Class-oriented Unions: Some Reflections Based on the Italian Case', pp. 129–51 in S. Clegg, G. Dow and P. Boreham (eds), *The State, Class and the Recession*, London: Croom Helm.

Rehbinder, Eckard (1981) 'Control of Environmental Chemicals under the Law of the Federal Republic of Germany', in H. Steiger (ed.), *Environmental Law and Chemical Substances*, Second European Symposium on Environmental Law, Giessen. Berlin: E. Schmidt Verlag.

Reynolds, Joel (1977) 'The Toxic Substances Control Act of 1976: An Introductory Background and Analysis', *Columbia Journal of Environmental Law*, 4 (1): 35–96.

Ridley, F. (n.d.) 'The Job Creation Programme: Administrative Problems of Implementation'. Paper presented to European Consortium for Political Research Workshops, University of Essex.

Riegert, Robert A. (1967) *Das amerikanische Administrative Law*. Berlin: Duncker and Humbolt.

Roche, W.K. (1982) 'Social Partnership and Political Control: State Strategy and Industrial Relations in Ireland', in M. Kelly, L. O'Dowd and J. Wickham (eds), *Power, Conflict and Equality*. Dublin: Turoe Press.

Rose, Joseph B. (1980) *Public Policy, Bargaining Structure and the Construction Industry*. Toronto: Butterworths.

Rugman, Alan (1981) *Inside the Multinationals*. New York: Columbia University Press.

Salisbury, R.H. (1979) 'Why No Corporatism in America?', pp. 213–30 in P.C. Schmitter and G. Lehmbruch (eds), *Trends Toward Corporatist Intermediation*. Beverly Hills and London: Sage Publications.

Sargent, Jane (1983) 'The Politics of the Pharmaceutical Price Regulation Scheme'. Berlin: International Institute of Management Discussion Paper IIM/LMP 83–13.

Saunders, C., Mukherjee, S., Marsden, D. and Donaldson, A. (1977) 'Winners and Losers: Pay Patterns in the 1970s', *PEP Broadsheet*, 43 (570).

Scase, R. and Goffee, R. (1980) *The Real World of the Small Business Owner*. London: Croom Helm.

Scase, R. and Goffee, R. (1982) *The Entrepreneurial Middle Class*. London: Croom Helm.

Schain, M. (1980) 'Corporatism and Industrial Relations in France', in P. Cerny and M. Schain (eds), *French Politics and Public Policy*. London: Methuen.

Scharpf, F. (1970) *Die politischen Kosten des Rechtsstaates*. Tübingen: Mohr.

Scharpf, F. (1984) 'Economic and Institutional Constraints of Full-employment Strategies: Sweden, Austria and West Germany, 1973–1982' in J.H. Goldthorpe (ed.), *Order and Conflict in Contemporary Capitalism*. Oxford: Clarendon.

Schindler, P. (ed.) (1979) *30 Jahre Bundestag: Dokumentation, Statistik, Daten*. Bonn: Presse und informationsamt.

Schmidt, M.G. (1982) 'Does Corporatism Matter? Economic Crisis, Politics and Rates of Unemployment in Capitalist Democracies in the 1970s', in G. Lehmbruch and P.C. Schmitter (eds), *Patterns of Corporatist Policy-Making*. Beverly Hills and London: Sage Publications.

Schmitter, P.C. (1974) 'Still the Century of Corporatism?' *Review of Politics* 36 (1) 85–131; reprinted as pp. 7–72 in P.C. Schmitter and G. Lehmbruch (eds), *Trends Toward Corporatist Intermediation*. Beverly Hills and London: Sage Publications, 1979.

Schmitterr, P.C. (1977) 'Modes of Interest Intermediation and Models of Societal Change in Western Europe', *Comparative Political Studies*, 10: 7–38; reprinted as pp. 63–94 of P.C. Schmitter and G. Lehmbruch (eds), *Trends Toward Corporatist Intermediation*. Beverly Hills and London: Sage Publications, 1979.

Schmitter, P.C. (1981) 'Interest Intermediation and Regime Governability in Contemporary Western Europe and North America' in S. Berger (ed.), *Organizing Interests in Western Europe: Pluralism, Corporatism and the Transformation of Politics*. Cambridge: Cambridge University Press.

Schmitter, P.C. (1982) 'Reflections on Where the Theory of Neo-corporatism Has Gone and Where the Praxis of Neo-corporatism May be Going', in G. Lehmbruch and P.C. Schmitter (eds), *Patterns of Corporatist Policy-Making*. Beverly Hills and London: Sage Publications.

Schmitter, P.C. (1983) '"Neo-Corporatism", "Consensus", "Governability" and "Democracy" in the Management of Crisis in Contemporary Advanced Industrial/Capitalist Societies'. Paper presented to OECD Expert Group on 'Collective Bargaining and Economic Policies', Paris.

Schmitter, P.C. (1984) 'Democratic Theory and Neo-corporatist Practice', Florence: European University Institute Working Paper no. 74, December.

Schmitter, P.C. (1985) 'Neo-corporatism and the State', in W.P. Grant (ed.), *The Political Economy of Corporatism.* London: Macmillan.

Schmitter, P.C. and Lehmbruch, G. (eds) (1979) *Trends Toward Corporatist Intermediation.* Beverly Hills and London: Sage Publications.

Schmitter, P.C. and Streeck, W. (1981) 'The Organization of Business Interests. A Research Design to Study the Associative Action of Business in the Advanced Industrial Societies of Western Europe'. Berlin: International Institute of Management, Discussion Paper IIM/LMP 81–13.

Schmitter, P.C. and Streeck, W. (forthcoming) *The Organization of Business Interests.*

Schwartz, Bernard (1962) *An Introduction to American Administrative Law.* Dobbs Ferry, NY: Oceana Publications.

Schwartz, Irvin and Marion, Larry (1977) 'How They Shaped Toxic Substance Law', *Chemical Week*, 27 April.

Schwerdtner, P. (1979) 'Trade Unions in the German Economic and Social Order', *Zeitschrift für die Gesamte Staatswissenschaft*, 135: 454–73.

Schwerin, D.S. (1980) 'The Limits of Organization as a Response to Wage–Price Problems', pp. 73–106 in Richard Rose (ed.), *Challenge to Governance: Studies in Overloaded Politics.* Beverly Hills and London: Sage Publications.

Seidman, Laurence S. (1978) 'Tax-Based Incomes Policies', *Brookings Papers on Economic Activity*, 2: 301–48.

Select Committee on Energy (1981) *First Report: The Government's Statement on the New Nuclear Power Programme*, Vol 1. Session 1980–81, HC 114–1. London: HMSO.

Sellier, F. (1970) 'L'évolution des negociations dans la sidérurgie et la métallurgie en France', *Droit Social*, 9–10.

Sen, Amartya K. (1974) 'Choice, Orderings and Morality', pp. 54–67 in Stephen Korner (ed.), *Practical Reason.* Oxford: Basil Blackwell.

Sen, Amartya K. (1977) 'Rational Fools: A Critique of the Behavioural Foundations of Economic Theory', *Philosophy and Public Affairs*, 6: 317–44.

Shonfield, A. (1965) *Modern Capitalism: The Changing Balance of Public and Private Power.* Oxford: Oxford University Press.

Solomos, J. (1980) 'The Political Economy of Energy Policy in Britain: A Critical Study of the Form and Functions of State Intervention 1960–1978'. DPhil. thesis, University of Sussex.

St Marc, P. (1961) *La France dans la CECA.* Paris: Fondation Nationale de Science Politique.

Statistics Canada (various years) *The Dairy Processing Industry*, Catalogue 32–209. Ottawa: Supply and Services Canada.

Stegemann, K. (1977) *Price Competition and Output Adjustment in the European Steel Market.* Tübingen: Mohr.

Stoffaes, C. (1978) *La Grande menace industrielle.* Paris: Calmann Levy.

Stonehouse, D. Peter (1979) 'Government Policies for the Canadian Dairy Industry', *Canadian Farm Economics*, 14 (1–2): 1–11.

Stora, B. (1979) *Crise, puissance, perspectives de la sidérurgie mondiale*. Paris: Economica.

Streeck, W. (1981) 'Qualitative Demands and the Neo-corporatist Manageability of Industrial Relations. Trade Unions and Industrial Relations in West Germany at the Beginning of the Eighties', *British Journal of Industrial Relations*, 14: 149–69.

Streeck, W. (1982b) 'Organizational Consequences of Corporatist Co-operation in West German Labour Unions', pp. 29–81 in G. Lehmbruch and P.C. Schmitter (eds), *Patterns of Corporatist Policy-Making*. Beverly Hills and London: Sage Publications.

Streeck, W. (1983) 'Between Pluralism and Corporatism: German Business Associations and the State', *Journal of Public Policy*, 3.

Streeck, W. (1984) 'Neo-corporatist Industrial Relations and the Economic Crisis in West Germany'. Florence: European University Institute, Working Paper no. 97.

Streeck, W. and Rampelt, J. (1982) 'Einstellungen und Erwartungen von Unternehmen gegenüber Wirtschaftsverbänden. Ergebnisse einer Befragung von Unternehmen in der Berliner Bauwirtschaft'. Berlin: International Institute of Management, Discussion Paper IIM/LMP 82–12.

Streeck, W. and Schmitter, P.C. (1984) 'Community, Market, State — and Associations? The Prospective Contribution of Interest Governance to Social Order'. Florence: European University Institute, Working Paper no. 94.

Stretch, J.A. (1969) 'Some Implications of the Industrial Training Act 1964', *The Training Officer*, 5 (2): 42–6.

Strinati, D. (1982) *Capitalism, The State and Industrial Relations*. London: Croom Helm.

Sueur, J.-J. (1983) 'Nationalisation et Industrie Sidérurgique', in L. Boy et al. *Sidérurgie et droit de crise*. Paris: PUF.

Suleiman, E.N. (1974) *Politics, Power and Bureaucracy in France: The Administrative Elite*. Princeton, NJ: Princeton University Press.

Sutcliffe, Charles (1982) 'Inflation and Prisoners' Dilemmas', *Journal of Post-Keynesian Economics*, 4: 574–85.

Tarantelli, E. (1983) 'The Regulation of Inflation in Western Countries and the Degree of Neo-Corporatism'. Florence: European University Institute, Summer School on Comparative European Politics.

Tarling, Roger and Wilkinson, Frank (1977) 'The Social Contract: Post-war Incomes Policies and Their Inflationary Impact', *Cambridge Journal of Economics*, 1 (4): 395–414.

Tavernier, G. (1968) 'Small Firms Versus the Industrial Training Act', *Personnel and Training Management*, January: 18–20.

Taylor, A. (1981) 'The Miners and the Labour Government'. Paper delivered to the Annual Conference of the Political Studies Association, Hull.

Taylor, R. (1980) 'The Training Scandal', *Management Today*, July.

Temin, Peter (1982) *Taking Your Medicine*. Cambridge, Mass.: Harvard University Press.

Terry, Michael (1985) 'Shop Stewards and Management: Collective Bargaining as Cooperation', in O. Jacobi et al., *Technological Change, Rationalization and Industrial Relations*. London: Croom Helm.

Traxler, Franz (1983) 'Prerequisites, Problem-solving Capacity and Restrictions of Self-regulation: A Case Study of Social Autonomy in the Austrian Milk Economy'. Paper presented to the Sixth Colloquium of the European Group for Organizational Studies, Florence, Italy.

TUC (1969) *Annual Report of the Trades Union Congress*. London: Trades Union Congress.

TUC (1974) *Collective Bargaining and the Social Contract*. London: Trades Union Congress.

TUC (1975) 'The Development of the Social Contract', pp. 346–64 in *Annual Report of the Trades Union Congress*. London: Trades Union Congress.

van Waarden, Frans (1983) 'Bureaucracy Around the State: Varieties of Collective Self-Regulation in the Dutch Dairy Industry'. Paper presented to Sixth Colloquium of the European Group for Organizational Studies, Florence, Italy.

Vickerstaff, S. (1983) 'Post-War Industrial Training in Britain: A Case Study of the Contradictions of Corporatism'. Paper presented to the Summer School on Comparative European Politics. Florence: European University Institute.

von Beyme, K. (1983) 'Neo-Corporatism: A New Nut in an Old Shell?' *International Political Science Review*, 4 (2): 173–96.

Walsh, Patrick J. (1984) 'The Rejection of Corporatism: Trade Unions, Employers and the State in New Zealand, 1960–1977'. PhD thesis, University of Minnesota.

Wassenberg, A. (1982) 'Neo-Corporatism and the Quest for Control: The Cuckoo Game', pp. 83–106 in G. Lehmbruch and P.C. Schmitter (eds), *Patterns of Corporatist Policy-Making*. Beverly Hills and London: Sage Publications.

Webber, D., Moon, J. and Richardson, J.J. (1984) 'State Promotion of Technological Innovation in France, Britain and Germany'. Paper presented to European Consortium for Political Research Workshops, Salzburg.

Weber, Jürgen (1977) *Die Interessengruppen im politischen System der Bundesrepublik Deutschland*. Stuttgart u.a.: Kohlammer.

Weber, Max (1978) *Economy and Society*, 2 vols. Berkeley and Los Angeles: University of California Press.

Weintraub, Sidney (1971) 'An Incomes Policy to Stop Inflation', *Lloyds Bank Review*, 99: 1–12.

Weintraub, Sidney (1978) *Capitalism's Inflation and Unemployment Crisis*. Reading, Mass.: Addison-Wesley.

Wilensky, H.L. (1976) 'The "New Corporatism", Centralization and the Welfare State', in *Sage Professional Papers in Contemporary Political Sociology*, vol. 2. Beverly Hills and London: Sage Publications.

Willman, Paul (1982) *Fairness, Collective Bargaining and Incomes Policy*. Oxford: Clarendon Press.

Wilson, F.L. (1983) 'Interest Groups and Politics in Western Europe: The Neo-Corporatist Approach', *Comparative Politics*, 16: 105–23.

Wilson, G.K. (1982) 'Why Is There No Corporatism in the United States?' in G. Lehmbruch and P.C. Schmitter (eds), *Patterns of Corporatist Policy-Making*. Beverly Hills and London: Sage Publications.

Wilson, Harold (1979) *Final Term*. London: Weidenfeld and Nicolson.

Winkler, J.T. (1975) 'Law, State and Economy: The Industry Act 1975 in Context', *British Journal of Law and Society*, 2 (2): 103–28.

Winkler, J.T. (1976) 'Corporatism', *Archives Européenes de Sociologie*, 17 (1): 100–36.

Winkler, J.T. (1977) 'The Corporatist Economy: Theory and Administration', in R. Scase (ed.), *Industrial Society: Class, Cleavage and Control*. London: Allen and Unwin.

Wolfe, A. (1977) *The Limits of Legitimacy*. New York: The Free Press.

Zysman, John (1977) *Political Strategies for Industrial Order.* Berkeley and Los Angeles: University of California Press.
Zysman, John (1983) *Governments, Markets and Growth: Financial Systems and the Politics of Industrial Change.* Ithaca, NY: Cornell University Press.

Index

Holmes, P.M., 16, 226, 231
House of Commons Treasury and Civil
  Service Committee, 86n
Housing and Construction Statistics, 149

IBM, see International Business
  Machines
ICL, see International Computers Ltd.
IG-Metall (IGM), 194, 195, 197, 198,
  199, 200, 201
Ilgen, T., 228
incomes policy, v, 2, 20, 26, 48, 65, 66,
  67, 72, 74–5, 76, 80, 83
  taxed-based (TIP), 71
  income redistribution, 77
individualism, 2, 3–4, 86, 87, 104, 201
  of interest associations, 24
industrial policy, 22–44, 27, 30, 31, 32,
  43–4, 45, 52, 85, 94
  'large scale restructuring', 22
  'positive adjustment policy', 22
  and Thatcherism, 92–3
industrial relations, 45, 67, 87, 100–4,
  166, 193, 196, 202, 206–7
  confrontationist, 101–2
  Thatcherite, 101
  'two nation' structure of, 85, 100–1,
  104
industrial training, 20, 50–64, 50n
inequalities, 92
  of power, 4, 7
inflation, 22, 65, 66, 69, 85, 90–1
  control, 89
  dis-inflation, 86, 88, 89, 90–3
  rate of in UK, 74, 75, 76, 80, 92
  real causes of, 92
  wage, 68, 73, 74, 76
information technologies
  state aid for, 98, 99
INMOS, 99
interest(s)
  class, 2, 48
  consumer, 11, 15
  exclusion, 8
  in firms, 18
  inter-class alliances, 15
  monopolies, 15
  'objective', 4
  organization, 2, 4, 25
  producer/provider, 11
  non-class, 3

representation, 8, 23
  sectoral, 13
  trans-sectoral, 53
interest groups, 3–4
International Business Machines, 98
international competitiveness, 29, 32, 43,
  77
International Computers Ltd., 96
international economy, the, 23
international pharmaceuticals industry,
  36–37
International Monetary Fund (IMF), 81
IRI, 211, 213
Irwin, F., 232
Italy, 10, 25, 192, 217, 219, 220
  ASSIDER, 214
  Cabinet conflict, 212
  'Cassa Integrazione Guadagni' (Wage
    Supplementation Fund), 213, 214
  CGIL-FIOM, 211, 213, 215
  CISL-FIM, 211, 215
  co-participation in, 213, 215
  'consigli di fabbrica' (workers'
    councils), 211-12
  Federazione Lavoratori
    Metalmeccanici (FLM), 209, 211,
    215, 219, 220
  FIAT dispute, 214
  industrial relations in, 211
  ISA, 214
  Japanese consultants in, 215
  Minister for State Holdings, 212
  Ministers of the Treasury and the
    Budget, 212
  trades unions and the state, 133
  steel industry, 209–16
  UIL-UILM, 211, 215

Jackman, R., 71, 232
Jacobi, O., 101, 227, 233, 240
Jacques, M., 87, 232
Japan(ese), 42n, 174, 215, 219
  capital, 139
  industrial policy in, 22–3
  'Japanization', 102, 102n, 208, 219
  steel producers, 192, 193
Jasonoff, S., 228
Jenkins, C., 53, 233
Jessop, B., 3, 8, 46, 51n, 87, 91, 85n, 233
Johansen, C.M., 46, 233

254   *Organized interests and the state*

Scharpf, F., 89, 188, 238
Scharpf, F.W., 30, 235
Schinder, P., 188, 238
Schmidt, M.G., 2, 10, 221, 238
Schmitter, P.C., v, vi, 2, 4, 6, 7, 8, 10,
    24n, 25, 26, 26n, 29, 31n, 39, 46, 46n,
    66, 94, 97, 106, 108, 122, 127, 147, 148,
    165, 169, 176, 190, 221, 223, 224–5,
    233, 234, 237, 238, 239, 240, 241, 243
Schneider, V., 9, 174, 243
Schwartz, B., 190, 239
Schwartz, I., 185, 239
Schwerdtner, P., 198, 239
Schwerin, D.S., 66, 67, 239
Scott, B.R., 203, 235
sector(al), 13, 18–20
    consciousness, 13, 216
    foreign control of, 28–29, 37
    interests, 62
    intervention, 94–100
    key industrial, 23
    policy, 85; see also under corporatism
    representation, 94, 100
    welfare and consumption, 14–15
Seidentrop, L., 232
Seidman, L.S., 71, 239
Select Committee on Energy, 239
self-enforcement
    delegated, 17
Sellier, F., 202, 206, 235, 239
Sen, A.K., 70, 71, 239
Shonfield, A., 136, 239
skill shortages, 52–3
Smith, B.C., 225, 237
'Smithsonian parities', 77n
social classes, 2, 3
    and state power, 3
'social closure, 8, 9, 206–7
social conflict, 25, 28
    reducing, 23
Social Contract, The, 67, 68, 72, 73, 73n,
    77–83, 89, 90, 126, 140, 142
    origins in the UK, 73
social democracy, vi, 26, 51, 52
Socialist Party, The French, 207
    government, 208, 209
    'social pacts', v
social reform, 52
Solomos, J., 128, 239
Soskice, D., 67, 231
Stahlwerke Peine Salzgitter, 195, 200

Starbuck, W.H., 236
state, the, 2, 6–7, 20, 25–6, 27, 106,
    133–4, 143–4, 165, 167–9, 220, 223–6
    autonomous nature of, 3, 5, 6–7, 16,
        25, 29, 41
    bilateral relations with industry, 95, 98,
        99, 203–206
    and class conflict, 121, 122–3
    coercion, 6–7
    'colonization' of, 134
    corporatism, 106–9, 114, 115, 121–6
    crisis of, 22
    delegation of authority, 38–9, 43
    differentiation from society, 29–30, 40–
        1, 42, 42n, 45
    directive role of, 6, 12
    and firms, 28–9, 95–6
    franchise, 16, 25
    host, 29
    and interest groups, 4, 6, 7, 9, 10, 24,
        25, 31, 45, 46–7
    interventionism, 16, 17, 29, 36, 45, 47,
        52, 55, 61, 89, 90, 94, 98, 109, 120,
        130, 132, 134, 170–1, 196, 199–201,
        204–6
    and levels of corporatism, 14, 16, 27,
        46–7, 107
    and producer groups, 11–12, 28, 38, 39,
        43
    and sectoral corporatism, 27–8, 29–30,
        46, 47, 50, 107
    sector of the economy, 26
    and social control, 4, 6, 25–6
    social provision by, 14, 87
    subsidy of research and development,
        98, 99
    and Thatcherism, 86–97
Statistics Canada, 32, 32n, 34n, 239
Stegemann, K., 195, 239
Steiger, H., 237
sterling, 52, 77, 77n, 81n, 88, 90
St Marc, P., 203, 239
Stoffaes, C., 205, 239
Stonehouse, D.P., 32, 239
'stop-go' policies, 51, 51n, 52, 89
Stora, B., 196, 204, 240
Strathclyde Research Project, 97
Streeck, W., v, vi, 2, 9, 12, 29, 31n, 94,
    97, 100, 101, 103, 104, 123, 145, 147,
    165, 169, 176, 190, 196, 197, 198, 200,
    201, 223, 239, 240, 243

Notes on contributors

Alan Cawson teaches politics in the School of Social Sciences, University of Sussex, and was a Jean Monnet Fellow at the European University Institute in 1984–5. He is the author of *Corporatism and Welfare* and is currently finishing a book on corporatism and political theory.

Philippe C. Schmitter is Professor of Political Science at the European University Institute, Florence. He is co-editor of *Private Interest Government: Beyond Market and State.*

Michael Atkinson and **William Coleman** teach in the Department of Political Science at McMaster University, where they are both engaged in research on business interests and industrial policy in Canada.

Sarah Vickerstaff is a temporary lecturer in Industrial Relations at the University of Kent. She recently obtained her PhD in sociology from the University of Leeds; the thesis was on 'The Limits of Corporatism: The British Experience'.

Jonathan Boston has worked in the New Zealand Treasury and is currently Lecturer in Political Science at Canterbury University, New Zealand. He gained his doctorate for research on the Social Contract and is the author of *Incomes Policy in New Zealand.*

Kevin Bonnett is Senior Lecturer in Sociology at the Cambridgeshire College of Arts and Technology. He is co-author of *Introductory Sociology*, and is currently finishing a book on corporatism and the monetarist reaction.

Noelle Burgi has recently completed a doctoral thesis on the organisation of the energy industry in Britain. She is scientific researcher at CNRS and teaches in the Political Science Department of the Sorbonne University (Paris I).

Wyn Grant is senior lecturer in politics at the University of Warwick. He is author of *The Political Economy of Industrial Policy* and *Independent Local Politics in England and Wales,* and co-author of *The CBI* and *The Politics of Economic Policy-Making.*

Wolfgang Streeck is Senior Research Fellow at the International Institute of Management in Berlin. He has written widely on trade unions, business associations, industrial relations and labour market policy. He is co-editor of *Private Interest Government: Beyond Market and State.*

Volker Schneider is completing doctoral research at the European University Institute, Florence on the chemicals industry in West Germany and the United States.

Martin Rhodes has just completed a doctoral thesis on the steel industry in France. He is currently Research Fellow in the Department of Politics at the University of Strathclyde.